Bite me too

By the not-so-sweet, tiny-bit-salty sisters
Julie Albert & Lisa Gnat

McArthur & Company

Toronto

First published in 2011 by
McArthur & Company
322 King Street West, Suite 402
Toronto, ON M5V 1J2
www.mcarthur-co.com

Library and Archives Canada Cataloguing in Publication

Albert, Julie, 1970-
    Bite me too: another stomach-satisfying, visually gratifying,
fresh-mouthed cookbook / Julie Albert & Lisa Gnat.

Includes index.
ISBN 978-1-77087-152-6

1. Cooking. 2. Cookbooks. I. Gnat, Lisa, 1972– II. Title.

TX714.A4583 2011   641.5   C2011-907658-6

The publisher would like to acknowledge the financial support of the Govern-
ment of Canada through the Canada Book Fund and the Canada Council for
our publishing activities. The publisher further wishes to acknowledge the
financial support of the Ontario Arts Council and the OMDC for our publishing
program.

Printed and bound in Canada

10 9 8 7 6 5 4 3 2 1

Dedicate me

To Lisa

Way to cook the book.
Love you and your whisk.

To Julie

I fill your stomach but you make my belly laugh.
Love you and your two cents' worth.

"Prepare to be amazed beyond all expectations. After all, it is what I do."

— Magic Mirror in *Snow White and the Seven Dwarfs*

BITE ME TOO may not be a fairy tale of seven heigh ho-ing dwarfs and tainted fruit (really, you can eat our apples), but it's a magical reflection of how my sister Lisa (she's the fairer one) and I (a tad wicked queen) live our lives and bring our passions for eating and feeding to the table every day. The pages of BITE ME TOO are packed with 176 foolproof and user-friendly recipes, inspiring photography, pop culture crack-ups and budget-friendly bashes. There's no magical kiss here – BITE ME TOO turns the fantasy of putting out a simple and satisfying meal, entertaining with ease and laughing in the kitchen into a reality.

"But I always say, one's company, two's a crowd and three's a party."

— Andy Warhol, artist

BITE ME TOO is the follow-up to our bestselling cookbook BITE ME. In this second rule-breaking, lick-the-bowl bonanza we're thrilled to have added great new features such as RSVP me, a "how-to" chapter on throwing exciting, easy and original parties. Much like our cooking, we believe in making entertaining accessible – your time, money and sanity are always key when putting together a Bite Me Bash.

"The world loves a spice of wickedness."

— Henry Wadsworth Longfellow, poet

Get ready to have some fun as you play your way through BITE ME TOO, a celebration of sisterhood, a marriage of cooking and art and a multi-sensory and fulfilling feast.

Thanks for Biting and be in touch —

Julie and, of course, *Lisa*

julie@bitemecookbook.com   lisa@bitemecookbook.com.

P.S. What's the ▓ at the bottom of some pages? Scan these QR codes with your smartphone or webcam and get linked to educational (and not so educational) BITE ME videos.

We're so alike, Lisa and I think we're twins born 2 years apart. However, when we dig a bit deeper there are quite a few differences. We're both convinced we could assemble the bigger roster of like-minded friends. Answer the questions below and scan the QR code to see whether you side with the sweet or salty sister.

In the '70s, I was busy

- ❑ Cleaning my Easy-Bake Oven
- ❑ Hanging Leif Garrett and Rex Smith posters
- ❑ Doing the Hustle
- ❑ Writing fan mail to Superman

The first thing I do in a hotel room is

- ❑ Disinfect the TV remote, faucets, doorknobs...
- ❑ Plop myself on the bedspread and check the room-service menu
- ❑ Change to a better room
- ❑ Find out where the closest pizza joint is

The song that best describes me is

- ❑ "Hells Bells" by AC/DC
- ❑ "The Joker" by Steve Miller Band
- ❑ "She's a Lady" by Tom Jones
- ❑ "Hard Headed Woman" by Cat Stevens

If I spill red wine on the white carpet, I instantly

- ❑ Blame it on a sibling and pour another glass
- ❑ Grab the deluxe carpet steamer and get to work
- ❑ Rearrange the furniture to cover the spot
- ❑ Blot, spray hydrogen peroxide and sprinkle baking soda

In my refrigerator, I always have

- ❑ A wedge of fresh Parmesan cheese
- ❑ Cans of full-octane Pepsi
- ❑ Face cream and film
- ❑ A tub of miso paste

The last thing I wrote was

- ❑ A grocery list
- ❑ "Bite Me" on a wall behind the school
- ❑ My name on a bake sale sign-up sheet
- ❑ A ditty to the tune of "The Addams Family"

I wake up in a cold sweat worried about

- ❑ Whether I do or don't split 10s in blackjack
- ❑ What I can add to pump up my pesto
- ❑ How to get the caramel inside the chocolate
- ❑ Where I put my *Saved by the Bell* board game

At midnight I can be found

- ❑ Color blocking my closet
- ❑ Putting the finishing touches to the kids' homework
- ❑ Whipping up muffins for morning
- ❑ On the phone asking, "Hi. Is your refrigerator running?"

If I won $10,000, I'd immediately head to

- ❑ Las Vegas
- ❑ The bank
- ❑ Buy a camel or a windmill
- ❑ Purchase 100-year-old balsamic vinegar

I wish I could

- ❑ Wink
- ❑ Be an octopus
- ❑ Dive without belly flopping
- ❑ Be invisible

If I rebelled, I would

- ❑ Stop using hand sanitizer
- ❑ Use a cake mix and canned icing
- ❑ Stay out after curfew with The Jets and The Sharks
- ❑ Get a tattoo of an ice cream with lightening bolts

My biggest pet peeve is

- ❑ "Reply to all"-ers
- ❑ Too many items in the Express Lane
- ❑ People who say "irregardless"
- ❑ Whistling, tapping and noisy eaters

Roasted Red Pepper Hummus with Pita Chips 14

Super Cool Chicken Nachos 15

Twice-Baked Mini Potatoes 17

Caramelized Onion & Gruyere Pizza 18

Crunchy Tortilla Chicken Wings 19

Polenta Crostini with Roasted Red Peppers & Olives 20

Amuse
me

Small Bites for your Bouche

Chinese Beef & Bok Choy Pot Stickers 22

Asian Shrimp Lettuce Wraps 23

Grilled Chicken Satays with Peanut Sauce 27

Quinoa, Roasted Red Pepper & Feta Wraps 28

Cheesy Chicken Quesadillas 29

Eggplant & Butternut Squash Bruschetta 30

Mini Meatball Subs 33

EXTRA BITE

Bring Me: Edible Gifts for Everyone on your List 24

ROASTED RED PEPPER HUMMUS with PITA CHIPS

INGREDIENTS

Pita Chips

3 tbsp olive oil

½ tsp ground cumin

¼ tsp kosher salt

5 (6-inch) white pita pockets

Red Pepper Hummus

2 cups canned chickpeas, rinsed and drained

1 cup jarred roasted red peppers, rinsed and drained

6 tbsp olive oil

¼ cup fresh lemon juice

1 tbsp chopped fresh flat-leaf parsley

1 small garlic clove, minced

½ tsp kosher salt

½ tsp ground cumin

¼ tsp freshly ground black pepper

⅛ tsp cayenne pepper

People just love to do "the drop-by." Is it the fun of catching me in a state of disarray or the joy in knowing they're getting this tasty roasted red pepper hummus dip with crunchy pita chips? Given how my hair can look very Nick-Nolte-mug-shot (Lisa's description), I'm guessing it's the latter, the fact that this delicious dip is my go-to quick and easy snack for unexpected visitors. A few pulses in the food processor and I've got a creamy, garlicky, lemony blend of chickpeas, roasted red peppers, olive oil and spices. Paired with my addictive baked pita chips – wedges seasoned with cumin and salt – it's no wonder they come a-knockin' at all hours.

DIRECTIONS

1) For the pita chips, preheat oven to 350°F. Line a baking sheet with aluminum foil and coat with non-stick cooking spray. In a small bowl, combine olive oil, cumin and salt. Split each pita open into 2 halves and brush rough sides with olive oil mixture. Cut each circle into 8 triangles. Place in a single layer on prepared baking sheet, oiled side up. Bake 13–15 minutes, until golden brown. Remove from oven and cool. Once completely cooled, these chips can be stored in an airtight container for up to 4 days. 2) For the hummus, in a food processor or blender, combine chickpeas, red peppers, olive oil, lemon juice, parsley, garlic, salt, cumin, black pepper and cayenne. Process until smooth. Cover and refrigerate until ready to serve with pita chips.

Serves 8–10

BITE ME BIT

"What knockers."

— Dr. Frederick Frankenstein (actor Gene Wilder) in the 1974 movie *Young Frankenstein*

SUPER COOL CHICKEN NACHOS

INGREDIENTS

Guacamole

2 ripe avocados, halved and peeled

1 tbsp fresh lime juice

¼ tsp ground cumin

¼ tsp kosher salt

pinch cayenne pepper

1 plum tomato, seeded and diced

1 tbsp chopped fresh flat-leaf parsley

Bean, Salsa & Cheddar Mash-Up

1½ cups canned black beans, rinsed and drained

2 tbsp butter

¼ tsp garlic powder

¼ tsp kosher salt

¼ cup salsa

½ cup shredded cheddar cheese

Chicken

1 tbsp olive oil

1 roasted deli chicken, breast meat only, cut into 1-inch cubes

¼ tsp ground cumin

¼ tsp chili powder

1 (300g) bag tortilla chips

3½ cups shredded cheddar cheese

Sour cream and salsa for dipping

I won't tell you who says it, but someone *like* our brother calls us Beavis and Butt-Head (Lisa is the latter). Fine with me. The snarky duo is credited with saying "Nachos Rule!" We couldn't agree more. We love the 3 Cs – chicken, chips and cheese – and if you think we're being total dolts for giving you a recipe for a most basic bar food, read on. This recipe is genius. It's a piled-high fiesta of crunchy tortilla chips, a delectable black bean, salsa and cheddar mash-up and chunks of chicken, all crowned with creamy guacamole. A platter of these matchless munchies and a cold pitcher of margaritas might have you too plastered with a silly grin and rubbing a satisfied stomach. Uh, huh, huh, huh, heh, heh, heh.

DIRECTIONS

1) For the guacamole, in a large bowl, mash avocados using a potato masher. Mix in lime juice, cumin, salt and cayenne. Fold in tomatoes and parsley. Place 1 of the avocado pits in the center of the guacamole to ensure guacamole won't brown before serving. Cover and let flavors blend for 1 hour at room temperature. 2) For the bean, salsa and cheddar mash-up, in a medium saucepan, combine beans, butter, garlic powder, salt and salsa over medium heat. Stir, cooking for 2 minutes. Remove from heat, add cheese and mash all together with a potato masher until coarse and chunky. 3) For the chicken, in a medium saucepan, heat olive oil over medium-high heat. Add chicken, cumin and chili powder, stirring well to combine flavors, and heat chicken, about 2 minutes. 4) Preheat oven to 350°F. Line a baking sheet with aluminum foil and coat with non-stick cooking spray. To assemble, spread out a single layer of chips on the baking sheet. Top with 1¼ cups cheddar cheese. Pile the remainder of the chips over the cheese and spoon bean, salsa and cheddar mash-up over top, then the chicken and the remaining cheddar cheese. Bake 10 minutes, until cheese has melted. Remove from oven and top center with guacamole. Serve immediately, accompanied with bowls of additional salsa and sour cream.

Serves 8–10 or 4 really big appetites

TWICE-BAKED MINI POTATOES

INGREDIENTS

26 Yukon Gold mini potatoes

1 tbsp olive oil

½ tsp chopped fresh thyme

½ tsp kosher salt

½ tsp freshly
ground black pepper

¾ cup sour cream

¼ cup milk

¼ cup freshly grated
Parmesan cheese

2 tbsp thinly sliced fresh chives

1 tbsp butter, softened

½ tsp kosher salt

¼ tsp freshly
ground black pepper

As a schoolgirl, I was an apple-shining keener. My yellow no. 2 pencils were permanently sharpened to a lethal conical point and my homework was always completed in full. I liked being prepared. I still do, so this appetizer is perfect for me. The ultimate finger food, these twice-baked, one-bite wonders can be made in advance – you just pop them in the oven for a second baking before the guests arrive. These tiny cheese and chive-stuffed taters get an A+ every time. Whew.

DIRECTIONS

1) Preheat oven to 425ºF. Line a large baking sheet with aluminum foil and coat with non-stick cooking spray. 2) Wash and dry potatoes. Place them in a large bowl and toss with olive oil, thyme, ½ tsp salt and ½ tsp pepper. Transfer to prepared baking sheet and bake until a fork easily pierces potatoes, about 25 minutes. Remove and let cool until you are able to hold them. Take each potato, slice the top off, and use a small spoon to carefully hollow it out. Place potato pulp in a medium bowl and mash to a chunky consistency. Add sour cream, milk, Parmesan, chives, butter, salt and pepper, mashing ingredients together. 3) Increase oven temperature to 450ºF. Generously spoon the filling into each potato shell. (Note: At this point, if you're preparing the potatoes in advance, allow them to cool, cover and refrigerate them. When ready to serve bring to room temperature.) Just before serving time, bake until slightly brown on top, 10–15 minutes.

Yield: 26 mini potatoes

BITE ME BIT

"I'm a potato and I'm so hip."

— from the 1976 Devo song "I'm a Potato"

CARAMELIZED ONION & GRUYERE PIZZA

INGREDIENTS

Pizza Crust

1 cup warm water

1 tbsp honey

1 pkg (2 ¼ tsp) active dry yeast

2½ cups flour

1 tsp kosher salt

1 tbsp olive oil

Caramelized Onions

2 tbsp olive oil

2 large red onions, cut in half and thinly sliced

2 tbsp brown sugar

¼ tsp kosher salt

yellow cornmeal, to dust baking sheets or pizza pans

2 tbsp olive oil1 tsp kosher salt

1 cup ricotta cheese

1 cup shredded Gruyere cheese

1 tsp chopped fresh thyme

This is pizza. I know it's pizza by its shape, yet, when I close my eyes and take a big bite, my tongue tells me that I'm devouring the finest *Soupe à l'oignon*. This rich and flavorful pizza has all the mouth-watering makings of a *magnifique* onion soup – the golden caramelized onions, the nutty, creamy and gooey Gruyere, and the fresh thyme atop a crisp homemade crust. Baked until bubbly, this winning combination of sweet onions and slightly salty cheese will, like traditional onion soup, stand the test of time. Only thing missing is the spoon.

DIRECTIONS

1) For the dough, place warm water in a small bowl and dissolve honey in it. Sprinkle yeast over water, cover and let stand 10 minutes. Place flour and salt in the bowl of an electric mixer. Using the dough hook attachment, add 1 tbsp olive oil and yeast mixture on low speed. Turn speed to medium and continue to mix for 4 minutes. Remove dough from bowl and knead by hand on a lightly floured surface for 5 minutes, until smooth and no longer sticky. Place in a large bowl that has been coated with non-stick cooking spray. Cover and let rise in a warm area for 1 hour. **2)** Meanwhile, to prepare caramelized onions, in a large skillet, heat 2 tbsp olive oil over medium-high heat. Add onions, brown sugar and salt, stirring frequently and cooking until onions are tender, about 15 minutes. **3)** Preheat oven to 500°F. Dust pizza pan or baking sheet with yellow cornmeal. After 1 hour and once the dough has doubled in size divide it in half and knead both balls on a lightly floured surface for 2 minutes. While working with 1 dough ball wrap the other in plastic wrap. On a lightly floured surface, roll dough into a 12-inch circle. Transfer to prepared pan. Brush with 1 tbsp olive oil and sprinkle with ¼ tsp salt. Spread with ½ cup ricotta cheese, top with half of the caramelized onions, sprinkle with ½ cup Gruyere cheese and finish with ½ tsp thyme and ¼ tsp salt. Bake 9–10 minutes, until edges are golden. Repeat with remaining pizza dough. Serve immediately.

Yield: 2 pizzas, for a total of 16 slices

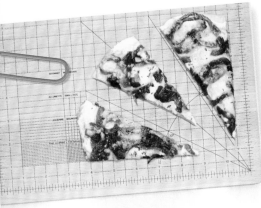

CRUNCHY TORTILLA CHICKEN WINGS

INGREDIENTS

3 lbs chicken wings, split, wing-tip removed

Marinade

2 cups buttermilk

1 large white onion, sliced

¼ cup fresh lemon juice

1 tsp ground cumin

1 tsp dried oregano

½ tsp cayenne pepper

½ tsp kosher salt

½ tsp freshly ground black pepper

Tortilla Coating

8 cups tortilla chips

1 cup flour

1 tsp ground cumin

½ tsp garlic powder

½ tsp freshly ground black pepper

¼ tsp kosher salt

¼ tsp cayenne pepper

4 tbsp melted butter

Spicy Wing Sauce

½ cup Louisiana-style hot sauce (we like Frank's)

¼ cup butter

2 tbsp honey

¼ tsp kosher salt

If you've read our first cookbook then you're painfully aware that my sister and her husband are football fiends. Yeah, yeah…go Dolphins, go…whatever. If I never hear another word about tailgating, TDs and tossing the pigskin, I'm good. However, there is one element of this sport I too adore, the excessive eating and serious snacking. Lisa recently created these tortilla-crusted wings specifically for Sunday showdowns. Marinated in a lemony buttermilk mixture these juicy, crunchy tortilla wings are baked to perfection and served up with a homemade spicy wing sauce. I love these wings, and, here's the kicker…I eat them while watching basketball. That'll show them.

DIRECTIONS

1) Place chicken wings in a large resealable plastic bag. In a large bowl, combine buttermilk, onions, lemon juice, cumin, oregano, cayenne, salt and pepper. Stir well to combine and pour over chicken wings. Let marinate in the refrigerator 6 hours to overnight. 2) For the coating, in a food processor, finely grind tortilla chips. Place in a large bowl with flour, cumin, garlic powder, pepper, salt and cayenne. Toss to combine. 3) Preheat oven to 425°F. Line a baking sheet with aluminum foil and place a cooling rack on top of the baking sheet for the wings to cook on. 4) Remove wings from buttermilk mixture, gently shaking off excess marinade. Dredge wings in tortilla chip mixture and make sure wings are coated all over. Place on prepared rack. Drizzle with 2 tbsp melted butter and bake 20 minutes. Turn wings over, drizzle with remaining 2 tbsp melted butter and cook 20 minutes more, until browned and cooked through. 5) For the wing sauce, in a medium saucepan, bring hot sauce, butter, honey and salt to a boil over medium heat. Turn heat to low and simmer 10 minutes. Serve with tortilla wings.

Serves 6–8

POLENTA CROSTINI with ROASTED RED PEPPERS & OLIVES

INGREDIENTS

Parmesan Polenta

3 cups water

1 cup yellow cornmeal

½ cup freshly grated Parmesan cheese

1 tbsp butter

½ tsp kosher salt

⅛ tsp dried basil

Roasted Red Pepper & Olive Topping

3 large red bell peppers

½ cup pitted and chopped Kalamata olives

2 tbsp olive oil

2 tsp chopped fresh basil

⅛ tsp kosher salt

⅛ tsp freshly ground black pepper

olive oil, for brushing polenta squares

fresh Parmesan curls, for topping

Do you know that if you mouth the phrase "olive juice," it looks just like you're saying "I love you"? I did it to Lisa the other day to thank her for showing me how to make such a strikingly elegant, from-scratch appetizer. Slightly intimidated, I set about putting together the Parmesan polenta and roasting the peppers, but, within minutes, my fears were put to rest – Lisa's good at giving directions so it was easy to get fantastic results. Crisp polenta squares serve as the perfect vehicle for the soft, sweet and aromatic oven-roasted peppers, along with the fruity, fleshy Kalamata olives. "Elephant shoes," Lisa (that's another one to try). Really, who says I can't be a class act?

DIRECTIONS

1) For the polenta, coat an 11 x 7-inch baking dish with non-stick cooking spray. In a medium saucepan, bring 3 cups of water to a boil over high heat. Slowly whisk in cornmeal, turn heat to low and stir continuously, 3–4 minutes, until mixture thickens. Remove from heat and stir in Parmesan cheese, butter, salt and basil. Transfer polenta to prepared baking dish and spread evenly to coat the bottom. Let polenta cool completely, 15–20 minutes. 2) For the topping, to roast the peppers, place oven rack 4 inches from top element and preheat to broil. Line a baking sheet with aluminum foil and coat with non-stick cooking spray. Cut peppers in half, remove ribs and seeds and arrange cut-side down on prepared baking sheet. Broil until pepper skin is blackened and blistered. Remove from oven and let cool slightly before peeling. Peel off skins, coarsely chop peppers and transfer to a medium bowl. Add olives, olive oil, basil, salt and pepper. Let stand at room temperature for 20 minutes allowing flavors to blend. 3) Meanwhile, preheat oven to 400°F. Line a baking sheet with aluminum foil and coat with non-stick cooking spray. Once polenta is set, cut into 2-inch squares. Slice each square lengthwise to make a thinner square. Brush both sides with olive oil and arrange in a single layer on prepared baking sheet. Bake 15 minutes, flip and bake another 15 minutes. Remove from oven and top each square with a spoonful of the red pepper andolive mixture followed by a Parmesan curl. Serve immediately.

Yield: 30–35 squares

BITE ME BIT

"You can lead a horticulture, but you can't make her think."

— Dorothy Parker, author and satirist, when challenged to use the word "horticulture" in a sentence

CHINESE BEEF & BOK CHOY POT STICKERS

INGREDIENTS

Beef & Bok Choy Filling

½ lb lean ground beef

¼ cup finely chopped bok choy

1 tbsp minced green onions

1 tbsp soy sauce

1 tbsp cooking sherry

1 tbsp vegetable oil

1 tsp sesame oil

1 tsp grated fresh ginger

1 tsp cornstarch

2 tbsp water

25 wonton wrappers

2 tbsp vegetable oil

½ cup water

Dipping Sauce

2 tbsp rice vinegar

2 tbsp soy sauce

¼ tsp sesame oil

We'd love to be invited to a Chinese New Year celebration. Why? Many reasons, not the least of which is the tradition of eating dumplings, a shape that symbolizes wealth. As well, we're intrigued by the practice of hiding a coin in a dumpling – the person who finds it has good luck for the year…trust me, we'd eat until we found that lucky coin. If this deters anyone from including us I'll make Lisa slip some cash in these zesty, zingy and satisfying beef, bok choy, green onion and ginger-filled pot stickers. Lightly pan-fried on one side and steamed to finish, these crispy, golden-bottomed treasure-troves are crowd-pleasers. *Xin nian kuai le!*

DIRECTIONS

1) For the filling, in a large bowl, combine ground beef, bok choy, green onions, soy sauce, sherry, vegetable oil, sesame oil and ginger. Stir well to combine, cover the bowl and refrigerate 30 minutes to allow flavors to develop. **2)** To assemble the pot stickers, lay out 1 wonton wrapper. In a small bowl, mix cornstarch and water. Dip your finger in the cornstarch and moisten the edges of the wrapper. Place 1 tbsp of the filling in the middle of the wrapper. Fold wrapper diagonally over the filling and pinch edges to seal shut. When all pot stickers are filled, in a large skillet, heat 2 tbsp vegetable oil over high heat. Add pot stickers and cook 1 minute, until bottom is golden. Add ½ cup water and cover the skillet immediately. Reduce heat to low and let them steam 10 minutes. Remove the lid, turn heat to medium for 1 minute longer and let the bottoms get crunchy and golden. Serve immediately. **3)** For the dipping sauce, in a small bowl, whisk rice vinegar, soy sauce and sesame oil. Serve with pot stickers.

Yield: 23–25 pot stickers

Learn how to strike it rich with pot stickers

ASIAN SHRIMP LETTUCE WRAPS

INGREDIENTS

Marinade

3 tbsp soy sauce

2 tbsp honey

1 tbsp fresh lime juice

1 tsp sesame oil

1 large garlic clove, minced

½ tsp minced fresh ginger

1 lb medium raw shrimp
(about 32 shrimp),
peeled and deveined

2 tbsp vegetable oil

2 tbsp chopped fresh basil

Rice

1 cup white rice

2 cups water

Tangy Marmalade Sauce

2 tbsp orange marmalade

2 tbsp honey

2 tsp soy sauce

16 Boston Bibb
(Butter lettuce) leaves

It can't be easy being our older brother. We two "twisted sisters" (a flattering moniker given to us by our dad) are constantly urging him to "cut to the chase" and "speed it up." So what if he likes to tell and retell the same, meandering, overly detailed stories and to recount his dreams? Shame on us. To make amends, Lisa created this refreshing roll, something we can "wrap up" for him. Crisp Boston Bibb lettuce is loaded with sautéed shrimp, white rice and a tangy marmalade sauce, resulting in a delicious bite. In fact, it's portable too, so he can bring it over to your house and tell you about the time he and Magilla Gorilla were chased by the Road Runner...

DIRECTIONS

1) For the marinade, in a medium bowl, whisk soy sauce, honey, lime juice, sesame oil, garlic and ginger. Add shrimp, toss with marinade, cover and refrigerate 30 minutes before cooking. 2) While the shrimp marinates rinse the rice in a strainer, drain and place in a medium saucepan. Add 2 cups water and bring to a boil over high heat. Turn heat to low, cover and simmer until rice is cooked, about 20 minutes. Remove from heat and allow rice to sit covered for 10 minutes before using in shrimp wraps. 3) For the marmalade sauce, in a small bowl, whisk marmalade, honey and soy sauce until well blended. Set aside. 4) To cook the shrimp, in a medium skillet, heat vegetable oil over medium-high heat. Add shrimp and cook, stirring 5–6 minutes until cooked through. Remove shrimp from heat, cut each shrimp in half and place in a medium bowl. Toss with basil. 5) To assemble rolls, place lettuce leaf on a plate, add about 3 tbsp rice, a small spoon of marmalade sauce, followed by 4 shrimp halves. Top with a small spoon of marmalade sauce and fold leaf together. Repeat with remaining lettuce, shrimp, rice and sauce.

Yield: 16 lettuce wraps

BITE ME BIT

"Whatever story you're telling, it will be more interesting if at the end you add, 'and then everything burst into flames.'"

— from Brian P. Cleary's 2010 book *You Oughta Know By Now*

Bring Me

How many scented soaps or #1 Teacher mugs does any one person need? None. That's why we think outside the bouquet when giving gifts and why we only give to others things we're dying and drooling to hold on to. Bring along (and share) these lethally addictive treats – they guarantee you'll always be invited back, that your kid will get an A+, that your mail will end up in the slot, that your haircut will be straight...

BROWN SUGAR & CARAMILK FUDGE

2 cups packed brown sugar
¾ cup butter
1 (10.5oz) can sweetened condensed milk
1 cup icing sugar
1 tsp vanilla extract
5 (52g) Caramilk Chocolate Bars

1) Line an 8x8-inch baking pan with parchment paper and coat with non-stick cooking spray. 2) In a medium saucepan combine brown sugar, butter and condensed milk. Whisk over medium heat, stirring often for 6 minutes. Remove from heat. 3) Using an electric mixer, beat icing sugar, vanilla and brown sugar mixture on medium speed for 4 minutes. Pour half in prepared pan, line with whole chocolate bars and top with remaining mixture. Refrigerate 2 hours before cutting into squares.

> **"The worst gift is a fruitcake. There is only one fruitcake in the entire world and people keep sending it to each other."**
>
> — Johnny Carson, TV host

HONEY-SPICED NUTS

2 tbsp butter, melted
2 tbsp honey
2 tbsp brown sugar
½ tsp chili powder
½ tsp paprika
½ tsp kosher salt
½ tsp ground cumin
¼ tsp dried oregano
⅛ tsp cayenne pepper
3 cups mixed nuts (pecans, almonds, walnuts)

1) Preheat oven to 300°F. Line a baking sheet with parchment paper.
2) In a large bowl whisk melted butter, honey, brown sugar, chili powder, paprika, salt, cumin, oregano and cayenne. Add mixed nuts and toss well. Place on prepared baking sheet and bake 30 minutes stirring every 10 minutes. Let cool completely before packaging nuts.

MARINATED OLIVES

1 cup large green olives (pitted or not), rinsed and drained
1 cup Kalamata olives (pitted or not), rinsed and drained
⅓ cup olive oil
3 tbsp apple cider vinegar
3 tbsp thinly sliced oil-packed sun-dried tomatoes
½ tsp ground cumin
¼ tsp crushed red pepper flakes

1) Place green and Kalamata olives in a glass bowl. In a medium saucepan combine olive oil, vinegar, sun-dried tomatoes, cumin and red pepper flakes over medium heat. Simmer 5 minutes, remove from heat and pour over olives. Cover and let marinate at room temperature for 2 hours. Can be refrigerated up to 1 week.

CHOCOLATE OREO POPS

30 Oreo cookies, finely crumbled
¼ cup flour
¼ cup packed brown sugar
2 tbsp cocoa powder
½ tsp vanilla extract
½ cup cream cheese, softened
¼ cup butter, softened
20–22 lollipop sticks
1 cup semi-sweet chocolate chips, melted

1) Line a baking sheet with parchment paper. In a large bowl combine Oreo crumbs, flour, brown sugar, cocoa powder and vanilla. Mix in cream cheese and butter until well blended. By heaping tablespoon, shape into round balls. Place on prepared baking sheet and refrigerate for 30 minutes. 2) Remove from refrigerator and place 1 lollipop stick in center of each ball. Roll each ball in melted chocolate and place back on baking sheet. Refrigerate to harden for 30 minutes.

GRILLED CHICKEN SATAYS with PEANUT SAUCE

INGREDIENTS

Marinade

½ cup soy sauce

1 large white onion, chopped

1 large garlic clove

1 tbsp grated fresh ginger

1 tbsp fresh lime juice

1 tbsp sugar

1 tbsp sesame oil

½ tsp ground cumin

4 boneless skinless chicken breast halves, cut into 3-inch strips

Peanut Sauce

½ cup smooth peanut butter

¼ cup packed brown sugar

¼ cup rice wine vinegar

2 tbsp soy sauce

2 tbsp water

¼ tsp cayenne pepper

15–20 wooden skewers, soaked in warm water for 20–30 minutes before threading on chicken

There's a food-on-a-stick frenzy sweeping the nation. Hit any State Fair and you'll find everything from impaled fried pickles to hot bologna. Jumping on the foodsicle Ferris wheel, I asked Lisa to shove spinach dip on a stick. She couldn't do it. However, she quickly appeased me with these flavorful, Thai-inspired chicken satays. Grilled until golden brown and dipped in a homemade peanut sauce, these sweet, salty and succulent portable bites make for great party food. Don't you just love her stick-to-it-iveness?

DIRECTIONS

1) For the marinade, in a blender, combine soy sauce, onion, garlic, ginger, lime juice, sugar, sesame oil and cumin, blending until smooth. Place chicken strips in a large resealable plastic bag, add marinade and toss to coat. Refrigerate at least 1 hour or overnight. 2) For the peanut sauce, in a food processor or blender, combine peanut butter, brown sugar, rice wine vinegar, soy sauce, water and cayenne. Blend until smooth, adding an extra tablespoon of water if necessary. Cover and refrigerate until ready to serve. 3) Preheat barbeque to medium-high heat. Thread chicken strips on prepared skewers and discard marinade. Grill 3–4 minutes per side. Serve with peanut sauce.

Serves 6–8

BITE ME BIT

"Those kids have a rare blood disease: Stick-it-to-da-man-noisis."

— Dewey Finn (actor Jack Black) in the 2003 movie School of Rock

QUINOA, ROASTED RED PEPPER & FETA WRAPS

INGREDIENTS

1 cup quinoa

1 tbsp olive oil

2 cups water

2 red bell peppers, halved and seeded

1 cup peeled, seeded and chopped English cucumber

1 cup diced feta cheese

1 tbsp chopped fresh flat-leaf parsley

Lime Cumin Dressing

2 tbsp olive oil

2 tbsp fresh lime juice

½ tsp ground cumin

½ tsp kosher salt

⅛ tsp sugar

16 round rice- paper sheets

Feta Dipping Sauce

½ cup feta cheese

⅓ cup sour cream

2 tbsp milk

2 tbsp olive oil

1 tbsp fresh lemon juice

¼ tsp dried oregano

¼ tsp kosher salt

I'm a modern girl. I like shiny, clean, new things. So, when Lisa suggested a quinoa (pronounced KEEN-wah) recipe, I balked. I mean, this ancient seed is older than Peru. And then I did a bit of digging. It was also considered "the gold of the Incas." I like gold. It increased the stamina of warriors. I like stamina. It's a "superfood," packed with protein, fiber and trillions of amino acids. I like trillions. As a result of my findings I gave these fantastically flavorful quinoa-stuffed rice-paper wraps a try and discovered that, yes indeed, much like 5,000-year-old quinoa, Lisa still has some value around here. Good job, relic.

DIRECTIONS

1) Place quinoa in a fine mesh sieve and rinse under cold water to remove the bitter outer coating. Shake to drain. In a deep skillet, heat 1 tbsp olive oil over medium heat. Add quinoa, stirring constantly to lightly toast, about 6 minutes. Add 2 cups water and heat to a boil. Reduce heat to low, cover and simmer until the liquid is absorbed, 13–15 minutes. Set aside to cool. 2) While the quinoa is cooking, set oven to broil. Place red peppers on baking sheet skin side up and roast under broiler until skins are charred. Remove from oven and when cool enough to handle, peel skins and slice peppers into strips. Place in a large mixing bowl. Add cucumber, feta and parsley. 3) For the dressing, in a small bowl, whisk olive oil, lime juice, cumin, salt and sugar. Pour over roasted pepper and feta mixture. Stir in quinoa and marinate 15 minutes. 4) To assemble the wraps, place 1 rice paper sheet in a shallow bowl or pie plate of hot water until just softened, about 1 minute. Lay wet rice paper sheet on tea towel. Place 4 tbsp quinoa salad in the middle of the wrap. Fold up the bottom of the rice paper placing it over the filling. Fold in the right side, followed by the left side and then the top, forming a tight cylinder. Repeat with remaining rice paper sheets and filling. Place finished wraps under a damp cloth to prevent them from hardening until ready to serve. 5) For the feta dip, in a blender, combine feta, sour cream, milk, olive oil, lemon juice, oregano and salt. Blend until well combined. Dip can be made ahead and refrigerated. Serve with quinoa wraps.

Yield: 16 large quinoa wraps

CHEESY CHICKEN QUESADILLAS

INGREDIENTS

1 tbsp olive oil

2 boneless skinless chicken breast halves, thinly sliced

½ tsp kosher salt

¼ tsp freshly ground black pepper

Vegetable Filling

1 tbsp olive oil

1 large red onion, halved and thinly sliced

1 large green pepper, diced

1 large red bell pepper, diced

1½ cups salsa

1 tbsp fresh lime juice

1 tsp ground cumin

1 tsp chili powder

¼ tsp kosher salt

8 (10-inch) flour tortillas

2 cups shredded Mexican blend cheese

Do cocktail parties make you sweat? Do you find people looking for escape routes as you prattle on about the weather and Slippers, your Siamese cat? Well, we're here to help make you a mingling maven. First, don't start conversations with "A priest, rabbi and leprechaun walk into a bar..." Second, lose the bone-crusher, limp fish or fingers-only handshakes. Finally, whip up a batch of these saucy, cheesy and zesty toasted tortilla triangles. One bite and you'll instantly be elevated to life-of-the-party. Just ask Lampshade Lisa.

DIRECTIONS

1) For the chicken, in a small skillet, heat 1 tbsp olive oil over medium-high heat. Add sliced chicken and season with salt and pepper. Cook 4–6 minutes or until cooked through. Set aside.
2) For the vegetable filling, in a large skillet, heat 1 tbsp olive oil over medium heat. Add onions and cook until softened, 3–4 minutes. Add diced green and red peppers, salsa, lime juice, cumin, chili powder, salt and cooked chicken. Cover over low heat for 10 minutes, stirring occasionally. **3)** To assemble quesadillas, heat a large skillet over medium heat. Coat with non-stick cooking spray and place 1 tortilla in the bottom of the pan, add ½ cup cheese and then a heaping ½ cup of the chicken mixture. Cover with a second tortilla. Cook until the tortilla starts to brown, about 2 minutes. Flip and cook 2 minutes more. Remove from pan and slice into 6 wedges. Repeat with remaining tortillas. Serve warm with sour cream and guacamole, if desired.

Yield: 48 small wedges

BITE ME BIT

"She's afraid that if she leaves, she'll become the life of the party."

— Groucho Marx, comedian

EGGPLANT & BUTTERNUT SQUASH BRUSCHETTA

INGREDIENTS

Toasted Garlic Bread

25 slices of French bread, ½ inch thick

3 tbsp olive oil

1 large garlic clove

¼ tsp kosher salt

Eggplant & Butternut Squash Topping

2 tbsp olive oil

1 small red onion, diced

2 cups diced, unpeeled eggplant

2 cups diced butternut squash

1 large garlic clove, minced

1 tbsp balsamic vinegar

1 tsp honey

¼ tsp kosher salt

¼ tsp freshly ground black pepper

1 cup ricotta cheese

We all know what not to bring a hostess: fresh-cut flowers, a bathroom scale, a re-gifted plastic pink flamingo. However, as the hostess, do you know what, apart from refills, you can give your guests? How about that welcoming, warm-and-fuzzy feeling that comes with delicious eats? This bruschetta will do all the work for you. Crusty French bread is rubbed with garlic, toasted and then topped with smooth, creamy ricotta and a chunky mixture of caramelized eggplant and butternut squash. Easily prepared in advance and assembled just before guests arrive, nothing says "gracious gourmet" more than a tray of these tasty bruschetta.

DIRECTIONS

1) Preheat oven to 400ºF. Place bread slices on a non-stick baking sheet. Brush one side with olive oil. Cut the garlic clove in half and rub the cut half on the oiled bread. Sprinkle bread slices evenly with salt. Bake 4 minutes, flip slices and bake 3 minutes more. Remove from oven and set aside. 2) For the topping, in a large skillet, heat olive oil over medium heat. Add onions, cooking for 2 minutes. Add eggplant and butternut squash, continuing to cook for 8 minutes, stirring frequently. Add garlic and continue cooking for 30 seconds. Add balsamic vinegar, honey, salt and pepper, cooking 2 minutes more. Remove from heat. 3) To assemble, spread each toasted slice of bread with a spoonful of ricotta cheese topped with eggplant/butternut squash mixture. Serve immediately.

Yield: 25 pieces

BITE ME BIT

"We were not allowed to say 'screw,' but we could say 'hump the hostess,' because 'hump' is in Shakespeare."

— Uta Hagen, actress

MINI MEATBALL SUBS

INGREDIENTS

Tomato Sauce

1 tbsp olive oil

1 large red onion, finely chopped

½ tsp kosher salt

¼ tsp freshly ground black pepper

1 large garlic clove, minced

1 (28oz) tin crushed tomatoes

1 (28oz) tin diced tomatoes

¼ tsp dried oregano

Meatballs

3 slices white bread, crust removed, torn into bite-sized pieces

½ cup milk

1¼ cups ground beef

1 large garlic clove, minced

1 large egg

½ cup freshly grated Parmesan cheese

2 tbsp chopped fresh basil

½ tsp kosher salt

½ tsp freshly ground black pepper

20 small dinner rolls/buns

1 cup shredded mozzarella cheese

½ cup freshly grated Parmesan cheese

There are so many promises made in cookbooks, with "yummy," "moist" and "easy" at the top of the list. Well, our mom says we can't lie, so here's the straight dope — these yummy, moist and easy mini meatball sandwiches are kid-sized bites that will satisfy the biggest appetites. After being simmered in homemade tomato sauce, flavorful meatballs are placed on small buns, covered in cheese and baked until bubbly. No empty promises here…just emptied platters.

P.S. Make a double batch of meatballs, freeze them and you've got a delicious dinner. We pinky swear.

DIRECTIONS

1) For the tomato sauce, in a large saucepan, heat olive oil over medium heat. Add onion, salt and pepper, cooking 5 minutes until softened. Add garlic and cook 30 seconds stirring constantly. Add tin of crushed tomatoes, tin of diced tomatoes and oregano. Turn heat to low and simmer 15 minutes. 2) For the meatballs, in a medium bowl, combine bread and milk, letting it stand for a few minutes. Add ground beef, garlic, egg, Parmesan, basil, salt and pepper. Mix with hands, just until combined. Roll mixture into about 20 meatballs the size of golf balls. Drop meatballs into prepared sauce and bring to a gentle simmer over medium-low heat for 30 minutes, until meatballs are cooked through. 3) To assemble the meatball subs, preheat oven to 400°F. Line a baking sheet with aluminum foil and coat with non-stick cooking spray. Arrange rolls on tray with the cut side up. Place 1 meatball on half of each roll, add a spoonful of sauce on top of the meatball and a tablespoon of mozzarella cheese. On the other half of the bun, put a small spoonful of sauce and 1 tsp of Parmesan cheese. Repeat with remaining meatballs. Bake 3 minutes or until cheese melts. Sandwich together and serve.

Yield: 20 mini meatball subs

BITE ME BIT

"I'm not smart enough to lie."

— Ronald Reagan, 40th President of the United States

Stock me

Addictively Steamy Soups

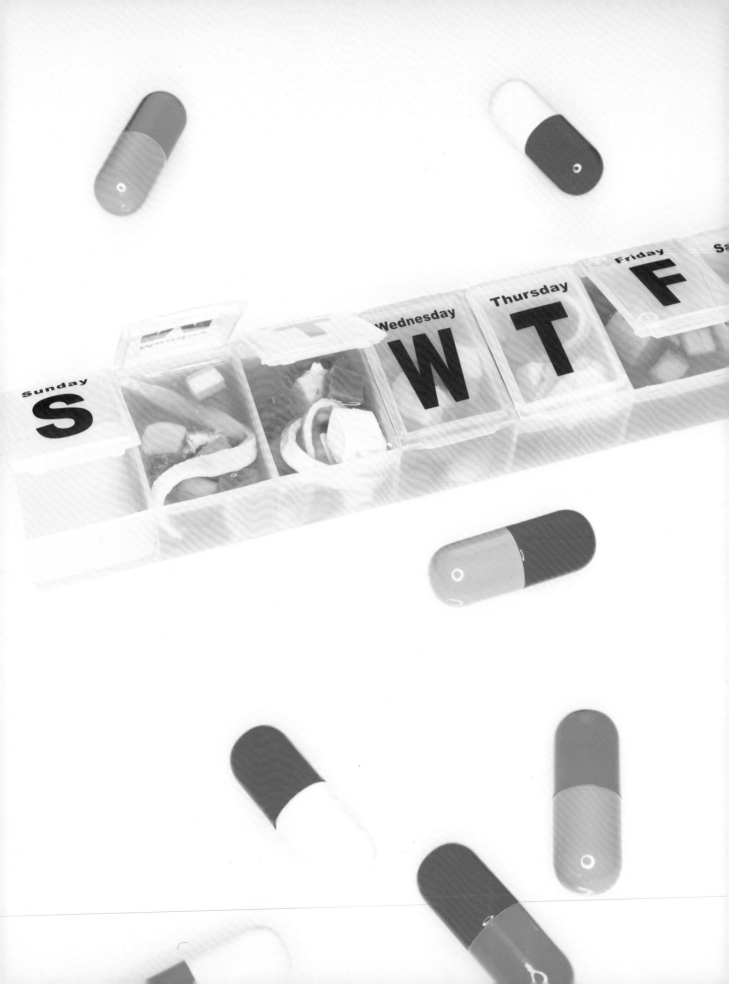

CURATIVE & CALMING CHICKEN NOODLE SOUP

INGREDIENTS

Homemade Noodles

1 cup flour

½ tsp kosher salt

2 large eggs

extra flour,
for kneading and rolling

Chicken Soup

1 (4 lb) whole chicken,
cut into 8 pieces

8 cups water

8 cups chicken broth

1 large white onion,
quartered

3 large carrots,
peeled and cut
into 2-inch pieces

2 large celery stalks, cut into
2-inch pieces

2 large garlic cloves, smashed

6 whole black peppercorns

½ cup fresh dill,
lightly packed

½ cup fresh flat-leaf parsley,
lightly packed

1 tsp dried thyme

1 tsp kosher salt

Over a decade ago, Lisa and I did yoga videos together in my living room. For many reasons this was futile (I'd talk to her the entire time), but there was one phrase we heard over and over and continue to repeat. "Fake it 'til you make it," said the bare-chested, bandana-wearing yogi Baron Baptiste. We've taken that lesson to heart – this chicken soup tastes like the it-took-all-day real McCoy, but it's full of shortcuts that allow you to whip together steamy, soul-saving soup at a moment's notice. With homemade noodles, you're adding an extra great touch to a flavorful, comforting soup already chock full of chunky chicken, carrots and celery. Who knew a bowl of heart-warming soup would lead us on a path to enlightenment, no sweat required?

DIRECTIONS

1) For the noodles, in a large bowl, combine flour and salt. Make a hole in the center and crack eggs into it. Using a fork, beat the eggs and gradually incorporate the flour. Turn dough out onto a well-floured surface and knead until smooth and no longer sticky. Divide dough in 2, wrap each half well with plastic wrap and refrigerate 30 minutes. 2) While the dough chills, in a large pot, combine chicken, water, chicken broth, onion, carrots, celery, garlic, peppercorns, dill, parsley, thyme and salt. Bring to a boil over high heat. Reduce to a gentle simmer for 1 hour. Skim soup if necessary during that time. 3) While the soup simmers, prepare the noodles. When ready to roll out the dough, work with one half at a time. On a floured surface, roll out as thin as possible. Be sure to move the dough between rolls to keep it from sticking, dusting with more flour if necessary. Using a sharp knife or pizza cutter cut dough into desired noodle length. Noodles can be cooked immediately or allowed to air dry on a cooling rack. When ready to cook, bring a large pot of lightly salted water to a boil. Add noodles, cooking 1–2 minutes. Drain and set aside. 4) Once the soup has finished cooking, remove chicken, carrots and celery and cut into bite-sized pieces. Into a large serving bowl, strain the remaining soup through a fine mesh sieve. Add cut-up chicken, carrots, celery and cooked noodles to soup.

Serves 10

POTATO LEEK SOUP with CROUTON CRUMBLE

INGREDIENTS

Crouton Crumble

3½ cups French bread cubes

2 tbsp olive oil

2 tbsp butter

1 tsp fresh thyme

½ tsp kosher salt

¼ tsp freshly ground black pepper

Potato Leek Soup

2 tbsp butter

2 cups chopped leeks, white and light-green parts only, washed well

1 large carrot, peeled and chopped

1 large garlic clove, minced

½ tsp kosher salt

¼ tsp freshly ground black pepper

2 fresh thyme sprigs

pinch cayenne pepper

4 cups peeled and diced Yukon Gold potatoes

4½ cups chicken broth

Big announcement. Lisa is a prospector and this is the beginning of the 21st century gold rush. This soup is liquid Au, atomic number 79, 24K, baby…buttery Yukon Gold potatoes are blended with flavorful leeks – a treasure trove in your bowl. What makes this smooth soup so precious? It's simple to make and satisfying enough to be a meal in and of itself. The sweet and savory flavor of leeks pairs perfectly with mild potatoes, and the hearty soup is topped with golden nuggets of toasted, crunchy French bread. Folks, if I can give you any advice, it's to always put your money on Lisa – she strikes it rich every time.

DIRECTIONS

1) For the crouton crumble, place the bread cubes in a food processor and pulse until the bread is pea-sized. In a medium skillet, heat olive oil and butter over medium heat. Add the breadcrumbs, thyme, salt and pepper. Cook 6–8 minutes stirring continuously until toasted. Remove from heat and set aside. 2) For the soup, in a large soup pot, heat the butter over medium heat. Add leeks and sauté for 4 minutes stirring often so leeks don't burn. Add carrots, garlic, salt, pepper, thyme and cayenne, cooking 2 minutes. Add potatoes and chicken broth, bringing to a boil over high heat. Reduce heat to low and simmer 15 minutes or until potatoes are tender. Remove from heat and discard thyme sprigs. Using a handheld or countertop blender, puree soup. Serve each bowl with crouton crumble over top.

Serves 4

BITE ME BIT

"Yellow-colored objects appear to be gold."

— Aristotle, philosopher

CAPTIVATING CARROT & PARSNIP SOUP

INGREDIENTS

2 tbsp butter

2 cups peeled and chopped parsnips

2 cups peeled and chopped carrots

1 large yellow onion, chopped

1 large garlic clove, minced

1 tbsp finely chopped fresh oregano

½ tsp kosher salt

¼ tsp freshly ground black pepper

4 cups vegetable broth

1 tsp fresh lemon juice

1 tsp soy sauce

At first, I felt kind of sorry for this soup. It isn't distinguished by having a fancy, hard-to-spell name like bouillabaisse or vichyssoise. It isn't known for being fattening or geographically significant like New England chowder, for being cold like gazpacho or for being labor intensive like duck consommé. No, carrot and parsnip soup isn't any of those things. Instead, it's quietly superior, thick enough to warm you to your toes but light enough to come before the main course. It's fresh in flavor, sweet carrots complemented by slightly spicy but equally sweet parsnips, delivering a soup rich in vitamins and minerals. Yes, this delicious, comforting carrot and parsnip soup is easy to make, a joy to eat and a breeze to spell.

DIRECTIONS

1) In a medium soup pot, melt butter over medium heat. Add parsnips, carrots and onions stirring occasionally for 10 minutes. Stir in garlic, oregano, salt and pepper, cooking an additional 10 minutes, until the entire mixture starts to brown and soften. Add vegetable broth and bring to a boil over high heat. Lower heat and simmer 20 minutes. Remove pot from burner and allow to cool slightly before blending. Using a handheld or countertop blender, puree soup to the desired consistency. Stir in lemon juice and soy sauce.

Serves 4–6

TOMATO, BASIL & COUSCOUS SOUP

INGREDIENTS

1 tbsp olive oil

1 tbsp butter

1 medium yellow onion, diced

1 large garlic clove, minced

2 tbsp flour

3 cups vegetable broth

1 (28oz) tin whole tomatoes, pureed with juices in food processor

2 tsp sugar

2 fresh thyme sprigs

¼ tsp kosher salt

¼ tsp freshly ground black pepper

1 cup Israeli couscous, uncooked

1¼ cups water

2 tbsp thinly sliced fresh basil

2 tbsp freshly grated Parmesan cheese

1 tbsp butter

It's cold, you're tired and soup is all you want right now. Before you reach for a can of preservative-, fat- and sugar-laden (sounds appetizing, huh?) soup, know that in just over 30 minutes, you can have a steaming bowl of healthy, homemade tomato greatness ready and waiting. Easy to make, this comforting tomato soup is flavored with onions, garlic, thyme, basil and Parmesan, pureed to a creamy (yet creamless) consistency. For an even more satisfying soup, Israeli couscous (plump pearls of toasted pasta) is added to fill you up and lend a chewy bite to your slurp. Soup's on!

DIRECTIONS

1) In a large soup pot, heat olive oil and butter over medium heat. Add the onions and cook 4 minutes, stirring often. Add garlic, cooking 30 seconds. Stir in the flour to coat the onion mixture, cooking 30 seconds more. Add vegetable broth, pureed tomatoes, sugar, thyme sprigs, salt and pepper. Bring to a boil, reduce heat to low and simmer covered for 30 minutes. 2) For the couscous, in a small saucepan, bring 1¼ cups water to a boil over high heat. Stir in couscous, reduce heat to low, cover and let simmer 8 minutes, stirring occasionally. Remove from heat and set aside. 3) When the soup is finished cooking, remove the thyme sprigs. Using a handheld or countertop blender, puree soup until smooth. Return to soup pot, stir in cooked couscous, basil, Parmesan and butter, reheating over low heat.

Serves 6

BITE ME BIT

"Couscous. The food's so nice, they named it twice."

— Dale Denton (actor Seth Rogen) in the 2008 movie Pineapple Express

FRESH CORN CHOWDER with CHEDDAR CRISPS

INGREDIENTS

Corn Chowder

6 ears fresh corn, shucked

6 cups water

1 tsp kosher salt

2 tbsp olive oil

1 medium yellow onion, diced

2 small garlic cloves, minced

2 medium carrots, peeled and diced

2 celery stalks, diced

1 medium red potato, peeled and diced

2 tsp chopped fresh thyme

½ tsp kosher salt

¼ tsp freshly ground black pepper

pinch cayenne pepper, optional

2 tbsp chopped fresh basil

Cheddar Crisps

1 cup grated sharp cheddar cheese

We are children of the corn. No, not Stephen King's murderous minors (a story that still haunts me), but instead, two girls who spent summers running between rows of corn in the fields. OK. Not really running between, but Lisa once had cornrows and it was super-funny. Truth is, we really did get our corn straight from the farmer's field and that was the inspiration for this full-flavored soup bursting with tender, sweet kernels. One spoonful and you'll quickly discover the beauty of the cob – a soup that is buttery and creamy without any butter or cream, a broth that relies solely on marvelous maize. If that's not Field-of-Dreams-ish enough for you, top a steaming bowl with these simple, one-ingredient lacey cheddar crisps. If you make it…they will devour it…

DIRECTIONS

1) For the soup, cut kernels off cobs and place in large bowl. Pull out 1 cup of corn and reserve for after pureeing the soup. Place the corncobs in a large soup pot with 6 cups water and 1 tsp salt. Bring to boil over high heat. Reduce heat to low, cover and simmer 30 minutes, occasionally stirring cobs. Discard cobs and strain corn broth into a large bowl. Set aside. 2) In a large soup pot, heat olive oil over medium-high heat. Stir in onion, cooking 3 minutes until softened. Add garlic, cooking 30 seconds. Reduce heat to medium-low, add carrots and celery and cook stirring occasionally, 4–5 minutes, until vegetables are tender. Add potatoes, thyme, salt, pepper and cayenne (if using), stirring well to combine. Add reserved corn broth and bring to a boil over high heat. Reduce heat to low, cover and simmer 20 minutes. Add only the corn from the large bowl, simmering an additional 10 minutes. Remove from heat and using a handheld or countertop blender, puree until desired consistency. Stir in 1 cup reserved corn and chopped basil. 3) For the cheddar crisps, preheat oven to 400°F. Line a baking sheet with parchment paper. Sprinkle cheddar in an even layer over parchment. Bake 8–10 minutes, until cheese starts browning and bubbling. Remove from oven, let cool and then break into uneven pieces to top soup.

Serves 4–6

Check out the world's best shucker

BUTTERNUT SQUASH SOUP with PARMESAN SAGE CROUTONS

INGREDIENTS

Butternut Squash Soup

1 (2 lb) butternut squash, peeled, seeded and cut into 1-inch chunks

2 tbsp olive oil

½ tsp kosher salt

¼ tsp freshly ground black pepper

1 tbsp olive oil

1 cup diced yellow onion

1 cup peeled and diced carrots

1 cup diced celery

2 tbsp finely chopped shallots

2 large garlic cloves, minced

1 tsp chopped fresh sage

1 tbsp apple cider vinegar

6 cups chicken broth

1 tbsp maple syrup

Parmesan Sage Croutons

3 thick slices rustic white bread

3 tbsp olive oil

2 tbsp freshly grated Parmesan cheese

1 small garlic clove, minced

2 tsp finely chopped fresh sage

½ tsp kosher salt

I was tired of butternut squash soup either teeming with cream or lacking in flavor. How to supercharge my soup? Easy. I turned to Lisa and said, "Yo Dawg, Pimp My Soup." And soup it up she did. First, the expert roasted the squash to bring out the sweetness and add depth of flavor. Second, she restored the health benefits of butternut squash by omitting fats, yet created a creamy and velvety-textured soup. Finally, the master brought sage to the party. Earthy in flavor, this herb worked beautifully in the silky soup and also atop the crunchy Parmesan croutons. Well done, Li'l Lee, well done.

DIRECTIONS

1) For the soup, preheat oven to 425ºF. Line a baking sheet with parchment paper. In a large bowl, toss butternut squash with 2 tbsp olive oil, salt and pepper. Pour onto prepared baking sheet and roast 25 minutes until very tender and lightly caramelized. Remove from oven and set aside. 2) In a large soup pot, heat 1 tbsp oil over medium heat. Add onions, carrots and celery, cooking until vegetables are softened, about 8 minutes. Add shallots, garlic and sage, stirring constantly for 1 minute. Add vinegar, stirring for 30 seconds. Stir in chicken broth, maple syrup and roasted squash. Over high heat, bring to a boil. Reduce heat to low and simmer for 15 minutes. Remove from heat and using a handheld or countertop blender, puree until smooth. Season to taste with salt and pepper. 3) For the croutons, preheat oven to 375ºF. Tear bread into pieces, about 1-inch each. In a large bowl, toss torn bread with olive oil, Parmesan, garlic, sage and salt. Spread in a single layer on a baking sheet and toast in the oven 10–12 minutes, until golden. Serve atop soup.

Serves 6

CHUNKY VEGETABLE BARLEY SOUP

INGREDIENTS

½ cup pearl barley, rinsed and drained

4 sprigs fresh thyme

4 sprigs fresh flat-leaf parsley

1 tbsp olive oil

1 medium yellow onion, chopped

2 small white potatoes, peeled and cut into small chunks

1 cup peeled and chopped carrots

½ cup chopped celery

1 large garlic clove, minced

¼ tsp kosher salt

¼ tsp freshly ground black pepper

8 cups vegetable broth

1 Parmesan rind, 2-inch piece

1 tbsp fresh lemon juice

freshly grated Parmesan cheese, for serving

How many bowls of vegetable soup have left you disappointed, sipping dull-as-dishwater broth speckled with bits and bobs of sad looking vegetables? I'm thrilled to let you know that those disenchanted days are behind you. This vegetable barley soup is a filling and flavorful bowl of steamy surprise. Loaded with chunky potatoes, carrots and celery, this soup also offers up pearl barley, a tender, nutty-flavored gem of a grain. If that doesn't restore your faith, the broth definitely will. Along with fragrant garlic, thyme and parsley, we put the Parmesan rind to great use, dramatically boosting the broth by adding a richness, creaminess and slight saltiness. Yes, spoon after spoon, you'll love how this soup magically "pops." Happy days are here again.

DIRECTIONS

1) Place the barley in a medium heatproof bowl and cover with boiling water. Leave to soak while vegetables are being prepared. 2) Tie thyme and parsley sprigs together using kitchen string or a few of the thyme stems. Set aside. 3) In a large soup pot, heat olive oil over medium heat. Add onions and cook to soften, about 3 minutes. Add potato, carrots, celery, garlic, salt and pepper. Stir frequently and cook until vegetables begin to soften, about 5 minutes. Add vegetable broth, thyme/parsley bundle and Parmesan rind. Bring to a boil over high heat. Reduce heat to low, add barley and simmer 20 minutes. Remove from heat and discard herb bundle and Parmesan rind. 4) Using a blender, puree 3 cups of the soup until smooth. Return to remaining soup along with lemon juice. Season with salt and pepper to taste and top each serving with Parmesan cheese.

Serves 6–8

BITE ME BIT

"I am a kind of paranoiac in reverse. I suspect people of plotting to make me happy."

– J.D. Salinger, author

STUNNING SPLIT PEA SOUP with FRESH DILL

INGREDIENTS

1 tbsp olive oil

1 large yellow onion, diced

2 large carrots, peeled and diced

1 large celery stalk, diced

1 large garlic clove, minced

2 tsp chopped fresh dill

½ tsp kosher salt

¼ tsp freshly ground black pepper

5½ cups vegetable broth

1½ cups green split peas

¼ cup sour cream

2 tbsp chopped fresh dill

Split pea soup is like oysters, octopus and mushrooms. Not seeing the link? Take a closer look. These foods won't win any beauty contests, but boy do they taste great. Though I'm a stickler for aesthetics, when it comes to my stomach, beautiful isn't always best (read: wedding cake). In the case of this homely soup, I'm awarding it the sparkling tiara and glittery sash – every bowl of this hearty, comforting vegetarian soup of split peas, carrots, onion and celery, laced with fresh dill and topped with a dollop of sour cream, is a pageant queen, swimsuit competition be damned.

DIRECTIONS

1) In a large soup pot, heat olive oil over medium-high heat. Add onions, carrots and celery, stirring frequently and sautéing until softened, about 5 minutes. Stir in garlic, dill, salt and pepper, cooking for 1 minute. Add vegetable broth and green split peas. Bring to a boil over high heat. Reduce heat to low and simmer covered for 1 hour, stirring often. Transfer mixture to a food processor or countertop blender and pulse until smooth. Return to pot and heat until hot. If soup becomes too thick, add stock or water as necessary. 2) To serve, in a small bowl, combine sour cream and 2 tbsp dill. Serve a dollop over each bowl of soup.

Serves 6

PASTA FAGIOLI SOUP

INGREDIENTS

2 tbsp olive oil

1 medium white onion, coarsely chopped

2 large carrots, peeled and coarsely chopped

1 large garlic clove, minced

6 cups chicken broth

1 (28oz) tin diced tomatoes

¾ cup dry pasta (small shape, such as mini shells macaroni)

1½ cups canned white kidney (cannellini) beans, rinsed and drained

1½ cups canned chickpeas, rinsed and drained

¼ cup freshly grated Parmesan cheese

2 tbsp finely chopped fresh basil

½ tsp kosher salt

¼ tsp freshly ground black pepper

Lisa can be willful. It's a fact. I have proof. Did you see bean recipes in the last book? Not a one, and don't think it wasn't for my lack of trying. Picture me on hands and knees, begging for a three-bean salad and bargaining for some baked beans – it was pointless because either she was legumaphobic or flat-out stubborn. Undeterred, I continued my campaign for BITE ME beans and was rewarded with this Pasta FaJulie, a hearty soup of pasta, beans and vegetables. I adore this Italian classic and with every scrumptious, heartwarming spoonful, I'm reminded that the Bean Battle was worth every scrap and skirmish.

DIRECTIONS

1) In a large soup pot, heat olive oil over medium heat. Add onions and carrots, cook 5 minutes to soften, stirring occasionally. Add garlic, stirring for 1 minute. Add chicken broth and tin of diced tomatoes with their juices. Bring to a boil over high heat. Reduce heat to low and simmer, partially covered, for 20 minutes. **2)** Meanwhile, in a small saucepan, cook pasta according to package directions. Drain and set aside. **3)** After soup has cooked for 20 minutes add white kidney beans and chickpeas, simmering partially covered for 10 minutes. **4)** Remove 2 cups of bean soup and place in food processor. Puree, return to soup pot and bring to a boil over high heat. Add cooked pasta, Parmesan, basil, salt and pepper, simmering 5 minutes. Serve with additional Parmesan cheese.

Serves 6

BITE ME BIT

"Just once I'd like someone to call me 'Sir' without adding, 'you're making a scene.'"

— Homer Simpson, patriarch, *The Simpsons*

CANNELLINI & KALE RIBOLLITA

INGREDIENTS

2 tbsp olive oil

1 medium yellow onion, chopped

1 large carrot, peeled and diced

1 large garlic clove, minced

¼ tsp kosher salt

¼ tsp freshly ground black pepper

1 tbsp tomato paste

½ cup dry white wine

1 (28oz) tin diced tomatoes

1½ cups canned white kidney (cannellini) beans, rinsed and drained

½ tsp dried Italian seasoning

4 cups chicken broth

1 (2-inch) piece Parmesan rind

3 cups chopped fresh kale, loosely packed, stems removed

1 tbsp chopped fresh basil

8 slices French bread, ½ inch thick

1 tbsp olive oil

Authentic Ribollita takes 3 days to make. We're all for authenticity, but we've taken some shortcuts with this classic Tuscan vegetable soup. Historically, Ribollita was considered a "peasant meal," a stew-like soup created to use up leftover minestrone soup and stale bread. The aristocrats didn't know what they were missing – this thick and hearty country soup is loaded with white beans, leafy greens, tomatoes and garlic, all poured atop crusty bread. All it takes is one hour for Lisa to make everyone feel very prosperous with this rich, luscious soup.

DIRECTIONS

1) In a large soup pot, heat olive oil over medium heat. Add onions and carrots, sautéing 5 minutes, stirring often. Add garlic, salt, pepper and tomato paste stirring for 30 seconds. Add white wine and continue cooking for 1 minute. Stir in diced tomatoes, white beans, Italian seasoning, chicken broth and Parmesan rind. Bring soup to a boil over high heat, reduce heat to low and stir in kale. Simmer uncovered for 25 minutes. Remove from heat and stir in chopped basil. **2)** Just before serving, preheat oven to 350°F. Brush French bread slices with 1 tbsp olive oil. Place on a baking sheet and bake slices 6 minutes, turn them and bake another 6 minutes, until beginning to brown. Place 2 slices of toast on the bottom of each bowl. Ladle soup over top and serve immediately.

Serves 4

ADAM'S AFRICAN SWEET POTATO SOUP

INGREDIENTS

2 tbsp olive oil

1 large white onion, diced

1 large garlic clove, minced

1 (1-inch) piece fresh ginger, grated

7 cups vegetable broth

2 large sweet potatoes, peeled and diced

2 large carrots, peeled and diced

1 (5.5oz) tin tomato paste

2 tbsp smooth peanut butter

1 tbsp chili powder

1 tsp kosher salt

⅛ tsp cayenne pepper

Lisa suffers from acute hairanoia. A serial chair-hopper who is suspicious of anyone who snips her tresses, she changes stylists and styles regularly. That said, it's a great surprise Lisa got, in addition to an excellent cut, this nutty sweet potato soup from a dear, departed stylist named Adam. A satisfying vegetarian soup, chock full of nutrients and warm spices, it's clear that if Adam cut as well as he cooked, he was worth sitting still for.

DIRECTIONS

1) In a large soup pot, heat olive oil over medium heat. Add onions, garlic and ginger, cooking 3–4 minutes to soften, but not brown.

2) Add vegetable broth, sweet potatoes, carrots, tomato paste, peanut butter, chili powder, salt and cayenne pepper. Bring to a boil over high heat. Reduce heat to low and simmer uncovered 30 minutes. Remove from heat and using a handheld or countertop blender puree until smooth.

Serves 4–6

BITE ME BIT

"I'm undaunted in my quest to amuse myself by constantly changing my hair."

— Hillary Rodham Clinton, U.S. Secretary of State

VIETNAMESE VEGETABLE & TOFU PHO

INGREDIENTS

Pho Vegetable Broth

9 cups vegetable broth

2 large celery stalks, roughly chopped

1 large carrot, peeled and roughly chopped

4 large shallots, peeled and roughly chopped

3 small garlic cloves, chopped

1 (1-inch) piece of fresh ginger, peeled and chopped

1 tbsp soy sauce

1 cinnamon stick

1 dried bay leaf

2 tsp coriander seeds

2 tsp cumin seeds

1 tsp anise seed

½ cup chopped fresh flat-leaf parsley, including stems

1 lb dried rice noodles, medium width

1 cup firm tofu, patted dry and sliced into 3-inch long, ½-inch thick pieces

2 cups bean sprouts

2 cups shredded napa cabbage

6 fresh basil leaves, cut into thin strips

1 lime, cut into 6 wedges

Before this recipe, I suffered from pho phobia. Not only did I say it wrong (it's pronounced "fah," not "foe"), but I also couldn't fathom how we'd bring Vietnam's national dish into our kitchens, how we'd do justice to this incredibly aromatic, flavorful and restorative treasure. Well, good thing I've got the Pho Queen (better than being the "Pho King"...say it fast and you'll know what I mean) on my side. After much research, spooning and slurping, Lisa has done it, replicating the steamy meal-in-a-bowl. Light yet filling, the soup teems with vegetables, tofu and rice noodles, all in an ambrosial broth infused with garlic, ginger, coriander, cinnamon and anise. Nothing to fear here – this easy-to-make soup is pho-freakin'-nominal.

DIRECTIONS

1) In a large soup pot, bring vegetable broth, celery and carrots to a boil over medium heat. Add shallots, garlic, ginger, soy sauce, cinnamon stick, bay leaf, coriander seeds, cumin seeds, anise seed and flat-leaf parsley. Reduce heat to low and simmer covered for 45 minutes. 2) While the broth is cooking, bring a large pot of water to a boil over high heat. Add noodles and cook 3 minutes. Drain and divide among 6 bowls. 3) For the tofu, heat a medium, non-stick skillet over high heat. Add tofu slices and cook 2 minutes, flip slices and cook 1 minute more, until golden brown. Remove from heat and set aside. 4) When the broth is ready, strain through a fine mesh sieve. Discard solids and return broth to pot, keeping hot until ready to serve. 5) To assemble each bowl, arrange bean sprouts, napa cabbage and tofu over noodles. Ladle hot broth over top, sprinkle with fresh basil and serve with lime wedge.

Serves 6

SAVORY BEEF & BARLEY SOUP

INGREDIENTS

1 tbsp olive oil

2 lbs stewing beef, cut into ¾-inch cubes, patted dry

¼ tsp freshly ground black pepper

1 medium yellow onion, chopped

2 large garlic cloves, minced

¼ cup chopped fresh flat-leaf parsley

1 tbsp chopped fresh thyme

1 cup dry red wine

2 cups peeled and sliced carrots

2 cups chopped celery

10 cups beef broth

2 cups water

1 cup pearl barley, rinsed and drained

Sophocles knew a thing or two about family (think: Oedipus) and food. The ancient Greek playwright had a philosophy when it came to what constituted a modern diet: bread, meat, vegetables and beer. Well, we think the tragedian would have jumped for joy had he had a bowl of this stick-to-your-ribs soup, chock full of tender beef, sweet vegetables and, of course, barley, the nutty-flavored base for beer. In a dark, rich broth, cubes of beef are simmered for hours, mingling with flavorful carrots, celery and pasta-like, fiber-rich pearl barley. We're pretty sure after dunking a crusty piece of bread in this hit-the-spot soup, the 5th-century BCE innovator would have stopped being such a downer and written a comedy or two.

DIRECTIONS

1) In a large soup pot, heat olive oil over medium heat. Add beef and brown in 2 batches if the pot isn't large enough to avoid crowding. Season with pepper and cook 5 minutes until beef is nicely browned on all sides. Stir in onions, garlic, parsley and thyme. Increase heat to medium-high and continue to cook for 3 minutes. Add wine, stir well and let wine reduce for 4 minutes. Stir in carrots, celery, broth and water. Bring to a boil over high heat, reduce heat to low and let simmer uncovered for 45 minutes. Add barley and continue cooking covered on low heat for 45 minutes more, until barley is tender. Serve with crusty bread for dunking.

Serves 8–10

WILD MUSHROOM SOUP

INGREDIENTS

1 (0.5oz/14g) package dried porcini mushrooms

2 cups boiling water

1 tbsp olive oil

1 tbsp butter

2 large garlic cloves, minced

1 medium yellow onion, diced

9 cups thinly sliced mushrooms (mixture of button, cremini, shiitake, chanterelle)

¼ cup chopped fresh flat-leaf parsley

1 tsp chopped fresh thyme

½ tsp kosher salt

¼ tsp freshly ground black pepper

1½ cups peeled and diced Yukon Gold potato

2½ cups chicken broth

Lisa and I always laugh when we watch *Dirty Dancing*, most of all when Baby screams to Johnny "You're WILD!" You've got to watch it – it's hi-lar. Anyway, when Lee gave me a bowl of this mixed mushroom soup, I was sure to tell her that she's WILD! I mean, who else could take a traditionally cream and butter-based wreck-of-a-soup and turn it into creamless, intensely flavored mushroom magic? Thickened with Yukon Gold potato, a mixture of dried porcini and fresh wild mushrooms deliver woodsy, earthy flavor to this pureed soup. No one puts mushrooms in the corner.

DIRECTIONS

1) Place dried porcini mushrooms in a medium bowl and cover with 2 cups boiling water. Let soak 20 minutes. Line a strainer with paper towel and drain mushroom liquid into a small bowl, reserving liquid. Rinse porcinis well, pat dry and chop, discarding any hard stems.
2) In a large soup pot, heat olive oil and butter over medium heat. Add garlic and onions, cooking 5 minutes, until onion is softened. Increase heat to high and add both dried mushrooms and mixed fresh mushrooms. Stir in parsley, thyme, salt and pepper, cooking 2 minutes. Add diced potato, reserved mushroom liquid and chicken broth. Bring to a boil, reduce heat to low and simmer 20 minutes. Remove from heat and let cool slightly before pureeing. Using a handheld or countertop blender puree soup and return to pot to reheat. Serve.

Serves 4–6

BITE ME BIT

"If Harry Potter's so magical, why can't he cure his own eyesight and get laid?"

— Frankie Boyle, comedian

Toss me

Swoon-Worthy Salads

CLASSIC CHUNKY POTATO SALAD

INGREDIENTS

6 large (2½ lbs) red potatoes, peeled and cut in half

2 tbsp olive oil

2 tbsp apple cider vinegar

1 cup chopped celery

2 large eggs, hard-boiled and chopped

2 dill pickles, chopped

Creamy Dill Dressing

¾ cup mayonnaise

½ cup sour cream

2 tsp chopped fresh dill

1 tsp Dijon mustard

1 tsp kosher salt

¼ tsp freshly ground black pepper

I'm still mad at Gus Van Sant and Celine Dion. Why couldn't they leave well enough alone? Did the original *Psycho* really require a remake and how much did we need to hear Celine Dion cover AC/DC? I'll tell you…no and not at all. We like to let classics bask in all their perfection, so Lisa created this old-fashioned life's-a-picnic potato salad, chock full of cold chunky potatoes, chopped celery, eggs and pickles, all tossed in a creamy dill dressing. Jeez. Next thing you know, someone will try to mess with *Knots Landing*.

DIRECTIONS

1) In a large pot, cover potatoes with lightly salted cold water and bring to a boil over high heat. Turn down to medium and cook until tender, about 15 minutes. Drain potatoes, cut into bite-sized pieces and place in a large bowl. Toss warm potatoes with oil and vinegar, allowing to cool for 20 minutes. Add celery, eggs and pickles, mixing to combine. 2) For the dressing, in a small bowl, whisk mayonnaise, sour cream, dill, Dijon, salt and pepper. Gently stir into potato mixture. Cover and chill before serving.

Serves 6–8

BITE ME BIT

"According to my jar of pickles, there's a 24-hour pickle hotline. I guess that's if you got brine problems that just can't wait until morning."

— Tim Steeves, comedian

THE CHOP CHOP SALAD

INGREDIENTS

Creamy Dressing

1 large egg

1 cup mayonnaise

¼ cup Heinz chili sauce

2 tbsp ketchup

2 tbsp sweet green relish

1 tbsp chopped green onions

1 tbsp fresh lemon juice

¼ tsp kosher salt

¼ tsp freshly ground black pepper

Chop Chop Salad

6 cups coarsely chopped iceberg lettuce

4 large carrots, peeled and diced

4 large celery stalks, diced

3 cups broccoli florets, cut into small pieces

2 cups cherry tomatoes, halved

1 cup radishes, diced

Though I adore her, I nearly karate chopped Lisa over this salad. It all started when she handed me the recipe and said, "This is a chop chop salad." "What? What?" I responded. She wasn't amused, but then again, neither was I. How could I describe a salad that sounds like it was named by an echo? Well, here it goes. Grab your knife knife and get chopping chopping because this isn't just a chopped salad, it's a chop chop of garden fresh, crisp vegetables all cut into confetti-sized pieces and held together with a creamy creamy Russian-style dressing. Carrots, broccoli, celery, cherry tomatoes and radishes bring great crunch crunch and flavor flavor to this everything-but-the-kitchen-sink, delicious delicious chop chop salad.

DIRECTIONS

1) For the dressing, place the egg in a small saucepan and cover with cold water. Bring to a boil over medium-high heat. Once boiling, remove pan from heat, cover and let sit 10–12 minutes. Place egg in a bowl of ice water. Once cooled, peel and place in food processor. Add mayonnaise, chili sauce, ketchup, relish, green onions, lemon juice, salt and pepper. Pulse until pureed and smooth. Cover and refrigerate until ready to dress salad. 2) For the salad, in a large bowl, combine chopped lettuce, carrots, celery, broccoli, tomatoes and radishes. Toss with dressing and serve immediately.

Serves 8

GREEN BEAN, TOMATO & ARUGULA SALAD

INGREDIENTS

1 lb fresh green beans, ends trimmed

2 cups arugula, lightly packed

1 cup cherry tomatoes, halved

1 cup mini bocconcini balls

1 tbsp thinly sliced fresh basil

Balsamic Vinaigrette

3 tbsp olive oil

2 tbsp balsamic vinegar

½ tsp Dijon mustard

½ tsp sugar

¼ tsp freshly ground black pepper

Let's face it. On their own, string beans are the Stuart Sutcliffe (aka the lost Beatle) of the vegetable world – no glory and few headlines. However, mix this crunchy, fiber-rich green vegetable with peppery arugula, juicy cherry tomatoes and mini bocconcini bites and watch a snap-worthy, Top 10 hit "Come Together" on your plate.

DIRECTIONS

1) For the beans, bring a large pot of lightly salted water to a boil over high heat. Reduce heat to low, add green beans, cover and cook until tender-crisp, 2–3 minutes. Drain and rinse with cold water to stop further cooking. Spread the beans out on paper towel and pat dry. 2) For the vinaigrette, in a small bowl, whisk olive oil, balsamic vinegar, Dijon mustard, sugar, salt and pepper. 3) To assemble the salad, in a large serving bowl, combine green beans, arugula, tomatoes, bocconcini and basil. Toss with balsamic dressing and season to taste with salt and pepper. Serve immediately.

Serves 6–8

BITE ME BIT

"We thought that if we lasted for two or three years, that would be fantastic."

— Ringo Starr, musician

THREE BEAN SALAD with CREAMY DILL DRESSING

INGREDIENTS

4 cups fresh green beans, ends trimmed

1½ cups canned chickpeas, rinsed and drained

1½ cups red kidney beans, rinsed and drained

1 cup sliced hearts of palm, rinsed and drained

2 large celery stalks, chopped

1 large red bell pepper, diced

Creamy Dill Dressing

1 small shallot, diced

¼ cup mayonnaise

2 tbsp olive oil

2 tbsp white wine vinegar

1 tbsp fresh lemon juice

1 tbsp coarse grain mustard

1 tbsp chopped fresh dill

1 tbsp chopped fresh flat-leaf parsley

¼ tsp ground cumin

¼ tsp kosher salt

¼ tsp freshly ground black pepper

I'm nostalgic for the '80s. I've tried to bring back a few phrases but haven't gotten great feedback saying "no doy" to the butcher and "chill pill" to my grandmother. Those are lame anyway. The one I really want to revitalize is "cool beans." This one is going to stick, fer sure. Why? Because beans are cool, especially the way Lisa makes them. While there are hundreds of variations on the traditional bean salad, none is quite as stellar as this one, a crunchy and healthy, make-ahead, dill-dressed salad of fresh, cooked green beans, chickpeas, kidney beans, hearts of palm, red peppers and celery. Wicked awesome for a crowd, this radically refreshing and très tasty salad is totally cool beans.

DIRECTIONS

1) For the green beans, bring a medium pot of water to a boil over high heat. Add green beans and turn heat to low. Cook 2 minutes, drain and immediately plunge into a bowl of ice water to stop cooking. Once cold, drain again and dry beans completely. Place in a large bowl along with chickpeas, kidney beans, hearts of palm, celery and red pepper. 2) For the dressing, in a food processor or blender, combine shallot, mayonnaise, olive oil, white wine vinegar, lemon juice, mustard, dill, parsley, cumin, salt and pepper. Pulse 2–3 times, until well combined. Pour over bean salad, toss well and refrigerate covered at least 2 hours allowing flavors to blend.

Serves 6

GRILLED CORN, TOMATO & AVOCADO SALAD

INGREDIENTS

Corn Salad

6 ears fresh corn, shucked

1 cup cherry tomatoes, halved

1 large ripe avocado, chopped

1 tbsp chopped fresh
flat-leaf parsley

1 tbsp chopped fresh basil

Honey Lime Dressing

3 tbsp olive oil

2 tbsp fresh lime juice

1 tbsp honey

½ tsp lime zest

¼ tsp kosher salt

¼ tsp freshly ground
black pepper

There are only a few table manners I care about – no texting, nose blowing or cud-like chewing. That's it. Which is a good thing, because when Miss Manners (aka Lisa) made this tri-colored, refreshingly light summer salad, I couldn't use the proper utensil. A fork wasn't letting me shovel in enough of the smoky, slightly charred sweet corn, ripe cherry tomatoes, creamy avocado and fresh herbs. Tossed in a honey-lime dressing, this delicious salad is easy to make and even easier to eat...with a spoon...and, if Lisa isn't watching, with a serving spoon, elbows firmly planted tabletop.

DIRECTIONS

Preheat barbecue to medium and lightly oil grill. Grill corn 8 minutes, turning occasionally, until tender and with some black specks. Once cool enough to handle, slice kernels off cobs and place in a large bowl with cherry tomatoes, avocado, parsley and basil. Toss to combine.

For the dressing, in a small bowl, whisk olive oil, lime juice, honey, lime zest, salt and pepper. Pour over corn mixture, tossing until evenly mixed. Cover bowl with plastic wrap and set aside for 10–20 minutes before serving, allowing flavors to blend.

Serves 6

BITE ME BIT

"You shut your mouth when you're talking to me!"

— Mrs. Kroeger (actress Rebecca De Mornay) in the 2005 movie *Wedding Crashers*

ORANGE, JICAMA & SPINACH SALAD

INGREDIENTS

Lime Cumin Dressing

¼ cup fresh lime juice

¼ cup olive oil

1 tbsp honey

1 tbsp chopped fresh
flat-leaf parsley

¼ tsp ground cumin

¼ tsp kosher salt

Salad

1 cup thinly sliced red onion

3 medium oranges, seedless

1 small jicama (about 1 lb),
peeled and cut into
matchstick strips

8 cups baby spinach

2 tbsp sesame seeds

I pay close attention to word pronunciation. Maybe that's because I lose faith when I hear someone, especially (EX-spesh-elly is a no-no) a leader of a country say NUKE-yoo-lar. That's why, when this salad came across my plate, I did a bit of digging into jicama (HICK-ah-mah), a popular root vegetable in Mexican cooking. While unattractive on the outside, once peeled, this crunchy tuber is a beauty. Not only is it excellent raw or cooked in salsas and stir-fries, but it also brings a refreshing twist to any salad. Tossed in a citrus and cumin dressing, this sweet, salty, spicy and textured salad of oranges, jicama, onions and baby spinach is going to become a regular on your mealtime schedule. That's SKE-jul, not SHED-yool.

DIRECTIONS

1) For the dressing, in a blender or food processor, combine lime juice, olive oil, honey, parsley, cumin and salt. Blend until smooth. Store covered in refrigerator until ready to use; can be made 3 days in advance. 2) For the salad, place the red onion slices in a small bowl of ice cold water. Place in refrigerator for 15 minutes as this will mellow the strong taste of the onions. 3) For the oranges, slice away peels, remove white pith and cut the segments out of the orange. Place in a large bowl. Add well drained and dried onions, jicama and baby spinach. Toss salad with enough dressing to coat lightly. 4) To toast the sesame seeds, place in a small skillet over low heat. Stir constantly until seeds are lightly browned, about 2 minutes. Sprinkle on salad.

Serves 6–8

BITE ME BIT

"President Bush has been silent on Schwarzenegger. Of course, he can't pronounce Schwarzenegger."

— David Letterman, TV host and comedian

POACHED EGG PANZANELLA SALAD

INGREDIENTS

Bread Croutons

4 cups crusty Italian or French bread, cut into 1-inch cubes

2 tbsp olive oil

¼ tsp kosher salt

¼ tsp freshly ground black pepper

Vinaigrette

¼ cup olive oil

2 tbsp rice vinegar

1 small garlic clove, minced

½ tsp Dijon mustard

½ tsp kosher salt

¼ tsp freshly ground black pepper

Salad

1½ cups English cucumber, seeded and cut into 1-inch cubes

8 large fresh basil leaves, thinly sliced

1 tbsp olive oil

1 medium red onion, sliced into ½-inch thick rounds

2 red bell peppers, quartered and seeded

6 plum tomatoes, quartered and seeded

Poached Egg

4–6 large eggs

2 tsp white vinegar

I always wanted to be on the debate team. Just ask my parents about the hours I spent formulating arguments and rebuttals. Well, here's one thing I can't dispute: rustic Italian cooking is perfect. Take for example this beautiful, brilliant bread salad (let's save the "Is it bread or salad?" squabble for another day), a Tuscan summer classic. Not only does it contain chunks of crusty bread, but it's also loaded with juicy tomatoes, crunchy cucumbers, fresh basil and grilled peppers and onions. Not only do the bread cubes soak up juices from the vegetables and tangy vinaigrette, but they also benefit hugely from the deep yellow yolk of the poached egg as it oozes greatness and mingles with bits in the bowl. In closing: no, man does not live by bread alone...man lives by a hearty bread salad bursting with flavor and fragrance. Case closed.

DIRECTIONS

1) Preheat oven to 375°F. Line a baking sheet with aluminum foil and coat with non-stick cooking spray. In a large bowl, toss bread cubes with olive oil, salt and pepper. Place on baking sheet and bake 10–12 minutes until dried out. Set aside. 2) For the dressing, in a small bowl, whisk olive oil, rice vinegar, garlic, Dijon, salt and pepper. 3) For the salad, in a large bowl, combine cucumber and basil. Preheat barbecue to medium-high heat and lightly oil grill. Brush both sides of onion slices and peppers with olive oil. Grill 3–4 minutes per side, removing from barbecue when slightly tender and lightly charred. Cut onion rings in half and peppers into 1-inch cubes. Add onions and peppers to the cucumber mixture. Add toasted bread and tomatoes to cucumber mixture. Pour dressing over top and toss to coat. Divide into individual servings. 4) For the poached egg, bring a medium saucepan of water to a boil over high heat. Reduce heat to medium and add vinegar. Working with eggs one at a time, crack each egg into its own small bowl. Give the water a quick whirl with a whisk right before adding eggs, as this will help eggs keep their shape. Slide each egg into the water. Poach for 3½ minutes. Remove with a slotted spoon, drain on paper towel and place 1 egg on top of each salad serving.

Serves 4–6

Get cracking and make the perfect poached egg

ASPARAGUS & EDAMAME ORZO SALAD

INGREDIENTS

1 cup orzo pasta

1 bunch asparagus, about 20 spears

¾ cup frozen shelled edamame

3 tbsp olive oil

3 tbsp freshly grated Parmesan cheese

¼ cup oil-packed sun-dried tomatoes, rinsed, drained and thinly sliced

1 tbsp chopped fresh basil

1 small garlic clove, minced

¼ tsp kosher salt

¼ tsp freshly ground black pepper

freshly grated Parmesan cheese, for serving

One of the most popular recipes in our first book was the Caprese Orzo Salad. Now, this shocked me. Yes, it's utterly delicious but, a) it's healthy (did you people not make it to the brunch and dessert sections?) and, b) it's super simple to make. We decided to follow The Kinks' advice and "Give the people what they want," so here it is, another scrumptious and easy-to-prepare pasta salad. In this destined-to-be-popular salad, tender orzo is combined with crunchy asparagus, protein-packed edamame, intense sun-dried tomatoes, freshly grated Parmesan, basil and garlic.

DIRECTIONS

1) In a medium saucepan, cook orzo in lightly salted boiling water for 10 minutes, or until tender. Drain well and place in large bowl.

2) For asparagus and edamame, bring a medium pot of water to a boil. Add both the asparagus and edamame, turn heat to low and cook 2 minutes. Drain and immediately plunge into a bowl of cold water. Drain and dry asparagus and edamame well. Cut each spear into 3 pieces and add both to the orzo. Add olive oil, Parmesan, sun-dried tomatoes, basil, garlic, salt and pepper, tossing well to coat. Cover and let stand at room temperature until ready to serve. Top each serving with Parmesan cheese.

Serves 4

BITE ME BIT

"La la, la la! You'll be popular! Just not quite as popular as ME!"

— from the 2003 original Broadway cast of *Wicked*

STACKED CAPRESE with ROASTED TOMATOES

INGREDIENTS

Roasted Tomatoes

6 plum tomatoes, halved and seeded

1 tbsp olive oil

2 tsp balsamic vinegar

¼ tsp kosher salt

¼ tsp freshly ground black pepper

Caprese Salad

6 large vine-ripened tomatoes, each cut into 3 slices

3 fresh buffalo mozzarella rounds, each cut into 4 slices

¼ cup fresh basil, cut into long, thin strips

6 tbsp olive oil

6 tsp good quality balsamic vinegar

¾ tsp kosher salt

¾ tsp freshly ground black pepper

You can save the airfare. Forget flying across the ocean to ogle leaning towers and wave Italy's green, white and red flag. We've got a sky-high, tricolored stack that'll satisfy your need for a *primo insalata grande*. *Sì*. Great salad. At the base we start with slices of sweet red vine-ripened tomatoes. Next are rounds of buttery buffalo mozzarella, a creamy-textured semi-soft cheese. Laid atop these snow-white circles are intensely flavored and vibrant slow-roasted tomatoes, followed by aromatic fresh basil. Think we're done? *Non, signore*. We continue building this soaring salad by adding more layers of the same, finished with a drizzle of fruity olive oil and savory balsamic vinegar. This kicked-up Caprese is simple – the only thing you'll need to worry about is the question, *"Ne voglio ancora,"* otherwise known as, "Are there any seconds?"

DIRECTIONS

1) Preheat oven to 275°F. Line a baking sheet with aluminum foil and coat with non-stick cooking spray. **2)** For the roasted tomatoes, lay cut side up on prepared baking sheet. Drizzle evenly with olive oil and balsamic vinegar. Sprinkle with salt and pepper. Place in oven and let them slow roast for 2 hours. Allow to cool before stacking in Caprese salad. These can be made ahead and refrigerated in a sealed container for up to 1 week. **3)** To assemble the salad, arrange 1 fresh tomato slice on a serving platter. Top with a slice of mozzarella, followed by 1 roasted tomato, 1 tsp basil, another fresh tomato slice, mozzarella, roasted tomato, basil and the final fresh tomato slice. Drizzle with 1 tbsp olive oil and 1 tsp balsamic vinegar. Sprinkle with ⅛ tsp salt and ⅛ tsp pepper. Repeat with remaining tomatoes. Serve immediately.

Serves 6

ROMAINE & RADISH SALAD with LEMON TAHINI DRESSING & GARLIC CROUTONS

INGREDIENTS

Garlic Croutons

3 cups French or Italian bread, cut into ½-inch cubes

2 tbsp olive oil

1 small garlic clove, minced

¼ tsp kosher salt

¼ tsp freshly ground black pepper

Lemon Tahini Dressing

½ cup plain yogurt

2 tbsp tahini

2 tbsp fresh lemon juice

2 tbsp honey

1 tbsp chopped fresh flat-leaf parsley

1 small garlic clove, minced

¼ tsp kosher salt

¼ tsp freshly ground black pepper

8 cups shredded romaine lettuce

2 cups cherry tomatoes

2 cups peeled and chopped English cucumber

½ cup radishes, trimmed and thinly sliced

Talk about a mouthful. First, there's the long name of the recipe. I tried to shorten it but couldn't omit any of the delicious elements. Second, this is one noisy salad. Just the romaine lettuce and cucumbers alone make it library-unfriendly. Add in the unexpected crunch of fresh radishes, with their mild-to-peppery bite, and you've got the makings of a symphony. Top it off with homemade crusty garlic croutons and toss it in a creamy lemon tahini dressing, and, well, you've got a full-blown crescendo on your hands. That is, until the thunderous applause begins.

DIRECTIONS

1) For the croutons, preheat oven to 375ºF. Line a baking sheet with aluminum foil and coat with non-stick cooking spray. In a small skillet heat olive oil over medium heat. Add garlic, stirring constantly for 30 seconds. Toss in the bread cubes, salt and pepper, stirring for 1 minute, until the bread cubes are well coated. Spread cubes on prepared baking sheet and bake 10 minutes stirring once halfway through cooking. Remove from oven and set aside to cool. 2) For the dressing, in a food processor or blender, combine yogurt, tahini, lemon juice, honey, parsley, garlic, salt and pepper, blending well to combine. 3) For the salad, in a large bowl, toss together shredded lettuce, tomatoes, cucumbers and radishes. Add croutons and dressing, tossing well. Serve immediately.

Serves 6

BITE ME BIT

"What the hell is a radish, anyway? It's like an apple did it with an onion."

— Dolph Starbeam on the TV show *The Simpsons*

TUNA NICOISE SALAD

INGREDIENTS

Lemon Basil Dressing

½ cup olive oil

2 tbsp fresh lemon juice

1 tsp minced shallot

1 tsp chopped fresh basil

½ tsp Dijon mustard

½ tsp honey

½ tsp kosher salt

¼ tsp freshly ground black pepper

Nicoise Salad

16 small red potatoes

2½ cups green beans, ends trimmed and halved

4 large eggs

8 cups loosely packed Boston lettuce, torn into bite-sized pieces

2 (6oz) cans solid white albacore tuna, drained and broken into chunks

1 cup canned white kidney (cannellini) beans, rinsed and drained

12 cherry tomatoes, halved

⅛ tsp kosher salt

⅛ tsp freshly ground black pepper

16 Nicoise olives

This famous salad first surfaced on the French Riviera. No big surprise there. I mean, who else, other than the chic French, could make canned tuna taste so *par excellence* and successfully combine such an array of gorgeous colors, complementary flavors and interesting textures? Nobody other than, perhaps, *ma soeur* Lisa, who tweaked this classic until it was *parfaite*. *Oui*, perfect. She ditched the anchovies, added creamy white beans to the potatoes, green beans, eggs, tuna, tomatoes and olives and tossed all of it in a delicious lemon basil dressing. Lisa certainly captured the *je ne sais quoi* of this main-course salad, but, *Mon Dieu!* it's time she took off the beret.

DIRECTIONS

1) For the dressing, in a blender, combine olive oil, lemon juice, shallots, basil, Dijon, honey, salt and pepper. Puree until smooth. **2)** For the salad, place potatoes in a large saucepan with enough water to cover them. Bring to a boil over medium-high heat. Reduce heat to medium and cook until tender, 15–20 minutes. Drain and let cool slightly. Slice each potato into 2 or 3 slices and place in a small bowl. Toss with 2 tbsp of the salad dressing. Set aside. **3)** For the green beans, bring a large saucepan of water to a boil over high heat. Reduce heat to low, add green beans and cook 2–3 minutes, until tender-crisp. Rinse under cold water and drain. Set aside. **4)** For the eggs, place eggs in a medium saucepan and cover with cold water. Bring to a boil over medium-high heat. Once boiling, remove pan from heat, cover and let sit 10–12 minutes. Remove eggs and place in bowl of ice water. Once cooled, peel eggs and cut into quarters. Set aside. **5)** Toss lettuce with a few tablespoons of dressing to lightly coat. Place on a large serving platter. In a small bowl, toss tuna with ¼ cup dressing. Place on top of lettuce in center of platter. Place white beans on lettuce beside tuna. In a small bowl, toss tomatoes with 1 tbsp dressing, salt and pepper and place in a mound on the lettuce. Place green beans in a small bowl, toss with 1 tbsp dressing and arrange in mound on lettuce. Place reserved potatoes in a separate mound on the lettuce. Scatter eggs and olives on platter. Drizzle extra dressing over salad. Serve immediately.

Serves 4

GREEK SALAD with SUGAR SNAPS

INGREDIENTS

Lemon Dijon Dressing

¼ cup olive oil

2 tbsp fresh lemon juice

½ tsp sugar

¼ tsp Dijon mustard

¼ tsp dried oregano

¼ tsp kosher salt

¼ tsp freshly ground black pepper

3 cups sugar snap peas, ends trimmed and stringed

2 cups seeded and cubed English cucumber

1 cup cherry tomatoes

1 large red bell pepper, cubed

1 cup cubed feta cheese

¾ cup Kalamata olives, pitted and halved

1 tbsp chopped fresh flat-leaf parsley

When I say, "It's all Greek to me," I'm being literal. Democracy, Olympics, philosophers and Goddesses, πω πω (oh my)! From history to culture to cuisine, I love all things Greek. Wait until you try this delicious, fresh salad Vassiliki (the Greek name I've given Lisa) created – it's the Mount Olympus of Greek salads, towering above all others. Crisp cucumbers, juicy tomatoes, crumbly feta and plump olives are further enhanced with the addition of crunchy, sweet sugar snaps. Tossed in a lemon Dijon dressing, this chunky country salad will have you too waving the blue and white flag. *Opa!*

DIRECTIONS

1) For the dressing, in a small bowl, whisk olive oil, lemon juice, sugar, Dijon mustard, oregano, salt and pepper. Set aside.
2) For the sugar snaps, bring a medium pot of lightly salted water to a boil. Turn heat to low, add sugar snaps and cook 2 minutes. Drain and immediately plunge into a bowl of ice water to stop cooking. Once cold, drain again and dry snap peas completely before adding to salad. 3) In a large bowl, combine cooked sugar snap peas, cucumber, tomatoes, red pepper, feta, olives and parsley. Toss well with dressing and let stand 10 minutes to combine flavors before serving.

Serves 4–6

TOMATO & MOZZARELLA PASTA SALAD

INGREDIENTS

Sun-Dried Tomato & Basil Vinaigrette

8 large fresh basil leaves, chopped

½ cup freshly grated Parmesan cheese

½ cup olive oil

6 tbsp red wine vinegar

1 tbsp fresh lemon juice

6 oil packed sun-dried tomatoes, drained and diced

1 small garlic clove, minced

2 tsp sugar

½ tsp kosher salt

Pasta Salad

¾ lb fusilli pasta

1½ cups fresh mozzarella cheese, cubed

1½ cups cherry tomatoes, halved

¾ cup freshly grated Parmesan cheese

¼ cup thinly sliced fresh basil

¼ tsp kosher salt

Tomato, tomahto. Lisa doesn't care how you say it. I do. It's tomato, and in the case of this deeply flavored pasta salad it's a double dose of the antioxidant-rich fruit. Oil-packed sun-dried tomatoes add a concentrated flavor and tangy twist to the basil vinaigrette, a dressing that works its way into the spiral pasta and coats cubed mozzarella cheese and sweet juicy cherry tomatoes. Bold, fresh and robust, this pasta salad is so delicious and popular that it'll fly out of the bowl like hot potatoes, or, if you're with Lisa, potahtoes.

DIRECTIONS

1) For the dressing, in a food processor or blender, combine basil, Parmesan, olive oil, red wine vinegar, lemon juice, sun-dried tomatoes, garlic, sugar and salt. Blend until smooth. Cover and let stand until ready to dress pasta. **2)** For the pasta, in a large pot of lightly salted, boiling water, cook fusilli until tender. Drain well and place in large mixing bowl. While pasta is still warm toss with sun-dried tomato dressing, mozzarella cheese, cherry tomatoes, Parmesan cheese, basil and salt.

Serves 6–8

SHRIMP PASTA SALAD with LEMON DILL DRESSING

INGREDIENTS

Pasta Salad

½ lb penne pasta

1 tbsp olive oil

½ lb medium raw shrimp, peeled and deveined

1 cup fresh or frozen green peas

1 cup peeled and sliced carrots, cut into thin rounds

1 large garlic clove, minced

¼ tsp kosher salt

¼ tsp freshly ground black pepper

Lemon & Dill Buttermilk Dressing

⅓ cup buttermilk

½ cup mayonnaise

1 tbsp chopped fresh dill

1 tbsp chopped fresh flat-leaf parsley

1 tbsp fresh lemon juice

½ tsp lemon zest

½ tsp kosher salt

¼ tsp freshly ground black pepper

⅛ tsp paprika

When the crickets chirp, ice cream melts and sidewalks sizzle, I know it's summer. I also know it's that fresh-cut grass and hot-tar time when the barbecue is fired up 24/7. With chicken and burgers flying off the grill I'm always looking for summertime sides that aren't too rich or heavy. Lisa, tired of me claiming cherry Popsicles can do the job, created this simply superb pasta salad. Crisp crustaceans, sweet and succulent green peas, crunchy carrots and tender penne are tossed in a tart lemon and fresh dill buttermilk dressing. Take your head out of the freezer chest – this aromatic, light and refreshing salad is the perfect dilly Dog Day cool down.

DIRECTIONS

1) Bring a large pot of lightly salted water to a boil, add penne and cook until tender. Rinse under cold water and drain. Place in a large bowl. 2) In a medium skillet, heat olive oil over medium-high heat. Add shrimp, continuously turning shrimp until just pink, about 2 minutes. Add green peas and carrots, stirring constantly until vegetables have softened slightly, 4 minutes. Add garlic, salt and pepper, cooking 1 minute more. Remove skillet from heat and allow mixture to cool slightly while preparing dressing. 3) For the dressing, in a medium bowl, whisk buttermilk, mayonnaise, dill, parsley, lemon juice, lemon zest, salt, pepper and paprika. Pour dressing over cooked pasta, adding shrimp and vegetable mixture. Toss well to coat.

Serves 4

BITE ME BIT

"Austria! Well, then. G'day mate! Let's put another shrimp on the barbie!"

— Lloyd Christmas (actor Jim Carrey) in the 1994 movie *Dumb & Dumber*

CRUNCHY ASIAN SLAW

INGREDIENTS

Noodles & Almond Topping

2 tbsp butter

2 (3oz) ramen noodle packages, crumbled, seasoning packs discarded

¼ cup slivered almonds

Asian Vinaigrette

3 tbsp rice vinegar

2 tbsp brown sugar

1 tbsp soy sauce

1 tbsp mirin

1 tsp sesame oil

⅓ cup vegetable oil

Slaw

6 cups thinly sliced napa cabbage

2 cups broccoli florets, cut in small pieces

1 cup canned or fresh mandarin orange segments, drained

½ cup grated carrots

½ cup water chestnuts, rinsed, drained and thinly sliced

¼ cup sunflower seeds

Lisa's Cabbage Patch Kid was named Mandarina Almondina Joy. What kind of name is that to give a chubby-cheeked doll adopted from Babyland General Hospital? Ludicrous. But, maybe it explains her love for cabbage, mandarins and slivered almonds. A stretch? Perhaps, but it works in all our favors when whipping up a batch of this joyfully bright and crunchy Asian coleslaw of napa cabbage, mandarins, broccoli, carrots, water chestnuts and sunflower seeds. This isn't the usual mayo-drenched horror show – this simple, sweet and tangy coleslaw is a refreshing, delicious and scrumptious salad. Now, if only I could get her to make something Surgeon Barbie can eat while driving her pink Corvette convertible.

DIRECTIONS

1) For the noodles and almonds, in a medium skillet, melt butter over medium heat. Add ramen noodles and almonds to skillet and cook, stirring until toasted, about 5 minutes. Remove from heat and set aside to cool. 2) For the dressing, in a small bowl, whisk rice vinegar, brown sugar, soy sauce, mirin and sesame oil. Whisk in vegetable oil until combined. 3) In a large bowl, combine napa cabbage, broccoli, mandarins, carrots, water chestnuts, sunflower seeds and ramen/almond mixture. Pour dressing over salad and toss to coat.

Serves 8–10

CHINESE CHICKEN NOODLE SALAD

INGREDIENTS

Noodle Salad

1 (14oz/400g) package fresh lo mein or chow mein noodles

2 tsp sesame oil

1 large red bell pepper, thinly sliced

1 large yellow pepper, thinly sliced

1½ cups chopped English cucumber, peeled and seeded

2 cups roasted deli chicken breast meat, shredded

¼ cup chopped fresh flat-leaf parsley

Peanut Dressing

½ cup smooth peanut butter

¼ cup soy sauce

¼ cup chicken broth

2 tbsp fresh lime juice

2 tbsp brown sugar

2 tsp finely grated fresh ginger

1 tsp hot chili sauce (Sriracha)

3 tbsp chopped peanuts, for garnish

Lisa is super-sick of wiping toaster pastry crumbs from my shirt. Determined to get me to sit down to a proper, nutritious, well-rounded lunch instead of eating on the go, she used her noodle and created a meal-in-a-bowl. This cold salad of fresh Chinese noodles, combined with crunchy vegetables and shredded deli-roasted chicken, all tossed in a super-saucy, so-good-it's-drinkable peanut dressing, fits the bill perfectly. Phew...my days of standing in front of the pantry deciding between chocolate-frosted and strawberry-filled are over.

DIRECTIONS

1) In a medium pot of lightly salted boiling water, cook noodles for 2 minutes. Drain and rinse under cold water. Transfer noodles to a large bowl and toss with sesame oil. Add red and yellow peppers, cucumber, chicken and parsley. 2) For the peanut dressing, in a food processor or blender, combine peanut butter, soy sauce, chicken broth, lime juice, brown sugar, ginger and chili sauce until smooth, about 20 seconds. Add to noodle salad tossing to coat. Garnish with chopped peanuts.

Serves 4–6

BITE ME BIT

"I saw the movie *Crouching Tiger, Hidden Dragon* and I was surprised because I didn't see any tigers or dragons. And then I realized why: they're crouching and hidden."

— Steve Martin, comedian, actor, author

PARMESAN-CRUSTED CHICKEN & ARUGULA SALAD

INGREDIENTS

Parmesan Chicken

3 boneless, skinless chicken breast halves, pounded to 1-inch thickness

¼ tsp kosher salt

¼ tsp freshly ground black pepper

1 tbsp olive oil

1 tsp Dijon mustard

½ tsp chopped fresh thyme

6 tbsp freshly grated Parmesan cheese

Creamy Basil Dressing

½ cup mayonnaise

½ cup sour cream

½ cup fresh basil leaves, lightly packed

½ cup freshly grated Parmesan cheese

2 tbsp fresh lemon juice

1 small garlic clove, minced

½ tsp kosher salt

Arugula Salad

4 large celery stalks, sliced

2 Granny Smith apples, cored and cut into ½-inch pieces

4 cups arugula, packed

Did you know that there are Facebook groups dedicated to hating salad? Now, I'm not one for love-ins, but I'm willing to bet that members of "green monster123" and "crucified crudités" have never sunk their teeth into this one: golden-baked Parmesan chicken, peppery arugula and crunchy apples are tossed together in a creamy basil and lemon dressing resulting in a delicious and sophisticated meal-worthy salad. It's time to press "like," you salad scorners, you.

DIRECTIONS

1) For the chicken, preheat the oven to 400°F. Line a baking sheet with aluminum foil and coat with non-stick cooking spray. Season the chicken with salt and pepper. In a small bowl, mix together olive oil, Dijon and thyme. Brush on top of chicken and sprinkle each breast with 2 tbsp Parmesan, pressing lightly to adhere. Bake 15 minutes until cooked through. Let cool slightly before chopping into bite-sized pieces. 2) For the dressing, in a food processor or blender, combine mayonnaise, sour cream, basil, Parmesan, lemon juice, garlic and salt blending until smooth. Cover and refrigerate until ready to use. 3) To assemble the salad, in a large bowl, combine cut up chicken, celery and apples and toss with dressing. Gently toss arugula into salad. Serve immediately.

Serves 4

SANTA FE CHOPPED SALAD with CORNBREAD CROUTONS

INGREDIENTS

Cornbread Croutons

1 cup cornmeal

⅓ cup flour

1 tsp kosher salt

1 tsp baking powder

¼ tsp baking soda

1 large egg

1 cup buttermilk

¼ cup butter, melted

2 tbsp butter

Avocado Buttermilk Dressing

1 large avocado, ripe

2 tbsp fresh lime juice

2 tbsp chopped fresh flat-leaf parsley

¼ cup mayonnaise

¼ cup buttermilk

¼ cup olive oil

1 tbsp canned chopped green chili peppers, drained

½ tsp ground cumin

½ tsp kosher salt

¼ tsp chili powder

¼ tsp freshly ground black pepper

Salad

2 tbsp olive oil

1½ cups frozen corn, thawed and patted dry

¼ tsp ground cumin

¼ tsp chili powder

¼ tsp kosher salt

1 cup canned black beans, rinsed and drained

2 large Granny Smith apples, cored and cut into bite-sized chunks

1 roasted deli chicken, breast meat diced

8 cups chopped iceberg lettuce

Not since iceberg lettuce has there been a more maligned ingredient than the humble crouton. Complaints about the salad topping range from "cut my gums" to "explode with a stab of the fork." Though I'm not a fan of stale, store-bought cubes of condensed sawdust, I remain cuckoo for croutons. Good thing my sister has her Masters of Croutonery. Lisa created this Santa Fe salad chock full of, you guessed it, homemade croutons. Baked to a golden brown, these addictive cornbread cubes are the crowning glory in an already flavorful, colorful, avocado-and-buttermilk dressed salad of chicken, crunchy apples, beans, roasted corn and…iceberg lettuce. We feel a comeback in the making for the crisp, light green leaves.

DIRECTIONS

1) For the cornbread croutons, place an empty 10-inch cast iron skillet in the oven and preheat to 400ºF. In a large bowl, combine cornmeal, flour, salt, baking powder and baking soda. Whisk in egg, buttermilk and melted butter, just until combined. Remove heated skillet from oven and add remaining 2 tbsp butter, swirling to coat pan. Pour in batter and bake 18 minutes, until golden. Let cornbread cool in skillet. 2) Lower oven temperature to 375ºF and line a baking sheet with parchment paper. Cut cornbread into 1-inch cubes and spread on parchment. Bake 15 minutes, stir and bake another 15 minutes until golden brown. Let cool before adding to salad. 3) For the dressing, in a food processor, combine avocado, lime juice, parsley, mayonnaise, buttermilk, olive oil, chopped chilies, cumin, salt, chili powder and pepper, blending until smooth and creamy. Cover and refrigerate until ready to use. 4) For the salad, in a large skillet, heat 2 tbsp olive oil over medium-high heat. Place corn in hot pan, stirring 3–4 minutes, until golden brown. Add cumin, chili powder and salt, cooking until spices are fragrant, about 30 seconds. Remove from heat and cool slightly. Transfer to a large serving bowl and add black beans, apples, chicken and lettuce. When ready to serve, toss with dressing and cornbread croutons.

Serves 6–8

WHEAT BERRY SALAD with MAPLE WALNUTS

INGREDIENTS

1 cup red spring wheat berries,
rinsed and drained

3½ cups cold water

1 tsp kosher salt

Vinaigrette

3 tbsp olive oil

2 tbsp balsamic vinegar

1 tsp fresh lemon juice

1 tsp kosher salt

½ tsp freshly ground
black pepper

1 cup peeled and chopped
English cucumber

½ cup dried cranberries

½ cup crumbled feta cheese

1 tbsp chopped fresh mint

1 tbsp chopped fresh
flat-leaf parsley

Maple-Glazed Walnuts

1 cup walnut halves

2½ tbsp pure maple syrup

⅛ tsp kosher salt

I used to spout the Julia Child line, "I just hate health food." Even walking into health food stores I'd be bowled over by that funky vitamin smell. Grossed me right out. Which makes it no surprise I was up-in-arms when Lisa suggested a wheat berry salad, wailing that I wasn't heading back into yeast-filled bulk bin stores to buy wheat berries. Turns out I didn't have to. Wheat berries are sold at regular, deodorized supermarkets. And, turns out they're unbelievably delicious. With a chewy texture, these hearty whole grains are nutritional powerhouses, rich in fiber, vitamins and minerals. Combined with tangy feta, cool mint, tart cranberries and sweet and salty walnuts they make a fresh, delicious, flavor-packed salad. OK, so I love health food. I just hate eating humble pie.

DIRECTIONS

1) In a medium saucepan, combine wheat berries, water and salt. Bring to a boil over high heat. Turn heat to low, cover and cook 1 hour or until berries are bursting and chewy. Remove from heat and drain excess water from wheat berries. Transfer to a large mixing bowl to cool. 2) For the vinaigrette, in a small bowl, whisk olive oil, balsamic vinegar, lemon juice, salt and pepper. Set aside. 3) Once wheat berries have cooled, add cucumber, dried cranberries, feta, mint and parsley to cooked wheat berries. Toss with dressing. 4) For the maple-glazed walnuts, heat a medium skillet over medium-high heat. Add walnuts, maple syrup and salt. Cook, stirring constantly for 3 minutes, until syrup is caramelized and nuts are lightly toasted. Immediately remove from pan and spread out on parchment paper to cool. Once cool, roughly chop and add to wheat berry salad. Serve immediately.

Serves 6

GIRL-MEETS-GRILL VEGETABLE PASTA SALAD

INGREDIENTS

2 large red bell peppers, halved and seeded

2 large zucchini, cut into ½-inch thick slices

12 thick asparagus stalks, bottoms trimmed

1 large red onion, peeled, cut into ½-inch thick wedges

2 tbsp olive oil

Balsamic Vinaigrette

2 tbsp olive oil

2 tbsp balsamic vinegar

1 tsp finely chopped fresh thyme

½ tsp kosher salt

¼ tsp freshly ground black pepper

¾ lb orecchiette (ear-shaped) pasta

Here's a little secret – Lisa has a mongo crush on Bobby Flay. How else can I explain her calling herself "Mistress Barbecue," tormenting me with "Throwdowns" and referring to her Goliath grill as "Q"? While Bobby might not light my fire, I'm thrilled she's still trying to impress him – flavorful grilled vegetables add incredible taste and texture to what could have otherwise been a boring, Bobby-less pasta salad.

DIRECTIONS

1) Preheat barbecue to medium heat. 2) In a large bowl, combine peppers, zucchini, asparagus and onion. Toss with 2 tbsp olive oil and set aside. 3) For balsamic dressing, in a small bowl, whisk 2 tbsp olive oil, balsamic vinegar, thyme, salt and pepper and set aside. 4) Place red pepper halves skin side down on preheated grill to blister skins. When the skins are black all over remove from grill and peel skins off when cool enough to handle. Cut peppers into large chunks and place in large mixing bowl. 5) Grill zucchini slices, asparagus and onion, about 3 minutes per side, until grill marks appear but vegetables are still firm. Remove from grill and cut asparagus and onions into large bite-sized pieces. Add all grilled vegetables to red peppers. Toss with balsamic dressing, marinating for 30 minutes. Meanwhile, bring large pot of salted water to a boil. Cook pasta until tender, stirring occasionally. Drain pasta and add to grilled vegetables. Season to taste with salt and pepper.

Serves 6–8

BITE ME BIT

"It is a secret?"

— Bobby Flay, chef and Grill Master

Pick me

Prize-Winning Vegetables

EXTRA BITE

FIERY OVEN FRIES

INGREDIENTS

Spiced Fries

4 large (about 2 lbs) russet
potatoes, unpeeled

1 tbsp olive oil

1 tsp paprika

1 tsp brown sugar

1 tsp kosher salt

1 tsp chili powder

¼ tsp garlic powder

Chipotle Ketchup

½ cup ketchup

1 tsp fresh lime juice

1 tsp sugar

¼ tsp ground chipotle chili powder

How many times has someone sworn to you "You can't taste the difference"? Ice cream vs. frozen yogurt? Coke vs. Pepsi? Of course you can taste the difference. Now, we're not big into making promises we can't keep, but trust us when we tell you that the only difference you're going to notice between our baked oven fries and the ones submerged in vats of oil is these figure-friendly spuds won't leave your lips and fingers glistening. Baked in spicy, smoky BBQ-flavored seasoning, these skin-on fries are crisp on the outside and soft on the inside, delicious when dipped in sweet-and-spicy chipotle ketchup. So, c'mon and join us for a great, guilt-free, French fry free-for-all.

DIRECTIONS

1) Preheat oven to 425ºF. Line a baking sheet with parchment paper.
2) Scrub potatoes and dry well. Cut the whole potato into ½-inch slices and then cut each slice into ½-inch strips, about 3-inches long. Place potato slices in a large bowl. Toss with olive oil, paprika, brown sugar, salt, chili powder and garlic powder. Spread potatoes in a single layer on prepared baking sheet. Roast 15 minutes, stir and return to oven for 10 minutes or until potatoes are tender and slightly crisp on the outside. 3) For the chipotle ketchup, in a small bowl, combine ketchup, lime juice, sugar and chipotle chili powder. Serve with fries.

Serves 4

BITE ME BIT

"I went into McDonald's yesterday and said 'I'd like some fries.' The girl at the counter said, 'Would you like some fries with that?'"

— Jay Leno, TV host and comedian

ROSEMARY ROASTED BABY POTATOES

INGREDIENTS

2 lbs mini white potatoes

2 tbsp olive oil

2 tbsp whole grain Dijon mustard

1 tbsp chopped fresh rosemary

1 tbsp fresh lemon juice

1 large garlic clove, minced

1 tsp kosher salt

½ tsp freshly ground black pepper

⅛ tsp cayenne pepper

I love rosemary, both Clooney and the herb. For our purposes I'll refrain from discussing that the former sings our toe-tapping anthem, "Sisters." Instead, I'll move on to the latter, a fragrant herb with a great rep. Known for improving memory, relieving muscle pain, curing indigestion and making hair grow (note: source not the AMA), rosemary is a powerful, needle-like leaf. In the culinary world this highly aromatic branch makes everything herbalicious, including this simple but satisfying side dish. Tossed with baby potatoes, Dijon mustard, lemon juice and garlic, rosemary boosts the flavor of these crispy-crusted, tender taters. Served up on a regular basis, "Come On-A My House" (sorry, it's the other Rosemary again) and taste this perfect combination of woody rosemary and golden brown potatoes.

DIRECTIONS

1) Preheat oven to 425°F. Line a baking sheet with aluminum foil and coat with non-stick cooking spray. 2) Cut potatoes in half, or if they're large, in quarters. Place in a large bowl and add olive oil, mustard, rosemary, lemon juice, garlic, salt, pepper and cayenne. Toss well to coat. Spread potatoes in a single layer on prepared baking sheet discarding any excess dressing. Roast potatoes 15 minutes, turn them and roast an additional 15 minutes until crusted on the outside and tender inside. Serve immediately.

Serves 4–6

BITE ME BIT

"I'm a hot little potato right now."

—Mugatu (actor Will Ferrell) in the 2001 movie *Zoolander*

FONTINA & KALE DOUBLE-STUFFED POTATOES

INGREDIENTS

4 large russet potatoes, scrubbed

2 tsp olive oil

½ cup water

4 cups chopped kale, loosely packed, thick ribs and stems discarded

2 tbsp butter, softened

¾ cup buttermilk

½ cup sour cream

1½ cups shredded Fontina cheese

2 tbsp finely chopped green onions

¾ tsp kosher salt

½ tsp freshly ground black pepper

6 tbsp freshly grated Parmesan cheese

The potato is a most versatile vegetable – it can be baked, boiled, fried, mashed, smashed and shredded – and yet, at times, the tuber can suffer from being a buffet bore. Well, here's one surprising spud, a brow-raiser, a potato bursting with pizzazz. Baked until tender, the russets are scooped out and mashed with leafy green kale, creamy Fontina cheese, buttermilk and sour cream, then put in the oven again until golden. Still not shocked? These potatoes can be prepped in advance and thrown in the oven for the second baking just before guests arrive. How's that for one exciting hot potato?

DIRECTIONS

1) Preheat oven to 400°F. Rub the outside of each potato with olive oil and pierce each with a fork several times. Bake 50–60 minutes, until fork tender. 2) While potatoes are baking, in a medium saucepan, bring ½ cup water to a boil over high heat. Reduce heat to low, add kale, cover and cook 2–3 minutes, until kale turns bright green. Drain, dry well and set aside. 3) Remove potatoes from oven and let cool until you can handle them. Cut potatoes in half lengthwise and scoop out flesh leaving ¼ inch potato flesh on bottom and sides of the potato skin. Place potato flesh in a large mixing bowl and mash with butter, buttermilk and sour cream until desired consistency. Gently fold in cooked kale, Fontina, green onions, salt and pepper. Discard 2 potato halves so you have more stuffing for the remaining 6 skins. Mound the mixture in potato shells, sprinkle each with 1 tbsp Parmesan and place on a baking sheet. Bake at 400°F for 15–20 minutes until golden on top.

Serves 6

BITE ME BIT

"If I woke up tomorrow with my head sewn to the carpet, I wouldn't be more surprised than I am now."

— Clark Griswold (actor Chevy Chase) in the 1989 movie *Christmas Vacation*

MASHED SWEET POTATOES with LIME & COCONUT

INGREDIENTS

3 large (about 2 lbs) sweet potatoes

½ cup coconut milk

1 tbsp fresh lime juice

½ tsp lime zest

½ tsp kosher salt

¼ tsp freshly ground black pepper

It's a bit tricky to make a simple vegetable side dish exciting. Just by their designation alone, side dishes are meant to be to the side, not the main event. Well, again, Lisa did the near impossible by creating an electrifying side dish, a star you're going to want to hitch your wagon to. Nutrient dense sweet potatoes are baked to bring their natural sweetness to the forefront. Then, the eye-catching orange flesh is mashed and mixed with rich coconut milk. In the final act, lime, its tart juice and zest, is added to elevate the creamy, flavorful mash. Tonight, these coconut-mashed sweet potatoes are going to outshine that *side dish* of steak.

DIRECTIONS

1) Preheat oven to 425°F. Pierce each sweet potato 3–4 times with a fork. Place on a baking sheet and bake 1 hour or until tender.

2) When cool enough to handle, cut potatoes in half and scoop out softened flesh into a medium bowl. Mash potatoes well and stir in coconut milk, lime juice, lime zest, salt and pepper.

Serves 4

BEST EVER ROASTED ROOT VEGETABLES with PISTACHIO CRUMBLE

INGREDIENTS

Roasted Veget ables

2 cups sweet potatoes, peeled and cut into 1½-inch pieces

1½ cups parsnips, peeled and cut into 1½-inch pieces

1½ cups carrots, peeled and cut into 1½-inch pieces

1½ cups turnips, peeled and cut into 1½-inch pieces

2 tbsp olive oil

½ tsp kosher salt

¼ tsp freshly ground black pepper

Honey Glaze

2 tbsp honey

2 tbsp butter

2 tsp chopped fresh rosemary

Pistachio Crumble

½ cup unsalted pistachios, shelled

¼ cup freshly grated Parmesan cheese

2 tbsp chopped fresh flat-leaf parsley

2 tsp fresh lemon juice

1 tsp olive oil

½ tsp honey

½ tsp chopped fresh rosemary

½ tsp lemon zest

¼ tsp kosher salt

Lisa told me that sometimes I exaggerate. Hurtful. I've never overstated anything in my whole, entire life. Take, for example, these roasted root vegetables. An exaggerator would say something like, "I eat vegetables to be healthy." I, on the other hand, would tell people that I eat this honey roasted, rosemary flecked medley of sweet potatoes, parsnips, carrots and turnips because the caramelized vegetables taste like candy. See, nothing amplified. An embellisher would say they enjoy the potassium in the pistachio crumble. Not me. In my understated way I'd tell you that the salty, nutty essence of the pistachios and the tart and tangy lemon work magically with the honey and rosemary, providing a satisfying crunch atop the tender vegetables. And that, my friends, is the honest truth.

DIRECTIONS

1) Preheat oven to 400°F. Line a baking sheet with parchment paper. Place sweet potatoes, parsnips, carrots and turnips in a large bowl and toss with olive oil, salt and pepper. Spread in a single layer on baking sheet and roast 40 minutes, stirring halfway through cooking time. **2)** While vegetables are roasting, prepare honey glaze. In a small saucepan melt honey and butter over low heat, stirring well to combine. Remove vegetables from oven after 40 minutes, brush with honey glaze and sprinkle with rosemary. Return to oven 10– 15 minutes more. **3)** For the pistachio crumble, place shelled pistachios in a food processor and pulse until coarsely ground. Transfer nuts to a small bowl and stir in Parmesan, parsley, lemon juice, olive oil, honey, rosemary, lemon zest and salt. Sprinkle over roasted vegetables just before serving.

Serves 4

BITE ME BIT

"I did not have 3,000 pairs of shoes. I had 1,060."

— Imelda Marcos, politician

SWEET SQUASH with MARSHMALLOW MERINGUE TOPPING

INGREDIENTS

8 cups peeled, seeded and diced butternut squash
2 tbsp butter, melted
1 tbsp brown sugar
½ tsp kosher salt

¼ cup milk, warm
3 tbsp butter, melted
2 tbsp brown sugar
½ tsp ground cinnamon
½ tsp kosher salt

Marshmallow Meringue

3 large egg whites
2 tbsp sugar
½ tsp vanilla extract
½ cup Marshmallow Fluff

Our grandmother, Alice, is brilliant, fabulous and funny. We're so lucky our kids have benefitted from her brains and beauty, but what they missed were the massive, marvelous meals we shared as we grew up in her steamy New York kitchen. We were always enchanted with her cooking and loved everything that came out of her magical, flower-print Corningware. Like an alchemist, she turned vegetables into candy, roasting butternut squash, mashing it with warm milk, melted butter, brown sugar and cinnamon and then topping it with a billowy cloud of marshmallow meringue. Doesn't get more dreamy than that, does it?

DIRECTIONS

1) Preheat oven to 400°F. Line a baking sheet with aluminum foil and coat with non-stick cooking spray. In a large bowl toss squash with 2 tbsp melted butter, 1 tbsp brown sugar and ½ tsp salt. Place on baking sheet in a single layer. Roast 25–30 minutes until tender, stirring halfway through bake time. Transfer squash to a large bowl and mash until slightly chunky. Stir in warm milk, 3 tbsp melted butter, 2 tbsp brown sugar, cinnamon and ½ tsp salt. Place in a 2-quart baking dish. Increase oven temperature to 425°F. 2) For the marshmallow meringue topping, place egg whites in the bowl of an electric mixer. Beat on medium-high speed until soft peaks form. Gradually add sugar and beat on high speed until stiff peaks form. Beat in vanilla on low speed. Gently fold marshmallow fluff into egg whites and spoon mounds of topping over the squash. Bake 5 minutes until meringue is lightly toasted.

Serves 6–8

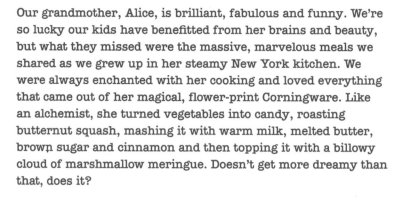

BITE ME BIT

"I had a dream last night I was eating a ten-pound marshmallow. I woke up this morning and the pillow was gone."

— Tommy Cooper, comedian

AIRY CARROT SOUFFLÉ with CRUNCHY PECAN TOPPING

INGREDIENTS

Crunchy Pecan Topping

½ cup chopped pecans

¼ cup packed brown sugar

2 tbsp butter, melted

Carrot Soufflé

6 large (about 1lb) carrots, peeled and each cut into 4 pieces

½ cup packed brown sugar

½ cup butter, melted

2 large eggs

1 tsp vanilla extract

3 tbsp flour

1 tsp baking powder

¼ tsp kosher salt

¼ tsp ground cinnamon

¼ tsp ground ginger

I apologize for using the scariest word in the culinary dictionary: soufflé. When you think of this classic French dish, do you picture yourself whipping egg whites into a frenzy, tip-toeing around and praying the fragile dome stays aloft? Well, here's a new way to picture yourself…cooking carrots, pureeing them with brown sugar, butter, eggs, vanilla and cinnamon and pouring it all into a casserole dish. Then, you get to top it with crunchy, sweet pecans and bake it for 40 minutes. During that time you can have a marching band play in your kitchen because this seductively sweet soufflé-pudding hybrid doesn't puff up much but still delivers the desired delicate and airy soufflé texture. See? The hardest thing about this side dish is deciding whether to serve it for dinner or dessert.

DIRECTIONS

1) Preheat oven to 350°F. Coat a 1-quart baking dish with non-stick cooking spray. 2) For the pecan topping, in a small bowl, combine pecans, brown sugar and melted butter. 3) For the soufflé, to a medium pot of boiling water, add carrot pieces and cook until fork tender, 10–15 minutes. Drain. 4) In a food processor, combine brown sugar, melted butter, eggs, vanilla extract, flour, baking powder, salt, cinnamon and ginger. Add cooked carrots, pulsing 2–3 times, until mixture is smooth. Pour into prepared baking dish and sprinkle evenly with pecan topping. Cook 40–45 minutes, until edges are golden. Serve hot or at room temperature.

Serves 4–6

A soufflé and a pudding collide in this sweet 'n easy dish

SPILLING the BEANS

Our Favorite Dishes & Future Wishes

Food We Loved at First Bite

Austin	Knuckle Sandwich at The Noble Pig
Boston	Famous Rumanian Pastramis andwich at Sam LaGrassa's
Chicago	Cinnamon Buns at Ann Sather
Chicago	Double Char Dog at The Wiener's Circle
Houston	BBQ Beef Potato at Potato Shack
Las Vegas	Twinkie Boy Milkshake at BLT Burger
Los Angeles	Yellow Brick Road pancakes at Griddle Café
Los Angeles	The entire menu at Pizzeria Mozza
Miami	Fried Oreos at Prime One Twelve
Miami	Crazy Moon Burger at La Moon
New York	Chocolate Pizza at Max Brenner
New York	Gravy Meatball Sliders at The Little Owl
New York	Matzo Ball Soup at Katz's Deli
Toronto	Roasted Marshmallow Ice Cream at Greg's Ice Cream
Toronto	Spaghetti at Scarpetta
Washington, D.C.	all 27 courses at Minibar
Washington, D.C.	Bill Cosby's Original Chili Half-Smoke at Ben's Chili Bowl

A Page from our TO-DO List

- Be the BITE ME sister team on *The Amazing Race*
- Share giggles with Anderson Cooper
- Watch Lisa Throwdown Bobby Flay with her biscotti
- Win a women's doubles table tennis trophy
- Sit front row at the Grand Sumo Tournament
- See Lisa milk a cow
- Teach Lisa how to ride a bike
- Watch Lisa run with the bulls
- Take an airboat ride in the Everglades
- Finally finish reading *Infinite Jest* and *War and Peace*
- Understand *Memento*, *Vanilla Sky* and *Inception*
- Go fly-fishing
- Visit the Galapagos Islands
- Open a Swiss bank account
- Have pho in Vietnam
- Say to someone, "Follow that car"
- Ring the bell at the NYSE
- Get hypnotized
- Wear a beekeeper's outfit
- Go storm chasing

HONEY DIJON ASPARAGUS & ALMONDS

INGREDIENTS

1 bunch asparagus, trimmed

Honey Dijon Vinaigrette

3 tbsp olive oil

2 tbsp rice vinegar

2 tsp fresh lemon juice

2 tsp honey

½ tsp Dijon mustard

¼ tsp kosher salt

¼ tsp freshly ground black pepper

¼ cup slivered or sliced almonds

We have great respect for asparagus – it's a nutrient-rich, versatile veggie that takes well to steaming, grilling, blanching or roasting – and while it's a regular at our tables, we sometimes want to dress it up a bit. The fleshy green spears are easily enhanced with the addition of this honey Dijon vinaigrette, a light, tangy dressing that perfectly balances the sweet with savory. To gussy things up even more, the tender-crisp stalks are sprinkled with lightly toasted almonds, providing a nutty crunch in every bite. Who knew that 6 inches growing out of the dirt could be so dignified?

DIRECTIONS

1) Bring a medium pot of water to a boil over high heat. Add asparagus and reduce heat to low, simmering 2–3 minutes until tender-crisp. Drain and rinse under cold water to stop further cooking. Pat dry with kitchen towel and arrange on a platter.

2) For the vinaigrette, in a small bowl, whisk olive oil, rice vinegar, lemon juice, honey, Dijon, salt and pepper. Spoon over asparagus.

3) For the toasted almonds, preheat oven to 350ºF. Place almonds in a single layer on a baking sheet. Roast 6–8 minutes shaking the pan frequently to prevent burning. Sprinkle over asparagus.

Serves 4

PANKO-CRUSTED BROCCOLI

INGREDIENTS

5 cups broccoli florets, stems removed

¼ cup flour

2 large eggs

¾ cup panko (Japanese breadcrumbs)

¾ cup freshly grated Parmesan cheese

1 tsp chopped fresh thyme

1 tsp lemon zest

¾ tsp kosher salt

¼ tsp freshly ground black pepper

2 tbsp olive oil

Creamy Lemon Dip

¼ cup sour cream

¼ cup mayonnaise

1 tbsp fresh lemon juice

1 tsp lemon zest

⅛ tsp kosher salt

I can't understand anyone who doesn't eat broccoli by the bushel. The wee green tree is a "miracle food," extolled for its anti-cancer, anti-inflammatory, anti-oxidant virtues. So, how do we best treat this crowned king-of-all-vegetables? Majestically. First, it takes a lovely plunge in a pot of boiling water. Next, it gets outfitted with a zesty Parmesan, panko and thyme coating. After a short stint in a sweltering oven, the crisp, tempura-style florets are dunked in a creamy lemon dip for a splendid finish. Now, if only this noble cruciferous vegetable could do something about my crow's feet, I'd be set.

DIRECTIONS

1) Preheat oven to 425ºF. Line a baking sheet with parchment paper and coat with non-stick cooking spray. 2) To a large pot of boiling water, add broccoli florets, cooking 2 minutes over low heat. Remove and immediately plunge into a large bowl of cold water. Drain well on a kitchen cloth. 3) For the coating, place flour in a shallow bowl. In a second shallow bowl, gently whisk eggs. In a third bowl, combine panko, Parmesan, thyme, lemon zest, salt and pepper. Working with a few pieces at a time, toss broccoli in flour, shaking off excess. Coat lightly in eggs and place in panko/Parmesan mixture, pressing lightly for crumbs to adhere. Repeat with remaining broccoli and place on prepared baking sheet. Drizzle broccoli with olive oil and bake 6–8 minutes, until golden brown. 4) While the broccoli bakes, prepare the dip. In a small bowl, whisk sour cream, mayonnaise, lemon juice, lemon zest and salt until combined. Serve with broccoli.

Serves 4

BITE ME BIT

"When I showed this to Brittany, she whimpered and thought I'd cut down a small tree where a family of gummy people lived."

— Sue Sylvester (actress Jane Lynch) discussing broccoli on the TV show *Glee*

ZUCCHINI FRIES with CARAMELIZED ONION DIP

INGREDIENTS

Zucchini Fries

3 medium zucchini, peeled and cut into 3-inch-long sticks

2 tsp kosher salt

¼ cup flour

2 large eggs, lightly whisked

1 cup panko (Japanese breadcrumbs)

½ cup freshly grated Parmesan cheese

1 tsp dried Italian herbs

2 tbsp olive oil

Caramelized Onion Dip

1 tbsp olive oil

1 large sweet onion, sliced

1 tsp brown sugar

¼ tsp kosher salt

1 tbsp apple cider vinegar

1 tbsp honey

1 tsp yellow mustard

½ cup mayonnaise

¼ tsp freshly ground black pepper

Creating a title for this recipe took some time to figure out. I decided to use my picky-eating kids as the focus group. At the first dinner, I lay down a platter of "zucchini strips." No takers. Next round, they became "zucchini spears." Again, no dice. It was time to pull out the big gun for this tough gang – I presented them with the newly named "zucchini fries." "Fries," they asked? And, before I could say, "Yuppers," the golden panko and Parmesan-crusted sticks were half gone. Baked until crisp, these addictive "fries" are dunked in a richly flavorful caramelized onion dip. Wait 'til they try my spinach fries...

DIRECTIONS

1) Place cut zucchini in a strainer, sprinkle with salt and toss to coat. Let drain 45 minutes. 2) Meanwhile, prepare onion dip. In a medium skillet, heat olive oil over medium-low heat. Add onions, brown sugar andsalt, cooking 10–15 minutes, stirring occasionally. Once onions are softened and golden, remove from heat and stir in cider vinegar. Place onion mixture in a food processor or blender. Add honey and mustard, blending until smooth. Place in a bowl and stir in mayonnaise and black pepper. Cover and refrigerate until ready to use. 3) Preheat oven to 425ºF. Line a baking sheet with parchment paper and coat with non-stick cooking spray. Remove zucchini from strainer, rinse very well under cold water to remove salt. Pat zucchini dry with a kitchen towel. Place flour in a medium bowl, eggs in another bowl and the panko, Parmesan and Italian herbs in a third bowl. Working one at a time, dip zucchini in flour, shaking off excess. Next, dip in egg and coat with panko mixture, pressing well to adhere crumbs. Place on prepared baking sheet and repeat with remaining zucchini. Drizzle entire sheet of zucchini with 2 tbsp olive oil. Bake 12 minutes, turn sticks and continue baking 6–8 minutes more, until golden brown and crispy. Serve immediately with caramelized onion dip.

Serves 4–6

BITE ME BIT

"I wish my name was Brian because maybe sometimes people would misspell my name and call me Brain. That's like a free compliment and you don't even gotta be smart to notice it."

— Mitch Hedberg, comedian

RICOTTA, BASIL & MINT ZUCCHINI BOATS

Lisa-the-Land-Lubber is cringing right now. I've called her cheesy, crunchy-topped zucchini masterpieces "boats." In my defense, these scooped-out zucchini, mounded high with creamy ricotta, Parmesan, basil and mint, *are* boats...lifeboats. Having saved me more times than I can count, this elegant, easy-to-make side dish is ideal for company because it can be prepared in advance, leaving me time to get three sheets to the wind. *Bon voyage*, Lisa.

INGREDIENTS

6 medium zucchini, halved lengthwise

Filling

2 tbsp olive oil

1 small yellow onion, finely chopped

1 large garlic clove, minced

2 cups ricotta cheese

½ cup freshly grated Parmesan cheese

¼ cup panko (Japanese breadcrumbs)

1 tbsp finely chopped fresh basil

1 tbsp finely chopped fresh mint

½ tsp dried oregano

½ tsp kosher salt

¼ tsp freshly ground black pepper

2 egg yolks, lightly beaten

2 tbsp olive oil

½ tsp kosher salt

Topping

¼ cup freshly grated Parmesan cheese

¼ cup panko (Japanese breadcrumbs)

2 tbsp olive oil

DIRECTIONS

1) Preheat broiler to high with the oven rack about 8 inches below the element. Line a baking sheet with aluminum foil and coat with non-stick cooking spray. **2)** For the zucchini, trim the ends of the halves. Scoop out zucchini seeds and discard pulp, leaving about ½ inch of pulp around the edges. Set aside. **3)** For the filling, in a medium skillet, heat 2 tbsp olive oil over medium heat. Add onion and cook 3–4 minutes until softened, stirring occasionally. Add garlic and sauté 1 minute until fragrant. Remove from heat and set aside. **4)** In a medium bowl, combine ricotta, ½ cup Parmesan, ¼ cup panko, basil, mint, oregano, salt, pepper and egg yolks. Stir in onion mixture. **5)** Rub prepared zucchini halves with 2 tbsp olive oil and season with ½ tsp salt. Place on baking sheet cut-side up. Place under broiler 3–5 minutes. Remove from oven and raise oven temperature to 375ºF. Stuff zucchini halves with even amounts of filling. If making ahead of time, cover and set aside. **6)** For the topping, in a small bowl, combine ¼ cup Parmesan and ¼ cup panko. When ready to serve, sprinkle each stuffed zucchini with mixture and drizzle with 2 tbsp olive oil. Bake uncovered 10–12 minutes until filling is hot and bubbly.

Serves 6

BITE ME BIT

"A lot of people ask me if I were shipwrecked and could only have one book, what would it be? I always say *How To Build A Boat*."

– Steven Wright, comedian

RATATOUILLE over SOFT PARMESAN POLENTA

INGREDIENTS

Ratatouille

6 cups 1-inch diced eggplant, peeled

4 cups 1-inch diced zucchini

1 tsp kosher salt

2 tbsp olive oil

1 tbsp olive oil

1 large yellow onion, cut into 1-inch pieces

2 large green peppers, cut into 1-inch cubes

2 large garlic cloves, minced

½ tsp kosher salt

½ tsp freshly ground black pepper

1 (28oz) tin diced tomatoes

2 tbsp chopped fresh flat-leaf parsley

2 tbsp chopped fresh basil

Soft Polenta

6 cups vegetable broth

1 cup water

1½ cups yellow cornmeal

2 tbsp butter

½ cup freshly grated Parmesan cheese

How, might I ask, can a Pixar movie cause people to instantly equate a delicious 17th-century French Provençal dish with an animated chef rat? Not a great association for ratatouille, but the Mediterranean stewed vegetables will always be number one in our minds. Eggplant, zucchini, onions, peppers and tomatoes are simmered with fresh herbs to make this traditional side dish an entrée-worthy international superstar. Move aside, Remy-the-Rodent...placed atop a creamy, soft Parmesan polenta, this full-flavored ratatouille is getting the star on the Hollywood Walk of Fame.

DIRECTIONS

1) For the ratatouille, place diced eggplant and zucchini in a colander. Toss with salt and let drain for 30 minutes. Rinse salt off and pat dry. In a large skillet, heat 2 tbsp olive oil over high heat. Add eggplant and zucchini, cooking 4 minutes until lightly browned. Remove from skillet and set aside. 2) Using the same skillet, heat remaining 1 tbsp olive oil over medium heat. Add onions and green peppers and cook, stirring frequently until softened, about 5 minutes. Stir in garlic, salt and pepper, cooking 1 minute. Add diced tomatoes, parsley and basil and bring mixture to a boil. Reduce heat to low and stir in eggplant/zucchini mixture. Simmer, partially covered, 45 minutes, stirring occasionally. While the vegetables cook, prepare the polenta. 3) For the polenta, in a large saucepan, bring broth and water to a boil over medium-high heat. Constantly whisk while adding cornmeal in a steady stream. Reduce heat to low and simmer gently, whisking occasionally to prevent lumps from forming. Cook 20 minutes until polenta is soft and creamy. Remove from heat and stir in butter and Parmesan. Serve hot topped with ratatouille.

Serves 6

BITE ME BIT

"I'm way too baked."

— from the 1996 Adam Sandler song "Mr. Bake-O"

BAKED EGGPLANT PARMESAN

I think my husband thought buying me a deep fryer meant more "greasy goodness" at home. Imagine his disappointment, en route to sizzle a Snickers bar, to discover I use the fryer to store the donut maker he got me. We're in a fryolator-free zone, where getting hit by spitting oil is a thing of the past. Lisa has cleaned up this Italian, grease-laden classic by turning on the oven. Slices of encrusted eggplant are baked to a golden crisp, then layered with zesty homemade tomato sauce, Parmesan and mozzarella cheese. Satisfying and healthful, this vegetarian dish has all the flavor and none of the fry...now, where am I going to stash the new Cinnamon Roll Bread Machine?

INGREDIENTS

Tomato Sauce

2 tbsp olive oil

1 large yellow onion, chopped

2 large garlic cloves

½ tsp dried oregano

½ tsp kosher salt

¼ tsp freshly ground black pepper

¼ tsp dried basil

1 (28oz) tin crushed tomatoes

1 (5.5oz) tin tomato paste

1 tsp sugar

Eggplant Parmesan

3 medium eggplants, about 2 lbs

1 tbsp kosher salt

⅓ cup flour

3 large eggs, lightly beaten

1½ cups breadcrumbs

1 cup freshly grated Parmesan cheese (divided)

¼ tsp kosher salt

¼ tsp freshly ground black pepper

¼ tsp garlic powder

3½ cups shredded mozzarella cheese

DIRECTIONS

1) For the tomato sauce, in a large saucepan, heat olive oil over medium-high heat. Add onions and cook 5 minutes, stirring often. Add garlic, oregano, salt, pepper and basil, cooking for 1 minute. Add crushed tomatoes, tomato paste and sugar. Bring to a boil over high heat. Reduce heat to low, partially cover and cook for 30 minutes, stirring occasionally. 2) Preheat oven to 425°F. Line 2 baking sheets with aluminum foil and coat with non-stick cooking spray. 3) For the eggplant, wash the outside skin and slice into ½-inch thick rounds. Place the slices in a large strainer, sprinkle with 1 tbsp salt, toss to coat and let sit 35-45 minutes. When finished, rinse eggplant slices with cold water, drain and dry well with paper towel. 4) Place flour in a large resealable plastic bag, add eggplant slices and toss to coat with flour. Place eggs in a medium bowl. In a large bowl, toss breadcrumbs, ½ cup Parmesan, salt, pepper and garlic powder. Dip each slice of eggplant in the eggs coating both sides and then in the breadcrumb mixture, coating both sides. Place in a single layer on prepared baking sheets and spray tops with non-stick cooking spray. Bake 13 minutes, flip the slices and continue to bake for another 13 minutes. Remove from oven and lower temperature to 350°F. 5) To assemble, coat a 13x9-inch baking dish with non-stick cooking spray. Cover the bottom of the dish with 1 cup of tomato sauce. Layer ⅓ of the eggplant over the sauce followed by ⅓ of the shredded mozzarella. Repeat twice more, starting with 1 cup of tomato sauce, until remaining eggplant, cheese and sauce have been layered. Sprinkle top with remaining Parmesan and bake 30 minutes.

Serves 8–10

MISO-GLAZED JAPANESE EGGPLANT

INGREDIENTS

Miso Glaze

3 tbsp sake

3 tbsp sugar

2 tbsp mirin

1 tsp fresh lime juice

4 tbsp white miso paste

4 Japanese eggplants

1 tbsp vegetable oil

1 tsp sesame seeds

I love it when I can describe a vegetable as tasting like crème brûlée. This dish, also known as *nasu dengaku* in Japanese restaurants, is eggplant transformed into a melty, creamy, sweet and salty treat. Long, narrow and glossy deep purple Japanese eggplants, with their delicate flavor and thin skin, lend themselves perfectly to being baked. Once tender, the flesh is topped with a nutty-tasting miso mixture and broiled until caramelized and bubbly. Whether using chopsticks or a dessertspoon to scoop it out, you're going to love this melt-in-your-mouth velvety vegetable.

DIRECTIONS

1) Preheat broiler to high heat. Line a baking sheet with aluminum foil and coat with non-stick cooking spray. **2)** For the miso glaze, in a small saucepan, combine sake, sugar, mirin and lime juice. Bring to a gentle boil over medium heat. Whisk for 2 minutes to dissolve sugar. Reduce heat to low and whisk in miso paste. Continue cooking 2 minutes, stirring often. Remove from heat and set aside. **3)** For the eggplants, slice each one in half lengthwise, leaving stems on. Using the tip of a sharp knife cut a crisscross pattern into the flesh of each eggplant piece. Brush the cut side with vegetable oil and place cut side down on prepared baking sheet. Broil 3 minutes, flip pieces over and cook another 3–4 minutes. Remove from oven and spread miso mixture thickly onto each eggplant and sprinkle with sesame seeds. Place back under broiler for 1–2 minutes, until glaze is bubbly; watch carefully so they don't burn.

Serves 4

BITE ME BIT

秋茄子は嫁に食わすな。

(Don't let your daughter-in-law eat your autumn eggplants.)

— Japanese Proverb

CHEESY SPINACH-STUFFED PORTOBELLO MUSHROOMS

INGREDIENTS

Red Pepper Pesto Sauce

2 large red bell peppers, halved and seeded

½ cup sliced almonds

¼ cup olive oil

¼ cup fresh basil leaves, packed

2 tbsp pine nuts

1 small garlic clove

½ tsp kosher salt

8 large portobello mushrooms

1 tbsp olive oil

⅛ tsp kosher salt

⅛ tsp freshly ground black pepper

Spinach Cheese Filling

1 tbsp olive oil

1 small white onion, finely chopped

1 small garlic clove, minced

1½ cups chopped fresh baby spinach

1½ cups whole milk ricotta cheese

½ cup shredded mozzarella cheese

½ cup freshly grated Parmesan cheese

3 tbsp breadcrumbs

¼ tsp kosher salt

¼ tsp freshly ground black pepper

While we sometimes sweat the small stuff (people with nose whistles, shriveled tiny stuffed mushrooms, etc.), we prefer to stuff the big stuff. And, by big stuff, we mean portobellos, the meatiest of meaty mushrooms. Considered the steak of vegetarians, these oversized, bold caps perfectly complement a mixture of fresh spinach, creamy ricotta, mild mozzarella and sharp Parmesan. Filled to the rim and baked until golden brown, the mounded mushroom sits atop a smooth puree of red pepper pesto. We have a feeling steakhouses across the country are going to be clamoring for this satisfying, flavorful, massive mushroom.

DIRECTIONS

1) For the red pepper pesto, preheat oven to broil. Place cut peppers on a baking sheet lined with aluminum foil and coated with non-stick cooking spray. Broil peppers until skin is blackened all over. Remove from oven and when cool enough to handle, peel skins off peppers. Place peppers, almonds, olive oil, basil, pine nuts, garlic and salt in a blender, pureeing until smooth, about 10 seconds. Set aside. **2)** Preheat oven to 400°F. Line a baking sheet with aluminum foil and coat with non-stick cooking spray. **3)** To clean the mushrooms, remove stems, wipe caps clean with a damp cloth and scrape out gills with a small spoon. Place mushrooms on baking sheet, gill side up. Brush mushrooms evenly with 1 tbsp olive oil and sprinkle each with salt and pepper. Place in oven, cooking 8 minutes. Drain any excess liquid from the mushrooms and let cool 20 minutes before filling. **4)** For the filling, in a medium skillet, heat 1 tbsp olive oil over medium heat. Add onions and garlic, stirring constantly until softened, 2–3 minutes. Remove from heat and place in large bowl. Add spinach, ricotta, mozzarella, Parmesan, breadcrumbs, salt and pepper. Combine well and divide mixture evenly among mushrooms, about ¼ cup per cap. Bake 10 minutes more until filling is heated through. To serve, place 2 generous tablespoons of red pepper pesto sauce on each plate and place mushroom on top. Serve immediately.

Serves 8

VEGETABLE & CHICKPEA CURRY

INGREDIENTS

2 tbsp vegetable oil

1 large yellow onion, thinly sliced

2 cups peeled and cubed Yukon Gold potato, about 2 large potatoes

1½ cups cubed butternut squash

1 large garlic clove, minced

1 tbsp tomato paste

1 tbsp curry powder

1 tsp grated fresh ginger

¼ tsp ground cumin

¼ tsp garam masala

¼ tsp ground cinnamon

¼ tsp kosher salt

¼ tsp freshly ground black pepper

2 cups cauliflower florets, cut into 1½-inch pieces

2 cups canned diced tomatoes, with liquid

1¼ cups vegetable broth

1 cup canned chickpeas, rinsed and drained

1 cup frozen peas

⅓ cup ground almonds

2 tbsp chopped fresh flat-leaf parsley

That darn food pyramid always had me questioning where to slot zucchini bread and pumpkin butter. Now the confusing triangle has been replaced with a USDA pre-portioned dinner plate, a circle that leaves absolutely no space for carrot cake. How, might I ask, is a girl supposed to fill her vegetable quota? Lisa answered that question with this quick and easy, healthy and extremely flavorful Indian-spiced vegetable dish. Meatless yet protein and fiber rich, this hearty dish is loaded with tender potatoes, squash, cauliflower, green peas and chickpeas, all stewed in an exotic-spice blend of curry, garam masala, cumin, cinnamon and ginger. Yah, well, here's a simple nutritional guideline – a huge bowl of this nutrient-dense, stew-like curry will power you through the day.

DIRECTIONS

1) In a large pot, heat vegetable oil over medium heat. Add onions, potatoes and butternut squash, cooking 5 minutes and stirring occasionally. Add garlic, tomato paste, curry powder, ginger, cumin, garam masala, cinnamon, salt and pepper, stirring well to combine. Add cauliflower and cook 1 minute. Stir in diced tomatoes and vegetable broth. Bring to a boil, reduce heat to low and simmer covered for 10 minutes. Remove pot cover and continue to cook another 10 minutes. Add chickpeas, frozen peas and ground almonds, cooking on low heat for an additional 10 minutes. Remove from heat and stir in parsley. Season to taste with salt and pepper.

Serves 6

NOT-SO-SUFFERIN' SUCCOTASH

INGREDIENTS

2 tbsp olive oil

1 large white onion, chopped

1 large garlic clove, minced

2 cups fresh corn kernels (3–4 ears)

2 cups fresh or frozen peas

2 cups frozen shelled edamame

1 cup chopped red bell pepper

½ tsp kosher salt

½ tsp freshly ground black pepper

2 tbsp thinly sliced fresh basil

You know I've hit rock bottom when I need to call on Sylvester, an animated cat, to help me write a recipe title. Truth is, the word "succotash" sounds, well, so suckish – it doesn't do justice to this healthy medley of corn, peas and edamame, nor does it speak to the sweet crunch of red peppers and slivers of fresh basil in this great summer staple. Th-th-th-that's all folks!

DIRECTIONS

1) In a large skillet, heat olive oil over medium heat. Add onion, sautéing until softened, about 4–5 minutes. Add garlic, constantly stirring for 1 minute. Add corn, peas, edamame and red pepper, stirring occasionally and cooking until vegetables are tender, about 10 minutes. Season with salt and pepper, remove from heat and stir in sliced basil.

Serves 6–8

BITE ME BIT

"Succotash my Balzac, dipshiitake."

— from the Jonathan Safran Foer novel *Extremely Loud & Incredibly Close*

ROASTED BRUSSELS SPROUTS with MAPLE DRESSING

INGREDIENTS

Brussels Sprouts

4 cups fresh Brussels sprouts, trimmed and halved

2 tbsp olive oil

¼ tsp kosher salt

⅛ tsp freshly ground black pepper

Maple Dressing

2 tbsp olive oil

1 tbsp apple cider vinegar

1 tbsp maple syrup

½ tsp Dijon mustard

¼ tsp kosher salt

¼ tsp freshly ground black pepper

If you've just finished eating something that involved the words "Grand Slam" or "Meat Lover's," I'll try, but there may be very little I can say to push you toward Brussels sprouts. While you're attempting to digest, let me appeal to your mind: in 1812, Thomas Jefferson introduced Brussels sprouts to the United States. Now, he may be better known for writing something called the Declaration of Independence and Statute of Virginia, but I think he had some great foresight launching these mini cabbages. Almost 200 years later, we're roasting these fiber- and vitamin-rich sweet emerald gems until golden-crusted. Tossed in a sweet and tangy maple mustard vinaigrette, these tender sprouts are going to have an entire nation jumping on the Brussels bandwagon.

DIRECTIONS

1) Preheat oven to 425°F. Line a baking sheet with aluminum foil and coat with non-stick cooking spray. In a large bowl, gently toss Brussels sprouts with 2 tbsp olive oil, salt and pepper. Place on prepared baking sheet in a single layer. Roast 10 minutes, flip Brussels sprouts and continue to cook 10 minutes more, until tender and golden. 2) While Brussels sprouts are roasting, prepare maple dressing. In a small bowl, whisk olive oil, cider vinegar, maple syrup, Dijon, salt and pepper. Remove sprouts from oven and place in a large bowl. Gently toss with maple dressing until well coated.

Serves 4

Fuel me

Energizing Pasta, Rice & Grains

ROASTED VEGETABLE MANICOTTI with CHUNKY TOMATO SAUCE

INGREDIENTS

Chunky Tomato Sauce

3 tbsp olive oil

½ cup chopped white onion

2 large garlic cloves, minced

1 (28oz) tin diced tomatoes, with juices

1 (6oz) tin tomato paste

½ cup dry red wine

1 tbsp brown sugar

½ tsp dried oregano

½ tsp kosher salt

¼ tsp freshly ground black pepper

1 tbsp fresh basil, cut into thin strips

kosher salt, to taste

Roasted Vegetable Manicotti

1½ cups chopped broccoli

1½ cups chopped cauliflower

1 cup peeled and chopped carrots

1 small onion, coarsely chopped

3 tbsp olive oil

¼ tsp kosher salt

¼ tsp freshly ground black pepper

3 cups coarsely chopped baby spinach

2 cups whole-milk ricotta cheese

1 cup shredded mozzarella cheese

1 cup freshly grated Parmesan cheese

2 large eggs

2 tbsp chopped fresh basil

2 tbsp chopped fresh flat-leaf parsley

½ tsp kosher salt

¼ tsp freshly ground black pepper

12 manicotti shells

¼ cup freshly grated Parmesan cheese

Oh yes. I have tricks up my sleeve. When I'm losing in Monopoly, I "borrow" money from the bank, when I'm getting clobbered in chess, there's a sudden "earthquake" that tilts the board, and, when I feel like being a dinnertime hero, I pull my favorite manicotti out of my sleeve. Manicotti, which translates to "sleeve" in English, is a large tube of pasta stuffed with sweet, roasted vegetables, topped with a homemade chunky tomato sauce and baked to cheesy perfection. Wait 'til you see what I pull out of my sleeve when I'm losing in Twister (hint: Charlie Horse and atomic wedgie) to Lisa.

DIRECTIONS

1) For the tomato sauce, in a large skillet, heat olive oil over medium heat. Add onion and cook, stirring often until softened, 4–5 minutes. Add garlic and cook for 30 seconds. Stir in tomatoes, tomato paste, wine, brown sugar, oregano, salt and pepper. Bring to a gentle boil. Reduce heat to low and simmer uncovered 15 minutes. Stir in fresh basil and season to taste with salt. Set aside until manicotti is ready to be assembled. 2) For the roasted vegetable filling, preheat oven to 350°F. Line a baking sheet with aluminum foil and coat with non-stick cooking spray. In a large bowl, combine broccoli, cauliflower, carrots, onion, olive oil, ¼ tsp salt and ¼ tsp pepper. Toss well and place on prepared baking sheet. Roast vegetables for 30 minutes, stirring after 15 minutes. When vegetables have softened, remove from oven and add chopped spinach, tossing well to combine. Place vegetables in a blender or food processor and pulse 2–3 times to coarsely chop. Place in a large bowl and add ricotta, mozzarella, Parmesan, eggs, basil, parsley, salt and pepper, stirring well to combine. 3) Cook manicotti shells according to package directions. Drain well before filling. 4) Increase oven temperature to 375°F. Spread 1½ cups tomato sauce on the bottom of a 13x9-inch baking dish. Fill a large resealable plastic bag or pastry bag with the manicotti filling. Cut an opening in one corner of your plastic bag and squeeze filling into the cooked shells. Arrange filled manicotti in baking dish. Top evenly with remaining 1½ cups tomato sauce and ¼ cup Parmesan cheese. Cover the dish with aluminum foil and bake 30 minutes. Cool 10 minutes before serving.

Serves 6–8

BITE ME BIT

"For many, immaturity is an ideal, not a defect."

— Mason Cooley, aphorist

LOADED VEGETABLE LASAGNA

INGREDIENTS

Tomato Sauce

1 tbsp olive oil

1 medium yellow onion, chopped

2 large garlic cloves, minced

1 (28oz) tin crushed tomatoes

1 (28oz) tin whole tomatoes

1 cup water

2 tbsp sugar

2 tsp chopped fresh basil

1 tsp kosher salt

9 lasagna noodles

Vegetable Filling

2 tbsp olive oil

2 cups zucchini, halved lengthwise and thinly sliced

12 asparagus spears, cut into 1-inch pieces

1½ cups sliced white mushrooms

1 medium yellow onion, diced

1 large garlic clove, minced

¼ tsp kosher salt

¼ tsp freshly ground black pepper

Cheese Filling

4 cups ricotta cheese

1 cup shredded Asiago cheese

½ cup freshly grated Parmesan cheese

2 large eggs, lightly beaten

½ tsp kosher salt

2 cups shredded mozzarella cheese

¼ cup freshly grated Parmesan cheese

A little effort goes a long way. This garden fresh lasagna is the perfect case in point. While we can all whip together a last-minute desperation lasagna in 10 minutes, the reviews are rarely raves. Not the case here. Take the time to create layers of homemade tomato basil sauce, thin-sliced zucchini, asparagus and mushrooms, tender noodles and a 4-cheese filling – the result is a full-flavored favorite. Perfect for feeding a crowd, this bubbly, cheesy and satisfying vegetarian (not an oxymoron since ardent meatarians always go back for seconds) is always a smash hit, a bestseller, a hot-ticket item.

DIRECTIONS

1) For the tomato sauce, in a large saucepan, heat olive oil over medium heat. Add onion and garlic, cooking 4 minutes. Stir in tomatoes, water, sugar, basil and salt. Bring to a boil, reduce heat to low and simmer 1 hour uncovered. Remove from heat and set aside. **2)** In a large pot of lightly salted, boiling water, cook lasagna noodles 4–6 minutes until almost al dente. Drain and set aside. **3)** For the vegetable filling, in a large skillet, heat olive oil over medium-high heat. Add zucchini, asparagus, mushrooms, onion and garlic, cooking 8 minutes, until slightly tender. Remove from heat and season with salt and pepper. Set aside. **4)** For the cheese filling, in a medium bowl, combine ricotta, Asiago, Parmesan, eggs and salt. Stir to combine. **5)** To assemble, preheat oven to 350°F. Coat a 13x9-inch baking dish with non-stick cooking spray. Spread 1 cup tomato sauce on bottom of baking dish. Place 3 noodles on top of sauce. Spread half the cheese mixture over the noodles followed by half the vegetable mixture (leaving any cooking liquid in the skillet). Top vegetables with 1 cup tomato sauce and sprinkle with 1 cup mozzarella. Lay 3 more noodles on top and spread remaining cheese mixture, followed by remaining vegetables. Top with 1 cup tomato sauce and 1 cup mozzarella. Lay remaining 3 noodles on top, cover with 1 cup tomato sauce and sprinkle with ¼ cup Parmesan. Bake 35 minutes uncovered and let stand 10 minutes before serving.

Serves 8

PERFETTO PASTA with ZUCCHINI & FRESH HERBS

INGREDIENTS

¾ lb pappardelle pasta

½ cup reserved pasta water

2 tbsp olive oil

4 small shallots, thinly sliced then roughly chopped

2 large zucchini, julienned into French fry size strips

2 small garlic cloves, minced

4 oil-packed sun-dried tomatoes, cut into narrow strips

1 tbsp fresh lemon juice

1 tsp lemon zest

½ tsp kosher salt

¼ tsp freshly ground black pepper

½ cup freshly grated Parmesan cheese

1 tbsp finely chopped fresh basil

1 tbsp finely chopped fresh mint

1 tbsp finely chopped fresh flat-leaf parsley

A lot of Italian words – *allora, boh, uffa* – get lost in translation. Not pappardelle. How apropos that the name for this wide ribbon pasta comes from the verb *"pappare,"* meaning, "to gobble up"? Get ready to polish off this garden-like pasta dish, a winning combination of powerful, broad noodles and gentle, fresh herbs. *Buon appetito.*

DIRECTIONS

1) Bring a large pot of lightly salted water to a boil over high heat. Stir in pasta and cook until tender. Reserve ½ cup pasta water and drain pasta well. **2)** For the zucchini mixture, in a large skillet, heat olive oil over medium heat. Add shallots and cook 2 minutes to soften. Add zucchini, stirring well to coat and continue cooking 3–5 minutes, until slightly tender. Add garlic and sun-dried tomatoes cooking until garlic becomes fragrant, about 1 minute. Remove from heat, stir in lemon juice, lemon zest, salt and pepper. Toss in cooked pasta, Parmesan, basil, mint, parsley and some of the reserved pasta water to moisten. Season with salt and pepper to taste. Serve immediately.

Serves 4

BITE ME BIT

"If only I was born Italian. All the best Yankees are Italian. My mother makes spaghetti with ketchup. What chance do I have?"

— Eugene Morris Jerome (actor Jonathan Silverman) in the 1986 movie *Brighton Beach Memoirs*

CREAMY GOAT CHEESE & BROCCOLI FUSILLI

INGREDIENTS

½ lb fusilli pasta

½ cup reserved pasta water

1½ cups broccoli florets

1 cup fresh or frozen green peas

2 tbsp olive oil

1 tbsp fresh lemon juice

4 oz soft goat cheese, crumbled

2 tbsp chopped fresh basil

½ tsp kosher salt

¼ tsp freshly ground black pepper

½ cup freshly grated Parmesan cheese, for topping

We're naughty. Eating chocolate after 10pm, secretly nicknaming people (Luigi, Hercules and Cauliflower Head, to name a few) and still getting sent away from the dinner table are tip o' the iceberg. We also crave cream sauces. With our stomachs and hips in mind, Lisa cooked up this creamy-but-creamless, buttery-but-butterless, rich-tasting vegetarian pasta. Fusilli, the ultimate corkscrew-shaped sauce catcher, is loaded with tender-crisp broccoli, sweet peas and fresh basil. When soft goat cheese is added the whole kit and caboodle gets melty and goolicious (fyi – this word was recently added to the dictionary), noodles and vegetables coated in creamy, tart and tangy goodness. This pasta dish is #@&ing awesome.

DIRECTIONS

1) Bring a large pot of lightly salted water to a boil over high heat. Cook pasta until tender and drain, reserving ½ cup of pasta water.

2) Bring a large pot of water to a boil over high heat. Turn heat to low, add broccoli and peas cooking for 1–2 minutes. Immediately put vegetables in a medium bowl of cold water to stop cooking. Drain well and return to pot along with cooked pasta. Over low heat, add olive oil, lemon juice, goat cheese, basil, salt and pepper, tossing pasta to coat. Add some of the reserved pasta water as needed to loosen the sauce. Serve immediately topped with a generous serving of Parmesan.

Serves 4

BITE ME BIT

"The main reason Santa is so jolly is because he knows where all the bad girls live."

— George Carlin, comedian

TGI Monday MUSHROOM FETTUCCINE

INGREDIENTS

2 tbsp butter

1 tbsp olive oil

6 cups sliced cremini mushrooms

2½ cups sliced shiitake mushrooms

2 large (about ½ cup) shallots, finely diced

2 large garlic cloves, minced

1 tsp minced fresh thyme

½ tsp kosher salt

¼ tsp freshly ground black pepper

¾ lb fettuccine

½ cup reserved pasta water

1 cup chicken broth

½ cup cream

¾ cup freshly grated Parmesan cheese

1 tbsp fresh lemon juice

½ tsp kosher salt

¼ tsp freshly ground black pepper

Bob Geldof wrote a song called "I Don't Like Mondays." While it was my schoolgirl anthem for my inevitable Sunday night "stomach ache," these days, it couldn't be further from the truth. I love Monday. Not to get all Motivational-Monday-Life-Coach-y on you, but I like the sense of possibility for the coming week, a fresh start after a carnivorous, wayward weekend. So, I start my week in a pure, clean and immaculate way with this meatless yet meaty mushroom fettuccine. The earthy flavors of tender, sautéed mushrooms, combined with shallots, garlic, thyme and Parmesan, make this creamy, cheesy pasta dish all the more Monday-rrific. Now Tuesday, that's a whole other story...

DIRECTIONS

1) In a large skillet, heat butter and olive oil over medium-high heat. Add both types of mushrooms and sauté 6–7 minutes, stirring often until golden brown. Add shallots, garlic, thyme, ½ tsp salt and ¼ tsp pepper. Cook 3 minutes, until shallots are soft. Transfer to a medium bowl and set skillet aside for step #3. **2)** For the pasta, bring a large pot of lightly salted water to a boil. Cook fettuccine until tender, stirring often. Reserve ½ cup cooking water before draining. **3)** Using the skillet you sautéed the mushrooms in, bring chicken broth to a boil over high heat, scraping up any browned bits. Stir in cream, bring back to a boil, then lower heat to a gentle simmer. Reduce sauce for 3 minutes. Remove from heat and stir in sautéed mushrooms. Add the pasta and just enough of the reserved pasta water for desired consistency. Add Parmesan, lemon juice, salt and pepper, stirring to combine. Serve immediately.

Serves 4–6

PENNE with ROASTED TOMATOES, SPINACH & BEANS

INGREDIENTS

Oven-Roasted Tomatoes

8 plum tomatoes, quartered and seeded

2 tbsp olive oil

¼ tsp kosher salt

¼ tsp freshly ground black pepper

½ lb penne pasta

½ cup reserved pasta water

2 tbsp olive oil

1 large garlic clove, minced

1½ cups canned white kidney (cannellini) beans

3 cups roughly chopped baby spinach

2 tbsp fresh lemon juice

2 tbsp fresh basil, cut into thin strips

¼ tsp kosher salt

¼ tsp freshly ground black pepper

¼ cup freshly grated Parmesan cheese

I was going to call this recipe "Garlic Penne with Other Delicious Things" but thought it would lessen the drama in what I'm about to reveal. Am I betraying Lisa by telling you she went to the annual Gilroy Garlic Festival to chase the dream of being crowned Miss Gilroy Garlic? Though she looks great for her age, she's a tad long in the tooth when competing with teenagers. Disappointment breeds her creativity, the result being this clove-tastic penne with ultra-flavorful, slow roasted plum tomatoes, leafy green spinach, creamy white beans, tart lemon juice and fresh basil. Honestly, I thought she had it in the bag, but can't say I'm sorry if this is what I get to eat when she loses.

DIRECTIONS

1) For the tomatoes, preheat oven to 300°F. Line a baking sheet with aluminum foil and coat with non-stick cooking spray. In a large bowl, toss cut tomatoes with olive oil, salt and pepper. Place on prepared baking sheet, cut side up, and bake 1½ hours. 2) Toward the end of the tomatoes roasting, cook the penne pasta in a large pot of lightly salted boiling water until tender. Drain pasta, reserving ½ cup of the cooking water. 3) Using the same large pot heat 2 tbsp olive oil over medium heat. Add garlic, stirring 30 seconds, until fragrant. Add cooked pasta, roasted tomatoes, white beans and spinach, cooking until spinach wilts, about 1 minute. Add lemon juice, basil, salt, pepper, Parmesan and some of the reserved pasta water as needed to loosen the sauce. Serve immediately.

Serves 4

BITE ME BIT

"You can never have enough garlic. With enough garlic, you can eat the *New York Times*."

— Morley Safer, reporter

Schlemiel! Schlimazel! FETTUCCINI BOLOGNESE!

INGREDIENTS

3 large celery stalks, chopped

3 large carrots, peeled and chopped

1 large red onion, quartered

4 large garlic cloves

1 rosemary sprig, leaves removed and roughly chopped

½ cup roughly chopped fresh flat-leaf parsley

1 tbsp dried oregano

2 lbs lean ground beef

1½ tsp kosher salt

1 tsp freshly ground black pepper

¾ cup dry white wine

2 (5.5oz) cans tomato paste

3½ cups beef broth

1½ lbs fettuccini

freshly grated Parmesan cheese for serving

Lisa was the only kid who had posters of Carmine "The Big Ragu" Ragusa lining her wall. I knew she had Shirley-envy (she insisted on calling me "Laverne" and her stuffed cat "Boo Boo Kitty"), but when she went to Italy to make her "dreams come true," I was more than a little concerned. Turns out, I didn't need to worry. She went to Tuscany to learn how to make a 3-day Ragu Bolognese, the quintessential Italian meat sauce. Since most of us don't have 72 hours to make dinner, Lisa adapted the satisfying sauce into this 1-hour rich and meaty classic, so full-bodied and fragrant that Lenny and Squiggy will be barging through the door at any minute.

DIRECTIONS

1) For the Bolognese sauce, in a food processor, combine celery, carrots, red onion, garlic, rosemary, parsley and oregano. Pulse 2–3 times to finely chop ingredients. 2) In a large pot, combine chopped vegetables with ground beef over high heat. Once mixture begins to boil, add salt and pepper, lower heat to a simmer, cover and cook 30 minutes, stirring occasionally. 2) After 30 minutes, increase heat to high and add white wine, letting it evaporate for 1 minute. Add tomato paste and beef broth. Bring to a boil, reduce heat to a simmer and cook uncovered for 30 minutes longer, stirring occasionally. 3) Meanwhile, for the pasta, bring a large pot of lightly salted water to a boil. Cook fettuccini until tender, drain and place in a serving bowl. 4) Toss with Bolognese sauce, with extra sauce served alongside or frozen for another meal. Serve with a sprinkling of freshly grated Parmesan cheese.

Serves 10–12

CHICKEN PICCATA LINGUINE

INGREDIENTS

Marinade

2 tbsp fresh lemon juice

2 tbsp olive oil

1 tsp lemon zest

3 boneless, skinless chicken breast halves

¾ lb linguine pasta

¼ tsp kosher salt

¼ tsp freshly ground black pepper

¼ cup flour

2 tbsp olive oil

Lemon Wine Sauce

2 tbsp butter

1 medium yellow onion, diced

2 large garlic cloves, minced

1 tbsp cornstarch

⅓ cup dry white wine

1¼ cups chicken broth

½ cup fresh lemon juice

2 tbsp capers, rinsed and drained

1 tbsp chopped fresh basil

½ tsp kosher salt

½ tsp freshly ground black pepper

½ cup freshly grated Parmesan cheese

Chicken piccata is one of our "go-to" recipes. Whether we're short on groceries (it uses simple ingredients I always have on hand) or time (it's easily whipped together), it's a classic that never fails to please. So, you can imagine how high I jumped when Lisa told me she'd added another element to this lickety-split lemon lover's supper. In a move of sheer genius she tossed sautéed tender chicken with linguine and a lemon-caper sauce. Stir in some fresh Parmesan and basil, and, there you have it – a speedy, satisfying dinner in a bowl.

DIRECTIONS

1) Place chicken breasts between 2 sheets of wax paper and pound to even thickness, about ½-inch thick. In a shallow dish, whisk lemon juice, olive oil and lemon zest. Add chicken and marinate at room temperature for 30 minutes. 2) While the chicken marinates, cook the pasta in a large pot of lightly salted boiling water until tender. Drain and set aside. 3) Remove chicken from marinade and season with ¼ tsp each salt and pepper. Place flour in a shallow dish. Dredge chicken in flour, shaking off excess. In a large skillet, heat olive oil over medium-high heat. Add chicken, cooking 3 minutes per side or until cooked through. Remove from skillet and slice into bite-sized strips. Set aside. 4) To make sauce, wipe skillet out and heat butter over medium heat. Add onions and garlic, cooking 5 minutes, stirring often. Sprinkle with cornstarch, cooking 1 minute more. Deglaze the skillet with white wine for 1 minute. Add chicken broth and lemon juice, bringing to a boil over high heat. Reduce heat to low, stir and simmer 4 minutes. Add capers, basil, salt and pepper, stirring to combine. Toss in cooked pasta and sliced chicken, cooking 2 minutes to heat through. Remove from heat and stir in Parmesan. Serve immediately.

Serves 4–6

BITE ME BIT

"You are my heroine! And by heroine, I mean lady hero. I don't want to inject you and listen to jazz."

— Liz Lemon (actress Tina Fey) on the TV show *30 Rock*

SUPREME SPINACH RISOTTO

INGREDIENTS

4½–5½ cups vegetable broth

2 tbsp olive oil

1 tbsp butter

1 medium yellow onion, chopped

1 cup chopped fennel

1½ cups Arborio or Carnaroli rice

½ cup dry white wine

8 cups loosely packed baby spinach, stems removed, chopped

½ cup freshly grated Parmesan cheese

Bow or curtsey, it's up to you. Risotto is "rice royalty," the king of the creamy, the sovereign of satisfaction in the grain world. Now, don't be all intimidated. You really can't go wrong. It's not a royal pain to make. All you have to do is stir. Yes, stir it a few times and you end up with top-ranking, regal rice. Blended with vibrant and nutrient rich spinach, subtle licorice flavored fennel, enhanced with white wine and Parmesan, this majestic meal is guaranteed to please the court.

DIRECTIONS

1) In a medium saucepan, bring vegetable broth to a simmer over low heat. Keep it warm throughout cook time. 2) In a large saucepan, heat olive oil and butter over medium heat. Add onion and fennel, cooking 5 minutes, until softened. Add the rice, stirring constantly to coat. Add wine and continue stirring as the rice absorbs the liquid. Add in 1 cup of vegetable broth, stirring frequently until the liquid is absorbed. Once absorbed, add another cup of broth to the rice. Repeat, making sure each addition of liquid is absorbed before adding the next. Continue for 18–20 minutes, until rice is creamy and tender. Once cooked, remove from heat and stir in spinach and Parmesan. Season with salt and pepper to taste.

Serves 4–6

A quick risotto lesson and 2 more recipes

BITE ME BIT

"I am an instant star. Just add water and stir."

— David Bowie, musician

SPAGHETTI alle VONGOLE

INGREDIENTS

2 lbs littleneck clams

1 lb spaghetti

2 tbsp olive oil

2 large shallots, minced

4 large garlic cloves, minced

½ tsp lemon zest

¼ tsp crushed red pepper flakes

¼ tsp dried oregano

1½ cups chicken broth

1 cup dry white wine

1 cup bottled clam juice

2 tbsp butter, melted

2 tbsp flour

¼ cup chopped fresh
flat-leaf parsley

freshly grated Parmesan cheese,
for garnish

Anything Elvis says, goes. When he sings, "do the clam," we do the clam. In this traditional vongole bianco, tender clams are combined with white wine, olive oil, garlic and chili peppers, delivering a light, simple, fresh-from-the-sea bowl of deliciousness. Yes, Elvis, we're gonna "Rock-A-Hula Baby," serving up this easy, clam-studded spaghetti in under 15 minutes. Only thing we're having trouble with is when the King croons about "Kissin' Cousins."

DIRECTIONS

1) Soak the fresh clams in water and change the water a few times to rid the clams of any sand. 2) Bring a large pot of lightly salted water to a boil. Add spaghetti and cook until tender. Drain and set aside. 3) In a large pot, heat olive oil over medium heat. Add shallots, garlic, lemon zest, red pepper flakes and oregano, stirring constantly and cooking 2–3 minutes. Add chicken broth, white wine and clam juice. Increase heat to medium-high and bring sauce to a boil. Add fresh clams, cover pot and steam them 4–5 minutes. After 5 minutes, discard any clams that haven't opened. With a large slotted spoon, remove clams and place on a plate. In a small bowl, whisk melted butter and flour. Over medium-high heat, add flour mixture to clam sauce, whisking constantly for 2 minutes. Reduce heat to low and add cooked spaghetti and parsley tossing well to coat. Serve in bowls and top each bowl with cooked clams in the shell. Sprinkle with freshly grated Parmesan cheese.

Serves 4

SPICY QUINOA PUTTANESCA

INGREDIENTS

Puttanesc a Sauce

1 tbsp olive oil

1 medium yellow onion, diced

2 large garlic cloves, minced

1 tbsp tomato paste

1 tsp chopped fresh thyme

¼ tsp crushed red pepper flakes

¼ tsp kosher salt

¼ tsp freshly ground black pepper

¼ cup dry white wine

½ cup Kalamata olives, pitted

½ cup store-bought roasted red peppers, drained and chopped

1 tbsp capers, rinsed and drained

1 (28oz) tin diced tomatoes

2 tbsp chopped fresh flat-leaf parsley

Quinoa

2 cups water

1 cup quinoa

Puttanesca is rumored to have originated among Napoli's nightwalkers. No surprise there. This sultry, spicy, aromatic red sauce of olives, capers and garlic is scandalously good. While The Oldest Professionals paired this kick-in-the-pants sauce with pasta, we've got a few tricks of our own. We've swapped noodles out for quinoa, the numero uno protein provider. There's nothing scandalous here...just two ladies of the night enjoying a seductively delectable bowl of quin-HO-a.

DIRECTIONS

1) For the sauce, in a large saucepan, heat olive oil over medium heat. Add onion and cook 5 minutes. Add garlic, cooking 30 seconds. Stir in tomato paste, thyme, red pepper flakes, salt, black pepper and white wine, cooking 1 minute. Add olives, roasted red peppers, capers and diced tomatoes. Bring to a boil over high heat. Reduce heat to medium and cook 15 minutes, stirring occasionally. Remove from heat and stir in parsley. 2) Meanwhile, to cook the quinoa, in a medium saucepan, combine water and quinoa. Bring to a boil over high heat. Reduce heat to low and cook uncovered for 15 minutes, stirring occasionally. Remove from heat and combine with puttanesca sauce.

Serves 4–6

BITE ME BIT

"Grown men should not be having sex with prostitutes unless they are married to them."

— Jerry Falwell, televangelist

BUTTERNUT SQUASH RICE PILAF

INGREDIENTS

2 tbsp olive oil

2 cups peeled, seeded and diced butternut squash

1 small white onion, diced

1 small garlic clove, minced

½ tsp ground cumin

½ tsp kosher salt

¼ tsp freshly ground black pepper

⅛ tsp cayenne pepper

1 cup long grain white rice

2 cups vegetable broth

¼ cup raw green pumpkin seeds (pepitas)

½ cup dried cranberries

2 tbsp chopped fresh flat-leaf parsley

½ tsp kosher salt

Our family dinners are often noisy and amusing, the table being a place where entertaining stories are told and secrets revealed. Boring rice can't possibly compete for attention, and that's why Lisa created this blaring and bejeweled rice pilaf. A trio of classic fall flavors – sweet roasted butternut squash, crunchy toasted pumpkin seeds, tart dried cranberries – jazz up bland white rice. Fragrant garlic and cumin further gussy things up, to say nothing of the unexpected kick delivered by a smidge of cayenne pepper. Forget politics and religion – everyone is going to be talking about this rousing rice.

DIRECTIONS

1) In a large saucepan, heat olive oil over medium heat. Add butternut squash and onion, cooking 8–10 minutes, stirring occasionally. Add garlic, cumin, salt, black pepper and cayenne, continuing to cook 30 seconds. Add rice and stir until well coated. Add vegetable broth and bring to a boil over high heat. Reduce heat to low, cover pan and cook 20 minutes until rice is tender and liquid is absorbed. 2) While the rice is cooking, place pumpkin seeds in a small skillet over low heat. Toast until lightly browned, 3–4 minutes. Remove from heat and set aside. 3) Once rice has finished cooking, remove from heat and let stand covered for 10 minutes. Remove cover and stir in cranberries, parsley, salt and toasted pumpkin seeds.

Serves 6

CHEESY MEXICAN RICE CASSEROLE

INGREDIENTS

1 tbsp olive oil

½ cup chopped yellow onion

1 small garlic clove, minced

½ cup diced green pepper

½ tsp ground cumin

½ tsp chili powder

¼ tsp kosher salt

1 cup long grain rice, uncooked

2 cups vegetable broth

¾ cups canned black beans, rinsed and drained

½ cup sour cream

½ cup shredded cheddar cheese

½ cup shredded Monterey Jack cheese

½ cup canned green chilies, chopped

2 tbsp freshly grated Parmesan cheese

It seemed so simple when I set out to write a poem about this easy cheesy, umpteen bean, nice rice casserole. Yet, my road to writing an ode has plateaued. Nothing relevant rhymes with epically creamy cheddar and Monterey Jack (knick-knack?), with baked black beans and green chilies (Achilles?), or with the perfect side dish for any Southwestern meal (unreal?). Though I enjoy to annoy I best be stopping before Lisa gives me a whopping nose bopping.

DIRECTIONS

1) Preheat oven to 425ºF. Coat a 1-quart baking dish with non-stick cooking spray. In a large saucepan, heat olive oil over medium heat. Add onions, garlic, green pepper, cumin, chili powder and salt. Cook stirring for 3 minutes, add rice and continue stirring for 1 minute. Stir in vegetable broth and bring to a boil. Cover, reduce heat to low and simmer 16–18 minutes, until liquid has been absorbed. Remove from heat and keep covered for 10 minutes. Place in a large bowl and cool slightly. **2)** Once rice has cooled slightly stir in black beans, sour cream, cheddar cheese, Monterey Jack cheese and green chilies. Spoon into prepared baking dish and sprinkle top with Parmesan. Bake 15–20 minutes until heated through and top is golden.

Serves 4–6

BITE ME BIT

"The poets have been mysteriously silent on the subject of cheese."

— G.K. Chesterton, author

CHINESE CHICKEN FRIED RICE

INGREDIENTS

Marinade & Sauce

4 tbsp soy sauce

3 tbsp mirin

2 tbsp sake

2 tbsp sugar

1 tbsp oyster sauce

2 boneless, skinless chicken breast halves, cut into bite-sized pieces

1 tsp vegetable oil

3 large eggs, lightly beaten

2 tbsp vegetable oil

1 small red onion, chopped

2 large carrots, peeled and diced

1 large garlic clove, minced

1 tsp finely grated fresh ginger

4 cups cold cooked white rice

1 cup frozen green peas

We avoid anything that pairs the words "day" and "old," a polite way of saying, "stinkin' stale." This dish is an exception to that rule — we *want* to use cold rice or the result will be a soggy, mushy mountain. Vibrant in color and bold in flavor, this stir-fried rice is loaded with chunks of protein rich chicken, crisp carrots, sweet peas, scrambled eggs and aromatic ginger. Sauced with a sweet-and-salty soy-mirin mixture, this simple fried rice is a wok wonder that beats greasy take-out every time.

DIRECTIONS

1) For the marinade, in a small bowl, whisk soy sauce, mirin, sake, sugar and oyster sauce. Pour 3 tbsp over cubed chicken and let marinate for 30 minutes. Set remaining sauce aside. **2)** In an 8-inch skillet, heat 1 tsp vegetable oil over medium heat. Add eggs, stirring gently but continuously, until mixture begins cooking. Stop stirring and cook 30–60 seconds more, until set. Slide eggs onto a cutting board and slice into ½-inch strips. Set aside. **3)** In a large skillet or wok, heat 2 tbsp vegetable oil over medium heat. Add onions and carrots stirring for 2 minutes. Add chicken and the marinade it's in, cooking 5–6 minutes, stirring continuously. Add garlic and ginger, cooking 30 seconds more. Stir in rice and remaining sauce, stirring well to coat. Add peas and cooked egg, cooking 2 minutes more, until peas are cooked and mixture is heated through.

Serves 6–8

Fowl
me
Provocative Poultry

COCONUT CHICKEN with APRICOT SAUCE

INGREDIENTS

Coconut Chicken

¼ cup flour

¼ tsp garlic powder

2 large eggs

1¼ cups panko
(Japanese breadcrumbs)

1 cup sweetened coconut flakes

½ tsp lime zest

4 boneless, skinless chicken breast halves

½ tsp kosher salt

¼ tsp freshly ground black pepper

Apricot Sauce

½ cup apricot jam

1 tbsp water

2 tsp fresh lemon juice

2 tsp soy sauce

1 tsp yellow mustard

Whether we were obsessing over Greg Brady's tiki necklace, Magnum's moustache, ukulele lessons or hula dance-offs, Lisa and I have always been consumed with all things Hawaiian. So, you can imagine our excitement when we heard that some coconuts have pearls in them. Don't you think we smashed many–a tropical fruit to smithereens? Turns out we're gullible. Nothing was found to make a necklace but a gem of an idea was born. Quick and simple to make (you don't want to miss a Hawaiian sunset, do you?), this chicken is baked in a panko-coconut coating until golden, juicy and crisp-crusted and served up with sweet 'n' salty apricot dipping sauce.

Mahalo, Lika (that's Lisa's island name).
Aloha Nui Loa, Kuli (that's mine).

DIRECTIONS

1) Preheat oven to 400°F. Line a baking sheet with parchment paper and coat with non-stick cooking spray. 2) For the chicken, in a shallow bowl, combine flour and garlic powder. In a second bowl, whisk eggs until well combined. In a third bowl, combine panko, coconut flakes and lime zest. Season chicken with salt and pepper. Dredge chicken in flour mixture, shaking off excess. Dip each breast into the eggs and then into the panko-coconut mixture, coating all sides and pressing well to adhere. Place on prepared baking sheet and bake 10 minutes per side, until golden and cooked through.
3) For the apricot sauce, in a food processor or blender, combine apricot jam, water, lemon juice, soy sauce and mustard until smooth. Serve with coconut chicken.

Serves 4

PARMESAN CHICKEN FINGERS with DIPPING TRIO

INGREDIENTS

Chicken Fingers

4 boneless, skinless chicken breast halves

2 large eggs, lightly whisked

1 cup freshly grated Parmesan cheese

1 cup panko (Japanese breadcrumbs)

½ tsp dried oregano

½ tsp kosher salt

¼ tsp freshly ground black pepper

¼ tsp paprika

¼ cup butter, melted

Honey Mustard Dip

¼ cup mayonnaise

1 tbsp Dijon mustard

1 tbsp honey

Parmesan Dip

3 tbsp freshly grated Parmesan cheese

¼ cup mayonnaise

2 tbsp sour cream

1 tbsp fresh lemon juice

⅛ tsp garlic powder

pinch of kosher salt

Sweet Ketchup Dip

½ cup ketchup

¼ cup honey

¼ tsp Worcestershire sauce

"All children, except one, grow up." J.M. Barrie didn't know me when he wrote the opening line of his 1904 play *Peter Pan*. I don't wear green tights, but I do have Tinker Bell (aka Lisa) fluttering over my shoulder, telling me what to do. She doesn't like it when I go out with a wet head, hides her face as I dig for my Shirley Temple maraschino and cringes when I order off the kids' menu. Methinks she's trying to hide me at home, creating these crunchy, golden-brown chicken fingers coated in a Parmesan-panko crust. Easy and family friendly, the baked strips are served up with a trio of delectable dipping sauces: honey mustard, creamy Parmesan and sweet ketchup. Tink really sprinkled her fairy dust on this one.

DIRECTIONS

1) For the chicken fingers, preheat oven to 425°F. Line a baking sheet with aluminum foil and coat with non-stick cooking spray. Cut each chicken breast into 4 or 5 lengthwise strips. Place eggs in a medium bowl. In another medium bowl, combine Parmesan, panko, oregano, salt, pepper and paprika. Dip chicken pieces in egg, letting any excess drip off, then dredge in Parmesan-panko mixture, pressing to adhere. Place on prepared baking sheet. Drizzle chicken strips with melted butter and bake 8 minutes. Flip the strips and bake another 8 minutes, until cooked through and crisp on the outside.
2) For the honey mustard dip, in a small bowl, whisk mayonnaise, Dijon and honey until combined. **3)** For the Parmesan dip, in a small bowl, whisk Parmesan, mayonnaise, sour cream, lemon juice, garlic powder and a pinch of salt until combined. **4)** For the ketchup dip, in a small bowl, combine ketchup, honey and Worcestershire sauce. All dips can be made ahead and refrigerated until ready to serve.

Serves 4–6

BITE ME BIT

"What if the Hokey-Pokey is all it really is about?"

— from the 2002 Jimmy Buffett album *Far Side of the World*

CHICKEN CACCIATORE

INGREDIENTS

4 boneless, skinless chicken breast halves

¼ tsp kosher salt

¼ tsp freshly ground black pepper

¼ cup flour

2 tbsp olive oil

1 tbsp olive oil

1 medium yellow onion, halved and thinly sliced

2 large garlic cloves, minced

4 medium carrots, peeled and cut into thin rounds

2 tbsp tomato paste

½ tsp dried rosemary

½ tsp dried oregano

¼ tsp kosher salt

¼ tsp freshly ground black pepper

¾ cup dry red wine

1 large red bell pepper, chopped

1 large green pepper, chopped

4 plum tomatoes, cut into quarters

¾ cup chicken broth

Though there are very few Italian recipes that aren't comforting, this one ranks up there with a crackling fire and *Seinfeld* repeats. Popular from Piedmont to Sicily, chicken cacciatore is a classic favorite with countless variations. Here, Lisa's version is rustic and hearty, teeming with tender chicken, luscious garlic and flavorful vegetables, all simmered in a rich red wine and tomato sauce. Made from common vegetables and pantry items, this stew-like, family-friendly dish goes from stove to table in under 30 minutes. Open wide. You're about to eat the equivalent of a big hug from Nonna.

DIRECTIONS

1) Season chicken with salt and pepper. Place flour in a shallow bowl and dredge each chicken piece to coat lightly. In a large skillet, heat 2 tbsp olive oil over medium-high heat. Add chicken and brown, 2–3 minutes per side. Remove from pan and set aside. **2)** Wipe out skillet and heat 1 tbsp olive oil over medium heat. Add onions, garlic and carrots, stirring occasionally and cooking 4–5 minutes until onion is tender. Stir in tomato paste, rosemary, oregano, salt and pepper, cooking 1 minute more. Add red wine, increase heat to medium-high and cook 2–3 minutes, to reduce slightly. Stir in red and green peppers, tomatoes and chicken broth. Bring to a simmer over medium heat and cook for 4 minutes. Return chicken to skillet, reduce heat to low and simmer covered for 15 minutes, until chicken is cooked through.

Serves 4

NEW CLASSIC CHICKEN with WHITE WINE & HERBS

INGREDIENTS

¼ cup flour

½ tsp paprika

½ tsp kosher salt

¼ tsp freshly ground black pepper

4 boneless, skinless chicken breast halves

2 tbsp olive oil

1 tbsp olive oil

1 large shallot, minced

1 large garlic clove, minced

½ tsp dried thyme

½ tsp dried oregano

½ tsp kosher salt

¼ tsp freshly ground black pepper

1 cup dry white wine

1½ cups chicken broth

2 tbsp cream

2 tsp cornstarch

1 tbsp roughly chopped fresh flat-leaf parsley

ox-y-mo-ron *noun* \ äk-s - mo r- än\
a combination of contradictory or incongruous words

Jumbo shrimp. Freezer burn. Pretty ugly. Do you, like many millions, rush to add "easy entertaining" to this list of opposite words? Not so fast. This sautéed chicken is at once simple *and* elegant. Yes, you read that right. With ingredients straight from your pantry you can throw this flavorful dish together on a moments notice. And, should that moment involve guests, prepare for them to be dazzled by terribly good, juicy chicken coated in a tantalizing white wine and herb pan sauce.

DIRECTIONS

1) Place flour, paprika, salt and pepper in a shallow dish. Place chicken between two sheets of wax paper and pound to even thickness, about ½-inch thick. Lightly coat chicken in flour mixture, shaking off excess. 2) In a large skillet, heat 2 tbsp olive oil over medium-high heat. Sauté chicken 4-5 minutes per side, until golden brown and cooked through. Remove from skillet and set aside. 3) For the sauce, wipe out skillet and add 1 tbsp olive oil over medium-low heat. Add minced shallot, cooking 1-2 minutes to soften. Add garlic, thyme, oregano, salt and pepper, stirring for 30-60 seconds until garlic and spices are fragrant. Stir in white wine and chicken broth. Turn heat to high, scrape up any browned bits on the bottom of the pan and bring to a boil. Reduce heat to medium-low, simmer and cook sauce 12-15 minutes. 4) In a small bowl, combine cream and cornstarch, mixing until smooth. Slowly add to sauce continually whisking until thickened, about 1 minute. Return chicken to pan along with any accumulated juices and heat through. Garnish with parsley and serve.

Serves 4

BRAISED CHICKEN with FENNEL & OLIVES

INGREDIENTS

4 boneless, skinless chicken breast halves

2 tbsp fresh orange juice

1 tbsp fresh lime juice

2 tsp chili powder

2 tsp paprika

1 tsp ground cumin

½ tsp dried oregano

½ tsp kosher salt

2 tbsp olive oil

1 tbsp olive oil

2 cups thinly sliced fennel

¼ tsp kosher salt

¼ tsp freshly ground black pepper

1 cup chicken broth

¼ cup fresh orange juice

½ cup thinly sliced dried apricots

½ cup Kalamata olives, pitted

1 tbsp chopped fresh flat-leaf parsley

"The whole is greater than the sum of its parts." Not sure if I have to credit Aristotle or gestaltis for this theory, but, whatever the case, I love it. It totally works with this chicken. Take a look down the diverse list of ingredients: fennel has a subtle licorice flavor, apricots are sweet and Kalamata olives offer a rich, meaty bite. On first glance it might seem these parts, though delicious on their own, don't work together, but that couldn't be further from the truth. These elements have great synergy, are the perfect balance of sweetness and acidity, of complementary textures and flavors. The sum of all parts is scrumptious. See, Dad? After all these years, Psych 101 paid off.

DIRECTIONS

1) Cut each chicken breast in half lengthways and place chicken in a medium bowl. In a small bowl, mix together 2 tbsp orange juice, lime juice, chili powder, paprika, cumin, oregano and ½ tsp salt. Pour over chicken and toss well to coat. 2) In a large skillet, heat 2 tbsp olive oil over medium-high heat. Add chicken and brown for 2 minutes on each side. Remove from skillet and set aside. 3) Wipe skillet out and heat remaining 1 tbsp olive oil over medium heat. Add fennel, salt and pepper and cook until softened, about 5 minutes. Return chicken and any accumulated juices to the skillet. Add chicken broth, orange juice, apricots and olives. Once mixture begins to boil, reduce heat to low, cover and simmer 10 minutes or until chicken is cooked through. Remove chicken from skillet and place on a serving platter, turn heat to high and reduce sauce for 2–3 minutes. Stir in parsley and pour over chicken.

Serves 4

BITE ME BIT

"After 10 years in therapy, my psychologist told me something very touching. He said, 'No hablo Ingles.'"

— Dennis Wolfberg, comedian

SPINACH, TOMATO & FETA STUFFED CHICKEN

INGREDIENTS

Marinade

¼ cup olive oil

1 large garlic clove, minced

½ tsp dried oregano

¼ tsp dried thyme

4 boneless, skinless chicken breast halves

Spinach, Tomato & Feta Stuffing

2 tbsp olive oil

1 medium yellow onion, diced

1 large garlic clove, minced

2 cups chopped baby spinach

1 cup crumbled feta cheese

¼ cup finely chopped sun-dried tomatoes

½ tsp chopped fresh thyme

½ tsp dried oregano

¼ tsp kosher salt

¼ tsp freshly ground black pepper

¾ cup panko (Japanese breadcrumbs)

2 tbsp olive oil

Tomato Relish

4 plum tomatoes, seeded and chopped

1 tbsp olive oil

2 tsp balsamic vinegar

¼ tsp kosher salt

⅛ tsp freshly ground black pepper

I asked Lisa to teach me a chicken dish that wouldn't fail to delight and impress. When she first gave me a copy of this recipe my head started to spin and I barely managed to choke out my most hated phrase, "Out of my league." However, Lisa fanned me and told me to "stuff it." Rude, but that offered up some effective motivation and technical accuracy. I calmed down and got to work, marinating the chicken in garlic and herbs, and creating a spinach, sun-dried tomato and feta filling. I could see the finish line and it looked restaurant-worthy. Once brimming with Mediterranean flavors, the chicken was panko-crusted, baked until golden and served with a tomato relish. Very much in my league, this chicken let me strut my stuff while my guests stuffed their faces. Victory.

DIRECTIONS

1) Place chicken in a large resealable plastic bag. In a small bowl, whisk olive oil, garlic, oregano and thyme. Pour marinade over chicken and refrigerate at least 2 hours. 2) For the stuffing, in a medium skillet, heat olive oil over medium heat. Add onions and cook 3 minutes to soften. Add garlic and continue cooking 30 seconds. Stir in spinach, cooking 1 minute more. Remove from heat and let mixture cool 5 minutes. In a large bowl, toss together feta, sun-dried tomatoes, thyme and oregano. Add onion-spinach mixture and combine well. 3) Preheat oven to 400°F. Line a baking sheet with aluminum foil and coat with non-stick cooking spray. Remove chicken from marinade and cut a long slit along the long edge of the chicken breast, going nearly through to the other side. Season both sides of the chicken with ¼ tsp each of salt and pepper. Fill pocket of chicken with stuffing, squeezing as much as you can inside. Place panko crumbs on a flat dish. Gently coat both sides of the stuffed chicken with panko. 4) In a large skillet, heat 2 tbsp olive oil over medium-high heat. Place chicken in skillet and cook 2–3 minutes to brown on one side. Place chicken on prepared baking sheet, flipping so browned side faces up. Bake 20 minutes or until cooked through. Let rest 5 minutes before serving. 5) For the tomato relish, in a small bowl, combine tomatoes, olive oil, balsamic, salt and pepper. Toss to combine and serve alongside stuffed chicken.

Serves 4

AU COURANT CHICKEN POT PIE

INGREDIENTS

5 boneless, skinless chicken breast halves

4 cups chicken broth

Biscuit Topping

2¼ cups flour

2 tsp baking powder

¼ tsp baking soda

1 tsp kosher salt

1 tsp sugar

¼ tsp freshly ground black pepper

½ cup butter, chilled and cut into ½-inch pieces

½ cup shredded sharp cheddar cheese

½ cup freshly grated Parmesan cheese

¾ cup cream

Vegetable Filling

1 tbsp butter

1 tbsp olive oil

1 large white onion, diced

½ lb (approx. 3 cups) cremini mushrooms, sliced

2 large carrots, peeled and chopped

1 celery stalk, chopped

2 tsp tomato paste

1 cup chopped zucchini

1 cup frozen green peas

¼ tsp kosher salt

¼ tsp freshly ground black pepper

This one is hot off the press. Chicken pot pie, the deep-dish American Dream, has left grandma's Formica-clad kitchen and is now a favorite among the in-crowd, lauded by the likes of fashionista Anna Wintour and celebrity chef Wolfgang Puck. Don't despair if you're not on the pages of *Vogue* or walking the red carpet anytime soon because all of us can enjoy the retro rage with this heartwarming, homey and family-friendly comfort food of saucy chicken and fresh vegetables topped with golden biscuits. Though it takes a bit of time to assemble, this pot pie, brimming with all the food groups, is easily worth the effort and will surely make a groupie of you too.

DIRECTIONS

1) For the chicken, in a large Dutch oven, cover chicken with broth and bring to a boil over high heat. Reduce heat to low, cover and cook 13 minutes or until chicken is no longer pink inside. Remove chicken and strain broth through a fine mesh strainer, reserving 2 cups of the broth. When the chicken is cool enough to handle, shred each breast into bite-sized pieces and place in large bowl. **2)** Preheat oven to 425ºF. Coat a 13x9-inch baking dish with non-stick cooking spray. Set aside. **3)** For the biscuits, line a baking sheet with parchment paper. In a large bowl, combine flour, baking powder, baking soda, salt, sugar and pepper. Cut in butter with your fingers until mixture resembles coarse oatmeal. Stir in cheddar and Parmesan. Add cream, stirring just until combined. Gather mixture into tablespoon-sized pieces (can be any shape) and place on prepared baking sheet. Bake 10 minutes, until lightly browned. Set aside.

Sauce

4 tbsp butter

½ cup flour

2 cups chicken broth (reserved)

1 cup whole milk

½ tsp minced fresh thyme

1 tbsp fresh lemon juice

½ tsp kosher salt

¼ tsp freshly ground black pepper

4) For the filling, in a large Dutch oven, heat 1 tbsp butter and 1 tbsp olive oil over medium heat. Add onions, mushrooms, carrots and celery, stirring frequently and cooking 6 minutes, until softened. Add tomato paste, stirring well to combine with vegetables. Add zucchini, cooking for 1 minute. Add frozen green peas, salt and pepper, cooking 1 minute longer. Remove from heat and add to shredded chicken.

5) For the sauce, in a large saucepan, melt butter over medium heat. Add flour and while continuously whisking, slowly add reserved 2 cups of chicken broth. Continue to whisk until the mixture is smooth, about 1 minute. Add milk and thyme, stirring until sauce has thickened. Remove from heat and stir in lemon juice, salt and pepper. Add sauce to chicken and vegetable mixture. Pour into prepared baking dish and scatter prepared biscuits evenly over filling. Bake at 425°F for 15 minutes, until heated through.

Serves 6

BITE ME BIT

"When the grandmothers of today hear the word 'Chippendales,' they don't necessarily think of chairs."

— Jean Kerr, author

CITRUS & HERB ROAST CHICKEN

INGREDIENTS

Citrus & Herb Rub

1 tbsp chopped fresh thyme

1 tbsp chopped fresh rosemary

1 tbsp kosher salt

1 tsp freshly ground black pepper

1 tsp lemon zest

1 tsp orange zest

3 tbsp canola oil

1 (3–4 lb) whole chicken

½ lemon, cut into quarters

½ orange, cut into quarters

2 large garlic cloves, smashed

1 small yellow onion, quartered

1 tbsp chopped fresh flat-leaf parsley, for topping

There's a reason roasting a whole chicken is super popular – it's a technique that requires minimal effort and skill in the kitchen yet yields impressive and tasty results. This moist masterpiece is no exception. Rubbed with herbs and citrus zest, the chicken is stuffed with flavor infusing onions, garlic, lemon and orange and then baked to a golden crisp. Simple and foolproof, this classic, taste-of-home tender chicken is a welcome addition to any novice cook's repertoire and a dependably delicious staple in any expert's kitchen.

DIRECTIONS

1) Preheat oven to 450ºF. Line a baking sheet with aluminum foil. 2) For the rub, in a small bowl, combine thyme, rosemary, salt, pepper, lemon zest, orange zest and canola oil. Stir well and set aside. 3) For the chicken, using a paper towel, pat the chicken dry before applying herb coating. Stuff the inside with lemon, orange, garlic and onion pieces. Rub the entire outside of the chicken with herb coating and place on prepared baking sheet. Cook 60–70 minutes, until a golden crust forms. Remove from oven and allow to rest a few minutes. Sprinkle with parsley before serving.

Serves 3–4

BITE ME BIT

"I've always said fashion is like roast chicken. You don't have to think about it to know it's delicious."

— Alber Elbaz, designer

PISTACHIO-CRUSTED CHICKEN with HONEY PEACH SAUCE

INGREDIENTS

Honey Peach Sauce

3 fresh peaches, peeled and chopped

2 tbsp fresh lemon juice

2 tbsp honey

1 fresh peach, peeled and diced

¼ tsp fresh thyme

Pistachio Chicken

4 boneless, skinless chicken breast halves

¼ tsp kosher salt

¼ tsp freshly ground black pepper

¼ cup flour

2 large eggs

1 tbsp Dijon mustard

1 tbsp olive oil

1 tbsp honey

1 small garlic clove, minced

½ tsp chopped fresh thyme

1 cup panko (Japanese breadcrumbs)

1 cup unsalted pistachios, shelled and coarsely chopped in food processor

¼ tsp kosher salt

We love assigning things and people theme songs. Coming up with one for this pistachio and peach chicken has been a doozy. At first, we considered Steve Miller's song "The Joker," because he sings about how he loves her peaches and wants to shake her tree. Um, no. This is a family show and it doesn't convey how perfectly the velvety-skinned, fragrant fruit works atop this crunchy crusted chicken. Next, thanks to our favorite filmmaker, Andrew Nisker, we turned to Peaches, a musician extraordinaire. Hmm. Neither her über-catchy "Diddle My Skittle" nor "Stick it to the Pimp" were going to do the job. Finally, we settled on the Peaches & Herb disco anthem "Shake Your Groove Thing." One bite of this juicy peach-topped chicken and you too will be "bumpin' booties" on the dance floor.

DIRECTIONS

1) For the peach sauce, in a blender, combine 3 chopped peaches, lemon juice and honey. Pulse until smooth. Transfer to a small saucepan and bring to a boil over medium heat. Reduce heat to low and simmer 15 minutes, stirring often. Remove from heat and stir in remaining diced peach and thyme. Set aside until ready to serve. 2) Line a baking sheet with aluminum foil and coat with non-stick cooking spray. Place chicken between two sheets of wax paper and pound to even thickness, about ½-inch thick. Season both sides of chicken with ¼ tsp each of salt and pepper. Place flour in a medium bowl. In another bowl, whisk eggs, Dijon, olive oil, honey, garlic and thyme. In a third bowl, combine panko, pistachios and ¼ tsp salt. Working with 1 chicken breast at a time, dredge in flour, shaking off excess. Dip in egg mixture and then coat in panko/pistachio mixture, pressing on both sides for crumbs to adhere. Place on prepared baking sheet. When all chicken breasts are coated, cover the baking sheet and refrigerate at least 1 hour. 3) When ready to bake, preheat oven to 500°F. Place tray in oven and immediately reduce oven temperature to 375°F. Bake 18–20 minutes, until cooked through. Slice and serve with honey peach sauce.

Serves 4

SWEET & SOUR CASHEW-CRUSTED CHICKEN

INGREDIENTS

Sweet & Sour Sauce

⅓ cup white vinegar

⅓ cup packed brown sugar

¼ cup ketchup

¼ cup water

1 tbsp cornstarch

2 tsp soy sauce

1 red bell pepper, cut into 1-inch pieces

1 cup canned or fresh pineapple chunks

Cashew Chicken

4 boneless, skinless chicken breast halves

¼ tsp kosher salt

¼ tsp freshly ground black pepper

¼ cup flour

1 large egg, lightly beaten

1 cup breadcrumbs

1 cup finely chopped unsalted cashews

¼ tsp kosher salt

2 tbsp olive oil

When Lisa sets a goal, she accomplishes it. She vowed to write a handful of nut-centric recipes, creations that would highlight the beauty of the hard-shell fruit. And, despite not covering off the chinquapin (aka bushy chestnut), she has been hugely successful. Here in the spotlight is the sweet, rich, kidney-shaped cashew. Chicken is encrusted with the nut, browned in the pan, baked until juicy and golden and then topped with a sweet and sour pineapple sauce. It's great, delicious, etc., but next time round, d'you think I can get The Nutcracker to develop more recipes around vodka?

DIRECTIONS

1) For the sauce, in a medium saucepan, combine vinegar, brown sugar, ketchup and water. Whisk over medium-high heat to dissolve sugar. In a small bowl, combine cornstarch and soy sauce. Once sauce comes to a boil, reduce heat to low and whisk in cornstarch-soy mixture, stirring for 30 seconds. Remove from heat and stir in red peppers and pineapple. Set aside. 2) Preheat oven to 375ºF. Line a baking sheet with aluminum foil and coat with non-stick cooking spray. 3) For the chicken, season chicken with ¼ tsp each of salt and pepper. Place flour in a small bowl. Place egg in another small bowl. In a medium bowl, combine breadcrumbs, chopped cashews and ¼ tsp salt. Dredge each chicken breast in flour, shaking off excess. Dip in egg and coat in cashew mixture pressing well to adhere. In a large skillet, heat olive oil over medium-high heat. Place coated chicken in the skillet and brown 2 minutes per side. Transfer to prepared baking sheet and bake 15–17 minutes until chicken is cooked through. To serve, slice each chicken breast into 4 pieces and spoon sweet and sour sauce over top.

Serves 4

BITE ME BIT

"I guess I went a little nuts."

— Charlie Sheen, actor

LUCKY #8 SAUCY LEMON CHICKEN

INGREDIENTS

Marinade

4 boneless, skinless chicken breast halves

2 tbsp oyster sauce

1 tbsp soy sauce

1 tbsp cornstarch

¼ cup cornstarch

1 large egg, lightly beaten

1 cup panko (Japanese breadcrumbs)

3 tbsp peanut oil

Lemon Sauce

2 tsp cornstarch

1 tbsp water

⅓ cup fresh lemon juice

⅓ cup honey

2 tbsp chicken broth

1 tbsp soy sauce

1 tsp lemon zest

1 lemon, thinly sliced for garnish

If Lisa were to open a Chinese restaurant, it would be called Imperial Happiness, she would be known as Little Dragon and I would be Lazy Susan. Diners sitting in red vinyl booths among bonsai and paper lanterns would get to devour #8 on the menu: Little Dragon's saucy, sweet and sour lemon chicken. Free of grease and MSG, this tender, panko-crusted chicken is browned and then sauced with a combination of tart lemon and sweet honey. For dessert, patrons would clutch tiny teacups and crack open fortune cookies dispensing invaluable advice… don't squat with spurs on.

DIRECTIONS

1) Place chicken between two sheets of wax paper and pound to even thickness, about ½-inch thick. In a shallow dish, whisk oyster sauce, soy sauce and 1 tbsp cornstarch. Place chicken in marinade, cover and refrigerate for 30 minutes. 2) Place ¼ cup cornstarch in a medium bowl, the lightly beaten egg in another bowl and the panko in a third bowl. Remove chicken from marinade and place in cornstarch, shaking off excess. Next, dip in egg, coating both sides and finally, encrust with panko crumbs, gently patting to adhere to both sides. Repeat with remaining chicken breasts. 3) In a large skillet, heat peanut oil over medium-high heat. Add chicken, cooking 7–8 minutes per side or until golden brown and cooked through. Remove from skillet and set aside. 4) For the lemon sauce, in a small bowl, combine 2 tsp cornstarch and 1 tbsp water and set aside. In a small saucepan, combine lemon juice, honey, chicken broth and soy sauce. Bring to a simmer over medium heat stirring continuously for 2 minutes. Whisk in cornstarch mixture and lemon zest, stirring 2 minutes more, until sauce thickens. To serve, slice chicken breasts into long strips and place on platter. Pour lemon sauce over chicken and garnish with lemon slices.

Serves 4

THRILL-SEEKERS' KUNG PAO CHICKEN

INGREDIENTS

Marinade

2 tbsp soy sauce

2 tbsp sherry cooking wine

1 tbsp cornstarch

1 tsp oyster sauce

3 boneless, skinless chicken breast halves, cut into 1-inch cubes

Kung Pao Sauce

¼ cup rice wine vinegar

¼ cup soy sauce

1 tbsp sugar

1 tsp hot chili sauce (Sriracha)

2 tsp cornstarch

1 tbsp water

1 tbsp vegetable oil

4 small dried red chili peppers

1 tsp vegetable oil

2 small garlic cloves, minced

1 tsp grated fresh ginger

2 large celery stalks, chopped

1 large red bell pepper, chopped

½ cup water chestnuts, rinsed, drained and thinly sliced

⅓ cup unsalted dry roasted peanuts

For many, eating Kung Pao chicken (aka Gong Bao Ji Ding) is the equivalent of riding the Kingda Ka coaster. Well, you can scrap that trip to Six Flags because our Kung Pao delivers all the high-flying thrills sans lineups, furry mascots and $9 sodas. Pull down the lap bar because this spicy, saucy Sichuan staple is going to knock your socks off with tender chunks of chicken speedily stir-fried with fiery chili peppers, crunchy vegetables and roasted peanuts. Buzzing with hot and sweet, salty and sour flavors, this intense chicken dish is as addictive, exciting and electrifying as riding a steep-and-deep chute-the-chute.

DIRECTIONS

1) For the marinade, in a medium bowl, whisk soy sauce, sherry, cornstarch and oyster sauce. Add cubed chicken and toss to coat, marinating 30 minutes. **2)** For the sauce, in a small bowl, whisk rice wine vinegar, soy sauce, sugar and chili sauce. Set aside. In another small bowl, combine cornstarch and water. Set aside. **3)** Place wok over high heat and add 1 tbsp vegetable oil. Add dried chili peppers and stir constantly for 30 seconds. Stir in chicken with marinade, stir-frying 3 minutes. Remove chicken and chilies from wok and set aside. **4)** In wok, heat remaining 1 tsp vegetable oil over medium-high heat. Add garlic and ginger, stirring constantly for 30 seconds. Add celery, red pepper and water chestnuts, stir-frying for 2 minutes. Return chicken and chilies to wok. Add sauce and bring to a boil. Stirring constantly, add cornstarch mixture and cook 1 minute, until sauce thickens. Stir in peanuts and serve.

Serves 4

BITE ME BIT

Mr. Wilhelm: You're a terrible liar, George. Look at you, you're a wreck! You're sweating bullets.

George: It's the Kung Pao. George likes his chicken spicy.

— from the TV show *Seinfeld*, episode #105

SWEET, SPICY & STICKY CHICKEN STIR-FRY

INGREDIENTS

Stir-Fry Sauce

¼ cup soy sauce

¼ cup water

¼ cup honey

2 tbsp brown sugar

1 tsp hot chili sauce (Sriracha)

2 tbsp cornstarch

2 tbsp water

2 tsp vegetable oil

1 small yellow onion, chopped

1 large yellow pepper, chopped

1 large red bell pepper, chopped

1 small garlic clove, minced

1 tsp grated fresh ginger

1 tbsp vegetable oil

4 boneless, skinless chicken breast halves, cut into ½-inch strips

1 tbsp cornstarch

How does Calgon, the bath and beauty brand, figure into this recipe? Well, let's start with their catchphrase we oft repeat: Calgon, take me away! What, other than a sandy Bahamian beach, takes us away from the bustle of the brood and the afterschool homework hustle? This stir-fry does a great job of answering the "What's for dinner?" question. A quick turn in the wok and you've got a chicken and vegetable stir-fry coated in a sweet, spicy and sticky mahogany glaze. Now, when the kids are clamoring for food, asking that age-old question, here's your easy answer: Ancient Chinese Secret.

DIRECTIONS

1) For the sauce, in a medium bowl, whisk soy sauce, water, honey, brown sugar and chili sauce. In a small bowl, dissolve cornstarch in water. Whisk into soy mixture. Set aside. 2) In a large skillet or wok, heat 2 tsp vegetable oil over medium-high heat. Add onions and peppers stirring 4–5 minutes until softened. Add garlic and ginger, stirring 1 minute. Remove vegetable mixture from pan and set aside. 3) Using the same pan, heat 1 tbsp vegetable oil over medium-high heat. Toss chicken strips with 1 tbsp cornstarch. Add chicken to skillet and brown on both sides, 1–2 minutes per side. Return onion and pepper mixture to skillet. Pour stir-fry sauce in skillet and cook 2–3 minutes, stirring constantly until thickened. Serve over rice.

Serves 4

MANGO & COCONUT CHICKEN CURRY

INGREDIENTS

5 boneless, skinless chicken breast halves, thinly sliced

½ cup coconut milk

½ tsp kosher salt

¼ tsp freshly ground black pepper

2 tbsp vegetable oil

1 large white onion, chopped

1 large red bell pepper, chopped

1 large garlic clove, minced

2 tbsp yellow curry powder, mild, medium or hot depending on your spice preference

2 tsp grated fresh ginger

½ tsp ground cumin

½ tsp kosher salt

¼ tsp freshly ground black pepper

1¼ cups water

2 tbsp apple cider vinegar

1 cup peeled and diced ripe mango

1½ cups peeled ripe mango, cut into 1-inch cubes

½ cup coconut milk

Attention, curry connoisseurs. Before you start with the poison pen letters, we know that this easy, aromatic, sweet and spicy mango and coconut curry isn't taken straight from Maa's (Mom in India) stove. But, hey, give us a break. Who needs "authenticity," or fenugreek seeds for that matter, when we can whip together this deliciously perfect, Indian-inspired curry of tropical mango, creamy coconut milk and kickin' spices?

DIRECTIONS

1) Place sliced chicken in a large resealable plastic bag, add ½ cup coconut milk, ½ tsp salt and ¼ tsp pepper and toss to coat. Marinate 1 hour. 2) In a large skillet, heat vegetable oil over medium heat. Add onions and red peppers, stirring until softened, about 4–5 minutes. Reduce heat to low, add garlic, curry powder, ginger, cumin, salt and pepper and stir continuously for 1 minute. Increase heat to high and add water and vinegar. Bring to a boil, reduce heat to low and add 1 cup diced mango cooking 15 minutes. Using a handheld or countertop blender, puree sauce until smooth. Return to skillet and bring back to a simmer. 3) Remove chicken from marinade and add to mango-curry sauce. Discard marinade. Over low heat, cover skillet and cook 10 minutes or until cooked through. Add remaining 1½ cups mango and ½ cup coconut milk. Stir to combine, cooking 1 minute longer.

Serves 6

BITE ME BIT

"I'm not a snob. Ask anybody. Well, anybody who matters."

— Simon Le Bon, musician

CHICKEN & ROASTED VEGETABLE CHIMICHANGAS

INGREDIENTS

Roasted Vegetables

2 medium zucchini, cut into ½-inch pieces

1 large red bell pepper, cut into ½-inch pieces

1 large green pepper, cut into ½-inch pieces

1 tbsp olive oil

1 tsp balsamic vinegar

1 tsp ground cumin

½ tsp dried oregano

¼ tsp kosher salt

¼ tsp freshly ground black pepper

2 cups deli roasted chicken, shredded

1 cup shredded Monterey Jack cheese

¾ cup salsa

¼ cup canned chopped green chilies, drained

6 (10- or 12-inch) flour tortillas

6 tbsp shredded Monterey Jack cheese

2 tbsp olive oil

salsa and sour cream, for serving

The secret password to our sister fort was never "open sesame." Entry was gained by whispering either "gobbledygook" or "whippersnapper." We've always loved words that are fun to say and here's one that's even better to eat than to utter: chimichanga. Traditionally a deep-fried burrito, our oven-baked version is a roasted vegetable, shredded chicken and gooey cheese-stuffed tortilla. These chimichangas, with their crisp, crunchy shell and creamy inside, have loads of…say it with us…razzmatazz.

DIRECTIONS

1) Preheat oven to 425°F. Line a baking sheet with aluminum foil and coat with non-stick cooking spray. 2) In a large bowl, toss zucchini, red pepper, green pepper, olive oil, balsamic vinegar, cumin, oregano, salt and pepper. Spread in a single layer on prepared baking sheet. Roast 15 minutes until vegetables are tender and start to become golden. Remove from oven and transfer to a large bowl. Add shredded chicken, Monterey Jack cheese, salsa and green chilies. 3) Line a baking sheet with aluminum foil and coat with non-stick cooking spray. Lay out all 6 tortillas on your counter. Place about ½ cup chicken and vegetable mixture in the center of each tortilla. Top each with 1 tbsp Monterey Jack. Fold opposite sides over the filling and roll up from bottom to close. Place seam side down on baking sheet. Brush tops and sides with olive oil. Place in 425°F oven for 15–20 minutes until golden brown and crisp. Serve with salsa and sour cream.

Serves 6

FIERY CHIPOTLE GRILLED CHICKEN

INGREDIENTS

Marinade

3 tbsp olive oil

1 tbsp fresh lime juice

1 tbsp honey

2 chipotle peppers in adobo sauce, chopped

2 small garlic cloves, minced

¼ tsp ground cumin

¼ tsp chili powder

¼ tsp kosher salt

¼ tsp freshly ground black pepper

6 boneless, skinless chicken breast halves

Chipotle Dipping Sauce

½ cup mayonnaise

1 chipotle pepper in adobo sauce, finely chopped

1 tbsp honey

1 tsp Dijon mustard

1 tsp fresh lime juice

¼ tsp kosher salt

¼ tsp freshly ground black pepper

Hi. I'm Julie and I'm a heat junkie. When I was young and innocent I got my fix from sinus-clearing wasabi and blistering Tabasco. Those days are long gone. Now to bring on the burn I turn to smoked, ripe jalapenos (aka chipotle peppers) canned in a spicy, vinegary red sauce. At my worst, I can be spotted loitering in the Mexican food aisle of my grocery store, stockpiling cans of chipotles. At my best, I'm downing piece after piece of this incredibly flavorful, eye watering, face flushing, head spinning and endorphin pumping grilled chicken with chipotle dipping sauce. I'm Julie and I never want to fan these flames.

DIRECTIONS

1) For the marinade, in a food processor, combine olive oil, lime juice, honey, chipotle peppers, garlic, cumin, chili powder, salt and pepper. Puree until well combined. In a large bowl, pour marinade over chicken and toss well to coat. Cover and marinate in refrigerator at least 1 hour, up to 8 hours. **2)** While chicken is marinating, in a small bowl, whisk mayonnaise, chipotle pepper, honey, Dijon, lime juice, salt and pepper. Cover and refrigerate until ready to use. **3)** Remove chicken from refrigerator 30 minutes prior to grilling, bringing to room temperature. Meanwhile, preheat barbecue to medium-high heat. Lightly oil the grill grate. Discard marinade and grill chicken 5–6 minutes per side until cooked through. Let rest 5 minutes before serving with chipotle dipping sauce.

Serves 6

BITE ME BIT

"When it hurts so bad, when it hurts so bad, why's it feel so good?"

— from the 1998 Lauryn Hill song "When It Hurts So Bad"

Grilling tips & chili pepper protocol

MASALA GRILLED CHICKEN with CUCUMBER RAITA

INGREDIENTS

Marinade

½ cup Greek-style plain yogurt

1 large garlic clove, minced

1 tbsp chopped fresh flat-leaf parsley

1 tbsp fresh lemon juice

2 tsp paprika

1 tsp garam masala

1 tsp ground cumin

1 tsp dried oregano

¼ tsp cayenne pepper

4 boneless, skinless chicken breast halves

¼ tsp kosher salt

¼ tsp freshly ground black pepper

Cucumber Raita

1 cup Greek-style plain yogurt

1 cup peeled, seeded and diced cucumber, divided

1 small garlic clove, minced

1 tsp fresh lemon juice

½ tsp ground cumin

½ tsp kosher salt

½ tsp freshly ground black pepper

2 tbsp chopped fresh flat-leaf parsley

We're told that variety is the spice of life. True, especially when we peek in our pantries. It's a whole new world in there, the Spice Route mapped out before our very eyes. We want to take your buds on a taste adventure, an expedition as simple as grabbing the Indian spice blend garam masala along with cumin, cayenne and paprika. Marinate chicken in a creamy yogurt, aromatic spice and zesty lemon mixture, then grill it to juicy perfection. Cucumber raita, a cool, creamy and refreshing condiment, perfectly complements the fragrant and flavorful chicken. Amazingly easy to make, you don't even have to pack your bags to spice things up a bit.

DIRECTIONS

1) For the marinade, in a medium bowl, whisk yogurt, garlic, parsley, lemon juice, paprika, garam masala, cumin, oregano and cayenne pepper. Place chicken and marinade in a large resealable plastic bag tossing to coat. Marinate refrigerated 4–24 hours. 2) Preheat barbecue to medium-high heat and lightly oil the grill grate. Remove chicken from marinade, shaking off excess and discarding marinade. Season each piece of chicken with salt and pepper. Grill 8–10 minutes per side until cooked through. Let rest 5 minutes before serving. 3) For the cucumber raita, in a food processor, combine yogurt, ½ cup of the diced cucumber, garlic, lemon juice, cumin, salt and pepper. Pulse 1–2 times to blend. Place in a medium bowl and stir in remaining ½ cup cucumber and chopped parsley. Serve with grilled chicken.

Serves 4

JERK CHICKEN with MANGO-MINT SALSA

INGREDIENTS

Marinade

½ cup chopped white onions

¼ cup fresh lime juice

3 tbsp olive oil

2 large garlic cloves, minced

2 tbsp grated fresh ginger

2 tbsp seeded and finely chopped jalapeno pepper

1 tbsp finely chopped fresh thyme

1 tbsp brown sugar

1 tsp lime zest

1 tsp ground allspice

1 tsp kosher salt

1 tsp freshly ground black pepper

¼ tsp ground cinnamon

6 boneless, skinless chicken breast halves

Mango Mint Salsa

2 ripe mangoes, peeled, pitted and diced

2 tbsp finely chopped red onion

2 tbsp fresh lime juice

2 tbsp olive oil

1 tbsp chopped fresh mint

½ tsp seeded and finely chopped jalapeno pepper

⅛ tsp kosher salt

⅛ tsp freshly ground black pepper

If I ever say you look like a fresh vegetable, I'm practicing my Jamaican patois, telling you that you're pretty. I'm working to master this language, one that lets me say, "Ah wah you a bodda me guthole fa?" instead of, "I don't know." So, in the spirit of my learning, I've also pushed Lisa toward Caribbean cooking. Sweet, hot, herbal and spicy, Jamaican jerk chicken has me hearing steel drums, mon. The chicken is marinated in a distinctively Caribbean mixture of lime juice, jalapenos (the authentic Scotch bonnet and habaneros are too atomic for us), thyme, cinnamon and allspice. Infused with the piquant spice blend, touched by the smokiness of the grill and served with a refreshing cool mint and sweet mango salsa, this jerk chicken is a tropical treat. *Mek wi nyam* (Let's eat)!

DIRECTIONS

1) For the marinade, in a food processor, combine onion, lime juice, olive oil, garlic, ginger, jalapeno, thyme, brown sugar, lime zest, allspice, salt, pepper and cinnamon. Process until well blended. Place chicken in a large shallow dish, add marinade and rub into chicken. Cover and marinate in refrigerator a minimum of 4 hours and as long as 24 hours, occasionally turning chicken to coat.
2) For the salsa, in a medium glass bowl, combine diced mango, red onion, lime juice, olive oil, mint, jalapeno, salt and pepper. Gently stir mixture and refrigerate 2–4 hours before serving. 3) Preheat barbecue to medium-high heat and lightly oil grill grate. Remove chicken from marinade, discarding marinade, and grill 6–7 minutes per side until cooked through. Serve with mango-mint salsa.

Serves 6

GRILLED CHICKEN with ROASTED SHALLOT SAUCE

INGREDIENTS

Marinade

2 tbsp soy sauce

2 tbsp fresh lemon juice

1 tbsp sesame oil

1 tbsp olive oil

1 large garlic clove, minced

2 tsp finely chopped fresh thyme

2 tsp finely chopped fresh rosemary

4 boneless, skinless chicken breast halves

¼ tsp kosher salt

¼ tsp freshly ground black pepper

Roasted Shallot Sauce

8 medium shallots, skin removed, left whole

1 tbsp olive oil

½ cup chicken broth

¼ cup dry white wine

1 tbsp soy sauce

1 tbsp balsamic vinegar

1 tsp finely chopped fresh thyme

2 tbsp light cream

Lisa hates close-talkers. I'm going to guess that has something to do with her aversion to people in her personal space. Though I'm not as militant as her, I still think of a certain boyfriend past as a giant garlic clove, so it thrills me my husband is a shallot man. Shallots have it all going on. Without the harsh bite and overpowering odor, these torpedo-shaped bulbs carry a slight taste of garlic mixed with the sweet flavor of onion. Roasted shallots lend elegance and richness to a spectacular sauce that tops this herb-marinated grilled chicken. This full-flavored dish won't have you reaching for the mouthwash, but, still, please take a giant step back when talking to Lisa (she told me to tell you).

DIRECTIONS

1) For the marinade, in a small bowl, whisk soy sauce, lemon juice, sesame oil, olive oil, minced garlic, thyme and rosemary. Place chicken in large resealable plastic bag, add marinade and toss to coat. Refrigerate 1–2 hours before grilling. 2) For the shallot sauce, preheat oven to 450°F. Place shallots in a small baking dish and toss with 1 tbsp olive oil. Cover the dish with aluminum foil and roast for 15 minutes. Turn the shallots and continue to cook covered another 15 minutes, or until shallots become soft and caramelized. Remove from oven and place shallots in a medium saucepan. Add chicken broth, white wine, soy sauce, balsamic vinegar and fresh thyme. Bring to a boil over medium-high heat. Add cream and cook 2 minutes longer. Place sauce in blender or food processor and blend until smooth. Sauce can be gently reheated when ready to serve. 3) For the chicken, preheat barbecue to medium heat and lightly oil grill grate. Remove chicken from marinade and discard marinade. Season the chicken with ¼ tsp salt and ¼ tsp pepper. Grill the chicken 8–10 minutes per side until cooked through. To serve, slice chicken and top with shallot sauce.

Serves 4

BITE ME BIT

"Conversational Distance, don't you hate these people that talk to you, they talk into your mouth like you're a clown at a drive-through?"

— Jerry Seinfeld, comedian, actor, author

HOISIN CHICKEN TORTILLA WRAPS

INGREDIENTS

Asian Sauce

⅔ cup hoisin sauce

3 tbsp rice vinegar

3 tbsp soy sauce

3 tbsp ketchup

2 tbsp brown sugar

½ tsp grated fresh ginger

2 boneless, skinless chicken breast halves

1½ cups broccoli florets

1½ cups shredded cabbage (red or white)

¾ cup grated carrots

⅓ cup couscous

½ cup water

pinch of salt

4 (10-inch) flour tortillas

Ever hear of a Nations United Wrap^{TM}? Didn't think so, because I just made it up. Don't get any ideas – I'm calling our lawyer tomorrow to make it ours. Now, what is it? How about a delicious handheld meal that crosses cultures and unites diverse cuisines? We start with chicken that has been coated and baked in a Chinese hoisin sauce mixture (including some North American condiments too!) and vegetables that have also been tossed in the sweet and salty sauce. Can you see it all coming together? Next, we prepare light and fluffy North African couscous and toss it in Asian sauce. Finally, it is all wrapped up in a Mexican tortilla. Grab it and don't let go because you've got a perfectly balanced and totally tasty world in your hand.

DIRECTIONS

1) Preheat oven to 375ºF. Line a baking sheet with aluminum foil and coat with non-stick cooking spray. 2) For the Asian sauce, in a small saucepan, bring hoisin, rice vinegar, soy sauce, ketchup, brown sugar and ginger to a boil over high heat. Reduce heat to low and simmer 5 minutes. Remove from heat. 3) Place chicken on prepared baking sheet and coat with ¼ cup of the Asian sauce. Bake 20 minutes, or until cooked through. Slice into long, thin strips. 4) While the chicken is cooking, in a small heatproof bowl, cover broccoli florets with boiling water. Let stand 5 minutes to soften. Drain well and place in a large bowl with cabbage and carrots. Toss with 2 tablespoons of Asian sauce. 5) For the couscous, in a small saucepan, bring ½ cup water and pinch of salt to a boil. Remove from heat and stir in couscous. Cover and let stand 5 minutes. Toss with 1 tbsp of the Asian sauce. 6) To assemble wraps, lay a tortilla on a plate. Place ¼ cup couscous down the center, along with slices from half a chicken breast and ½ cup of the vegetable mixture. Drizzle with Asian sauce, wrap up tortilla and serve.

Serves 4

OVEN ROASTED TURKEY BREAST with GRAVY

INGREDIENTS

4 large carrots, peeled and chopped

4 large celery stalks, chopped

1 large white onion, chopped

4 large garlic cloves

1 (3lb) boneless turkey breast

1 tbsp olive oil

1 tbsp brown sugar

1 tsp paprika

1 tsp garlic powder

1 tsp kosher salt

½ tsp ground cumin

½ tsp chili powder

½ tsp freshly ground black pepper

½ cup chicken broth

½ cup dry white wine

Turkey Gravy

1 cup drippings from the roasting pan

1 cup chicken broth

2 tbsp cornstarch

¼ cup water

I *love* making a whole turkey, look forward to wrestling with the slippery 18-pound bird, fighting my kids for the wishbone and carving it up for all to enjoy for days and days and days. So, when Lisa said we're just putting a breast in this book, I balked. What good is turkey without struggling to get it made and without endless hours spent sitting oven-side? I'll tell you what it is – easy. This turkey breast is rubbed with a spicy, slightly sweet mixture and then baked atop vegetables, white wine and broth until beautifully browned, tender and juicy. Served with silky gravy made from the pan juices, the flavorful slices of white meat from the turkey breast make me long for the glory days of disposing of giblets...not.

DIRECTIONS

1) Preheat oven to 350°F. Coat a small roasting pan with non-stick cooking spray. Arrange carrots, celery, onion and whole garlic on the bottom of the roasting pan. Rinse turkey breast, pat dry and set on top of the vegetables in the pan. Brush turkey with olive oil.

2) In a small bowl, combine brown sugar, paprika, garlic powder, salt, cumin, chili powder and pepper. Lift skin on the turkey breast and spread mixture evenly under the skin. Add chicken broth and white wine to the bottom of the pan. Push a meat thermometer into the thickest part of the breast, lightly cover with aluminum foil and make a small hole for the meat thermometer to pop through. Roast until thermometer reads 170°F, starting to check at 1½ hours. Cooking time will be closer to 2 hours. Remove from oven and let rest in roasting pan 15 minutes before placing on cutting board.

3) For the gravy, using a very fine mesh strainer, pour 1 cup of liquid from the roasting pan and place in a medium saucepan. Discard vegetables. Add chicken broth to saucepan and bring to a boil over medium heat. In a small bowl, combine cornstarch and water. Slowly add to boiling broth mixture while constantly whisking. Reduce heat to low and continue to whisk until gravy thickens, 8–10 minutes. Slice turkey and serve with gravy.

Serves 4

BITE ME BIT

"How many sarcastic pills you take this morning?"

— Phil Weston (actor Will Ferrell) in the 2005 movie *Kicking & Screaming*

ASIAN TURKEY BURGERS

INGREDIENTS

Turkey Burgers

¼ cup soy sauce

2 tbsp hoisin sauce

1 tbsp rice vinegar

1 large garlic clove, minced

1 tsp grated fresh ginger

¼ tsp freshly ground black pepper

¼ tsp cayenne pepper

1½ lbs lean ground turkey

½ cup panko
(Japanese breadcrumbs)

1 tbsp olive oil

Creamy Sesame Spread

1 tsp sesame seeds

2 tbsp sour cream

2 tbsp mayonnaise

2 tsp soy sauce

½ tsp sesame oil

¼ tsp cayenne pepper

6 hamburger buns

lettuce and sliced tomato, optional

Let's talk turkey. Don't do the carnivore-cringe. Turkey burgers have gotten a bad rap over the years, labeled dry, beige, bland, blah and blech punishment for the meat eater. Well, the suffering is over – turkey burgers can be juicy, tasty and immensely satisfying. Flavored with savory hoisin, soy, ginger and garlic, these heart-healthy burgers are grilled to tender perfection and topped with a spicy sesame spread. How's that for a bold and beneficial burger?

DIRECTIONS

1) In a large bowl, combine soy sauce, hoisin, rice vinegar, garlic, ginger, black pepper and cayenne pepper. Add ground turkey and panko and mix just until incorporated. Form into 6 turkey burgers and place on a tray, cover and refrigerate for 2 hours. The cold ensures the burgers won't fall apart while grilling. 2) Preheat barbecue to medium-high heat and lightly oil grill grate. Brush both sides of the burgers with 1 tbsp olive oil. Place on grill and cook 7–9 minutes per side or until burger reaches internal temperature of 165ºF in the center. 3) For the sesame spread, place sesame seeds in a small skillet over low heat. Stir for 2 minutes until seeds are golden. Remove from heat. In a small bowl, whisk sour cream, mayonnaise, soy sauce, sesame seeds, sesame oil and cayenne pepper. Spread on each side of the buns, place grilled burger on bun and top with lettuce and tomato.

Serves 6

Roasted Cod with Basil & Walnut Pesto 163

Pecan-Crusted Cod with Sweet Citrus Glaze 164

Cornflake Tilapia with Tartar Sauce 165

Crunchy Dill-Crusted Salmon 166

Teriyaki Salmon & Vegetable Stir-Fry 167

Sesame Roasted Salmon with Wasabi Dip 168

Hook
me

Alluring Fish & Seafood

Grilled Tuna with Orange & Avocado Salsa 170

Red Snapper with Roasted Red Pepper Aioli 171

Lemon Halibut with Carrots & Leeks 172

Kickin' Cajun Halibut 174

Primo Fish Tacos with Chipotle Lime Dressing 175

Seared Scallops with Spinach & White Wine 176

Chef Binkley's Sweet & Sour Shrimp 177

ROASTED COD with BASIL & WALNUT PESTO

INGREDIENTS

Basil & Walnut Pesto

⅓ cup walnuts

1 cup fresh basil, roughly cut

1 large oil-packed, sun-dried tomato, chopped

1 small garlic clove

¼ tsp kosher salt

¼ tsp freshly ground black pepper

½ cup olive oil

½ cup freshly grated Parmesan cheese

Cod

4 (6oz) cod fillets

¼ tsp kosher salt

¼ tsp freshly ground black pepper

12 oil-packed, sun-dried cherry tomatoes

¼ cup coarse fresh breadcrumbs (from 2 slices of white bread, crusts removed and pulsed 2–3 times in food processor)

4 tsp olive oil

Cod is the blank canvas of fish. Lisa loves transforming mild cod into a masterpiece. Here, as the Picasso of Pesto, she artfully juxtaposes the firm white fish with a vibrant, colorful and highly tasty topping of nutty walnuts, flavor-packed sun-dried tomatoes, basil, garlic and Parmesan. Her skill and creativity don't end there – she tops it all off with sweet, slow roasted cherry tomatoes and crunchy breadcrumbs. The rave reviews are in – this is her *chef d'oeuvre*.

DIRECTIONS

1) For the pesto, preheat oven to 400°F. Place walnuts on a baking sheet and bake 6 minutes. Let cool slightly and then place in food processor with basil leaves, sun-dried tomato, garlic, salt and pepper. Process until finely chopped. With the motor running, slowly pour in olive oil and process until mixture is well combined. Transfer to a bowl and stir in Parmesan. Cover and refrigerate until ready to use. **2)** For the fish, preheat oven to 450°F. Line a baking sheet with aluminum foil and coat with non-stick cooking spray. Rinse cod and pat dry. Season fillets with salt and pepper. Place on prepared baking sheet and spread each fillet with 1 tbsp pesto, top each piece with 3 sun-dried cherry tomatoes and sprinkle 1 tbsp breadcrumbs over each piece. Drizzle fish with olive oil and roast 9–10 minutes until fish is opaque and cooked through. Serve immediately.

Serves 4

PECAN-CRUSTED COD with SWEET CITRUS GLAZE

This fish had me hook, line and sinker. I'm a sucker for mild and versatile cod, a fan of anything crusted in crunchy pecans and an enthusiastic eater of all things orange. This fish has it all, marinated in OJ, coated in a pecan crust and drizzled with a sweet and tangy orange glaze. Baked until tender, cod is elevated from special-of-the-day to catch-of-the-decade.

INGREDIENTS

Marinade

4 (6–8oz) cod fillets
¼ cup orange juice
1 tsp orange zest
¼ tsp kosher salt
¼ tsp freshly ground black pepper

Pecan Crust

¾ cup chopped pecans
¼ cup flour
2 large eggs
¾ cup panko (Japanese breadcrumbs)
¼ tsp kosher salt

Orange Honey Glaze

¼ cup orange juice
2 tbsp honey

DIRECTIONS

1) Place cod in a large resealable plastic bag. In a small bowl, whisk orange juice, zest, salt and pepper. Pour over cod and marinate at room temperature for 20 minutes. 2) Preheat oven to 375°F. Place pecans on a small baking sheet and cook 3–5 minutes, watching carefully, until toasted. Remove from oven and set aside. 3) Increase oven temperature to 425°F. Line a baking sheet with aluminum foil and coat with non-stick cooking spray. Place flour in a shallow bowl. In another bowl, gently whisk eggs. In a third bowl, combine panko, salt and toasted pecans. Remove cod from marinade and dredge both sides in flour, shaking off excess. Dip cod in eggs and then coat in pecan-panko mixture pressing well to adhere to both sides. Place on prepared baking sheet and cook 10–12 minutes. 4) For the glaze, in a small saucepan, heat orange juice and honey over medium heat. Once mixture comes to a gentle boil, simmer 3 minutes. Remove from heat and drizzle over cooked cod just before serving.

Serves 4

CORNFLAKE TILAPIA with TARTAR SAUCE

INGREDIENTS

Tartar Sauce

½ cup mayonnaise
2 small dill pickles, chopped
1 tbsp fresh flat-leaf parsley
1 tsp capers, rinsed and drained
1 tsp fresh lemon juice
⅛ tsp freshly ground black pepper

4 (6oz) tilapia fillets
¼ tsp kosher salt
2 tbsp fresh lemon juice

¾ cup crushed cornflakes
½ cup breadcrumbs
1 small garlic clove, minced
1 tbsp chopped fresh flat-leaf parsley
½ tsp dried thyme
½ tsp kosher salt
¼ tsp freshly ground black pepper
pinch of cayenne pepper
¼ cup butter, melted

When people say, "I like it because it doesn't taste like fish," there's a good chance they're talking about tilapia. Short of coating it in anchovies, you can safely serve this lean, mild-flavored fish to any fish-a-phobic diner. Snow white and firm, tilapia is a protein-packed fish that takes on any surrounding flavors. In this quick and easy recipe, tilapia is baked in a crisp crust until golden and crunchy on the outside and tender and moist on the inside, and served with a creamy tartar sauce. My days of duking it out over cereal box prizes aren't over – I'll pinch and push if it means getting the last piece of this cornflake tilapia.

DIRECTIONS

1) For the tartar sauce, in a blender, combine mayonnaise, pickles, parsley, capers, lemon juice and pepper. Pulse 2–3 times to combine. Refrigerate at least 1 hour before serving. **2)** For the tilapia, preheat oven to 400°F. Line a baking sheet with aluminum foil and coat with non-stick cooking spray. Pat the tilapia dry with paper towel, place on baking sheet, season with ¼ tsp salt, drizzle lemon juice evenly over each fillet and set aside. **3)** In a large bowl, combine cornflakes, breadcrumbs, garlic, parsley, thyme, salt, pepper and cayenne pepper. Add melted butter and mix until well combined. Divide the mixture among the fillets and press down lightly to adhere. Bake 15 minutes or until the crumbs are golden and the fish flakes easily with a fork. Serve immediately with tartar sauce.

Serves 4

BITE ME BIT

"Confidence is going after Moby Dick in a rowboat and taking the tartar sauce with you."

— Zig Ziglar, author

CRUNCHY DILL-CRUSTED SALMON

INGREDIENTS

4 (6oz) salmon fillets, skin removed

½ cup mayonnaise

2 tbsp coarse grain mustard

2 tbsp fresh lemon juice

2 tbsp chopped fresh dill

1 tbsp chopped fresh flat-leaf parsley

1 tsp lemon zest

½ tsp kosher salt

¼ tsp freshly ground black pepper

1¼ cups panko (Japanese breadcrumbs)

2 tbsp olive oil

Being rhythmically challenged (Lisa does the cadaver dance while I'm prone to whip out the Elaine Benes "little kicks"), we shudder at anything involving the phrase "two-step." That is, until now. Elegant and easy, this two-step crusted salmon, the ideal pairing of fish and dill, makes it effortless to keep perfect tempo.

DIRECTIONS

1) Preheat oven to 450°F. Line a baking sheet with aluminum foil and coat with non-stick cooking spray. Rinse salmon fillets and pat dry with paper towel and set aside. 2) In a small bowl, combine mayonnaise, mustard, lemon juice, dill, parsley, lemon zest, salt and pepper. Place panko crumbs in a shallow dish. Spread mayonnaise mixture over fish, coat in panko, lightly pressing to adhere. Place on prepared baking sheet and drizzle each fillet with ½ tbsp olive oil. Bake 10 minutes, until the crumbs are golden and the fish is cooked through. Serve with lemon wedges.

Serves 4

BITE ME BIT

"I would imagine that if you could understand Morse code, a tap dancer would drive you crazy."

— Mitch Hedberg, comedian

TERIYAKI SALMON & VEGETABLE STIR-FRY

INGREDIENTS

Teriyaki Sauce

½ cup soy sauce

½ cup sake

¼ cup mirin

2 tbsp brown sugar

1 tsp grated fresh ginger

2 tbsp cornstarch

2 tbsp water

Salmon Marinade

4 (6oz) salmon fillets

2 tbsp soy sauce

2 tbsp rice vinegar

2 tbsp brown sugar

1 tsp sesame oil

½ tsp grated fresh ginger

Vegetables

1 tbsp peanut oil

¼ cup diced shallots

1 large garlic clove, minced

3 cups chopped bok choy

2 cups snow peas, ends trimmed, sliced in half

1 large red bell pepper, chopped

1 large yellow pepper, chopped

We're going to gloss over the health benefits of eating salmon (rich in omega-3s, protein, iron) because there's nothing drool worthy about "fatty acids." Instead, we're going to concentrate on the pink fillets we marinate in a Japanese mixture of soy sauce, rice vinegar, ginger and sesame oil and then bake in a homemade, rich and deep-mahogany-colored teriyaki sauce. Then, we'll mention that crunchy bok choy, snow peas and peppers are stir-fried to glistening, crisp perfection in the sweet and tangy teriyaki sauce and served beneath the beautifully glazed salmon. Oh yes, much sexier and tastier than reminding you that salmon will slow down the build up of atherosclerotic plaque.

DIRECTIONS

1) For the teriyaki sauce, in a medium saucepan, combine soy sauce, sake, mirin, brown sugar and ginger. Bring to a boil over medium heat. In a small bowl, dissolve cornstarch in water. Whisking constantly, add cornstarch mixture to saucepan and reduce heat to low. Cook 3 minutes, until thickened. Remove from heat and set aside. 2) For the salmon, place fillets in a large resealable plastic bag. In a small bowl, whisk soy sauce, rice vinegar, brown sugar, sesame oil and ginger. Pour over salmon and marinate 30 minutes in the refrigerator. 3) Preheat oven to 425°F. Line a baking sheet with aluminum foil and coat with non-stick cooking spray. Remove salmon from marinade and place on baking sheet skin side down. Spoon 1 tbsp prepared teriyaki sauce over each fillet. Bake 10 minutes. 4) For the vegetables, in a wok or large skillet, heat peanut oil over high heat. Add shallots and garlic, stirring constantly for 1 minute. Add bok choy, snow peas and peppers. Stir-fry 3–4 minutes until vegetables are tender-crisp. Add 3 tbsp teriyaki sauce, stir to coat and remove from heat. 5) To serve, place a scoop of vegetables on each plate, top with salmon and drizzle with any remaining teriyaki sauce. Serve immediately.

Serves 4

SESAME ROASTED SALMON
with WASABI DIP

INGREDIENTS

Marinade

2 tbsp orange juice

2 tbsp honey

2 tbsp soy sauce

1 tbsp olive oil

1 small garlic clove, minced

1 tsp grated fresh ginger

½ tsp lime zest

4 (6oz) salmon fillets, skin removed

¼ tsp kosher salt

⅛ tsp freshly ground black pepper

1½ tbsp sesame seeds

Wasabi Dip

¼ cup mayonnaise

2 tsp soy sauce

1 tsp wasabi paste

1 tsp fresh lime juice

Socks on, socks off. Socks on, socks off. Sensei Lisa said this Asian-inspired salmon would knock my socks off and straight into next week. The sage master wasn't wrong. Marinated in a soy-citrus mixture and topped with nutty-flavored sesame seeds, the salmon is roasted to golden-crusted tender perfection. She wowed me even more with the addition of her spicy wasabi dip, but, can she, like Julie-san, karate chop the cap off a beer bottle while blindfolded and standing on one foot? I think not.

DIRECTIONS

1) For the marinade, in a small bowl, whisk orange juice, honey, soy sauce, olive oil, garlic, ginger and lime zest. Place the salmon in a large resealable plastic bag. Add marinade, turn to coat and refrigerate 1 hour. 2) Preheat oven to 425°F. Line a baking sheet with aluminum foil and coat with non-stick cooking spray. Remove salmon from marinade and discard marinade. Place salmon on baking sheet and season each fillet with salt and pepper. Sprinkle tops evenly with sesame seeds, pressing lightly to adhere. Bake 10 minutes or until fish is flaky. 3) For the wasabi dip, in a small bowl, whisk mayonnaise, soy sauce, wasabi and lime juice until combined. Serve with salmon.

Serves 4

BITE ME BIT

"If people knew how hard I worked to get my mastery, it wouldn't seem so wonderful at all."

— Michelangelo, artist

GRILLED TUNA with ORANGE & AVOCADO SALSA

INGREDIENTS

Tuna

4 (6–8oz) center-cut tuna fillets, about 1-inch thick
2 tbsp fresh lime juice
2 tbsp olive oil
¼ tsp kosher salt
¼ tsp freshly ground black pepper

Orange & Avocado Salsa

½ cup red onions, thinly sliced
2 tbsp olive oil
1 tbsp fresh lime juice
1 tsp honey
¼ tsp kosher salt
¼ tsp freshly ground black pepper
2 large navel oranges, peeled and sectioned
1 avocado, ripe yet still firm, peeled and diced

I've cheated on my butcher. Though I cherish the hours spent discussing rubs and won't ever forget the intensive tenderloin training, I've strayed from his pasture over to the fishmonger's fillets. Tuna is beefy. Its dark-red flesh carries no fishy taste, has a meaty texture and is packed with protein. That's not all. When I long for the thrill of the grill, this lean fish delivers. Marinated in lime juice and olive oil, these simply seasoned tuna steaks are char-grilled and served with a refreshing salsa of juicy oranges, creamy avocado and tangy red onions. I know. After this, I can just forget my all access pass to the Beltway Beef Convention.

DIRECTIONS

1) Place tuna in a large resealable plastic bag. In a small bowl, whisk lime juice, olive oil, salt and pepper. Pour over tuna and marinate 30 minutes in the refrigerator. 2) For the salsa, place onion slices in a small bowl and fill with ice water. Let stand 30 minutes. Drain well. In a medium bowl, whisk olive oil, lime juice, honey, salt and pepper. Add oranges, avocado and red onions. Toss well to combine. Don't prepare more than 30 minutes before serving as avocado will start to discolor. 3) Preheat barbecue to medium-high heat. Lightly oil grill grate and grill tuna 3 minutes per side for rare. To serve, spoon salsa on top of tuna.

Serves 4

BITE ME BIT

"I'm sorry I ate your fish, okay?"

— Otto West (actor Kevin Kline) in the 1988 movie *A Fish Called Wanda*

RED SNAPPER with ROASTED PEPPER AIOLI

INGREDIENTS

Roasted Red Pepper Aioli

¼ cup jarred roasted red peppers, drained, patted dry and chopped

¼ cup mayonnaise

1 tbsp olive oil

1 small garlic clove, minced

1 tsp fresh lemon juice

1 tsp fresh lime juice

¼ tsp sugar

¼ tsp kosher salt

4 (6–7oz) red snapper fillets, about ½-inch thick

1 tbsp olive oil

½ tsp kosher salt

¼ tsp freshly ground black pepper

¼ tsp garlic powder

¼ tsp paprika

⅛ tsp cayenne pepper

Snapper Foster. That's what I wanted to name this mouthwatering fish dish. Lisa wouldn't let me. She wasn't swayed that this was my secret shout-out to The Hoff (as in David Hasselhoff) and the swoon-worthy character he played on *The Young and the Restless* during my impressionable preteen years. Nor did it help that I vowed to compare the flavor-packed aioli, a mix of roasted red peppers, garlic and olive oil, to his *Baywatch* swim trunks. So, here's my Lisa-friendly intro: Snapper is a popular (just like Snapper Foster) white fish with a sweet and nutty flavor (sounds like DH, huh?). It's versatile (DH, again) and is great grilled and topped with roasted red pepper aioli (look how he runs in the sand!), perfect for every night (like *Knight Rider* reruns).

DIRECTIONS

1) For the aioli, in a food processor or blender, combine roasted red peppers, mayonnaise, olive oil, garlic, lemon juice, lime juice, sugar and salt. Blend until almost smooth. Transfer aioli to a small bowl, cover and refrigerate before serving. This can be made up to 2 days in advance. 2) For the red snapper, preheat barbecue to medium-high heat and lightly oil grill grate. Brush each fillet with olive oil. In a small bowl, combine salt, pepper, garlic powder, paprika and cayenne pepper. Evenly season both sides of the red snapper. Place snapper on grill skin side down, close the lid and grill for 4 minutes. Turn fish, close lid and continue to cook 4 minutes or until fish flakes easily with a fork. Serve drizzled with red pepper aioli.

Serves 4

LEMON HALIBUT with CARROTS & LEEKS

INGREDIENTS

4 (6–7oz) halibut fillets

1 tsp lemon zest

1 tsp grated fresh ginger

1 tsp olive oil

½ tsp kosher salt

¼ tsp freshly ground black pepper

2 tbsp olive oil

4 medium leeks, white and light-green parts only, halved lengthwise, thinly sliced and rinsed well

1½ cups peeled carrots, thinly sliced on the diagonal

¼ tsp kosher salt

¼ tsp freshly ground black pepper

1 cup vegetable broth

4 fresh thyme sprigs

¼ cup fresh lemon juice

Lisa told me I have to write this intro like a grown-up because this halibut is "sophisticated." Did she think I'd haul out the whoopee cushion? Ahem. Ladies and Gentlemen, halibut is a lovely, firm white fish. It is made all the lovelier when placed atop sautéed leeks and carrots and oven braised in a delightful mixture of vegetable broth, thyme and lemon juice. Not only is it a healthy and delicious dish but it also presents wonderfully to esteemed company, or, in my case, to an uncouth, immature 40-something-year-old.

DIRECTIONS

1) Preheat oven to 375ºF. Pat halibut fillets dry with paper towel. In a small bowl, combine lemon zest, ginger, 1 tbsp olive oil, salt and pepper. Pat mixture evenly over one side of each fillet. Set aside.

2) In deep ovenproof skillet, heat 2 tbsp olive oil over medium heat. Add leeks and carrots, stirring often for 5 minutes, until softened. Season with ¼ tsp salt and ¼ tsp pepper. Add vegetable broth, cover and cook over medium heat for 6–8 minutes, until leeks and carrots are tender. Remove from heat and arrange fish on top of vegetables with the lemon/ginger side face up. Top each fillet with 1 sprig of thyme. Pour lemon juice evenly over fish and cover the fish with a piece of parchment paper, then cover the skillet with the lid. Bake 13–15 minutes or until just cooked through. Discard thyme sprigs, transfer fish to serving plate and serve alongside leeks and carrots.

Serves 4

KICKIN' CAJUN HALIBUT

INGREDIENTS

Spice Mixture

2 tbsp olive oil

2 tsp paprika

1 tsp dried thyme

½ tsp dried oregano

½ tsp kosher salt

½ tsp freshly ground black pepper

⅛ tsp cayenne pepper

4 (6–8oz) halibut fillets

1 tbsp olive oil

Well, butter my butt and call me a biscuit. Miss Lisa has brought Louisiana north with this deliciously spicy fish. With a simple rub of paprika, thyme, oregano and cayenne pepper, mild halibut becomes zip-a-dee-doo-dah, I reckon. Easy and quick to make, the spice-rubbed fish hits the skillet and develops a nice, blackened crust and is then finished to moist perfection in the oven. I declare, this is the best dang fish outside the Bayou.

DIRECTIONS

1) Preheat oven to 400ºF. Line a baking sheet with aluminum foil and coat with non-stick cooking spray. 2) For the spice mixture, in a small bowl, whisk 2 tbsp olive oil, paprika, thyme, oregano, salt, pepper and cayenne pepper. Set aside. 3) Pat halibut fillets dry with paper towel. Brush spice mixture over the top of each piece of fish. Heat a large skillet over high heat. Add 1 tbsp olive oil and place fillets seasoned side down in the skillet. Cook 1–2 minutes or until the crust on the bottom is very brown. Place fish on baking sheet browned side up. Bake 8 minutes or until cooked through. Serve with fresh lemon or lime wedges.

Serves 4

PRIMO FISH TACOS with CHIPOTLE LIME DRESSING

INGREDIENTS

Marinade

4 (6oz) cod, tilapia or any white, flaky fish fillets

2 tbsp olive oil

2 tbsp fresh lime juice

1 tsp lime zest

1 tsp ancho chili powder

1 tsp ground cumin

¼ tsp kosher salt

¼ tsp freshly ground black pepper

Chipotle Lime Dressing

½ cup sour cream

½ cup mayonnaise

2 tbsp fresh lime juice

½ chipotle pepper in adobo sauce, more if you like it extra spicy

¼ tsp kosher salt

¼ cup roughly chopped fresh flat-leaf parsley

8 (8-inch) flour tortillas

2 cups shredded green cabbage

2 cups shredded purple cabbage

Gremmie. Barney. Hanging 2. These are all terms that have been used to describe Lisa atop (and under) her surfboard, getting nailed by waves and swallowing Neptune Cocktails. She may not be Gidget but she did manage to bring something back from her last trip to Baja – inspiration to create these totally off-the-wall, gnarlatious fish tacos. Baked instead of fried, these healthy, fresh tacos are filled with citrus-marinated white fish, drizzled with spicy chipotle lime dressing and topped with shredded cabbage. Cowabunga, Lisa – you finally conquered the Big One.

DIRECTIONS

1) Preheat oven to 375ºF. Line a baking sheet with aluminum foil and coat with non-stick cooking spray. Place fish in a shallow dish. To make the marinade, in a small bowl, whisk oil, lime juice, lime zest, chili powder, cumin, salt and pepper. Pour over fish and marinate 20 minutes. **2)** For the dressing, in a food processor, combine sour cream, mayonnaise, lime juice, chipotle pepper and salt. Puree mixture for 10 seconds. Place in serving bowl, stir in parsley, cover and refrigerate until ready to assemble. **3)** Remove fish from marinade and place on prepared baking sheet. Bake 9–11 minutes until fish is cooked through. Let fish rest for 5 minutes and then flake with a fork. Leave oven on to heat tortillas. **4)** To assemble, divide tortillas into 2 stacks and wrap in aluminum foil. Place in heated oven for 3–5 minutes to heat through. Divide the flaked fish among the tortillas and garnish with green and purple cabbage. Drizzle with chipotle dressing and roll up around fillings. Serve immediately.

Serves 4

BITE ME BIT

"Then, after I've gotten rid of Batman and Robin for good, I will rule the waves. Me, the Joker, king of the surf and all the surfers."

— The Joker (actor Cesar Romero) on the TV show *Batman*

SEARED SCALLOPS with SPINACH & WHITE WINE

INGREDIENTS

1½ lbs large sea scallops

2 tbsp olive oil

¼ tsp kosher salt

¼ tsp freshly ground black pepper

1 tbsp butter

¼ cup minced shallots

½ cup dry white wine

6 cups baby spinach, loosely packed

1 tbsp fresh lemon juice

4 large basil leaves, thinly sliced

When I took a survey of why people rarely make scallops at home, the answer was consistent – scared stiff. Now, c'mon. Who's bigger, you or the little white shellfish? Grab the skillet and get going because in less than 10 minutes you'll have plump scallops sitting atop a mound of white wine, shallot and lemon-flavored baby spinach. Quickly sautéed in a sizzling pan, the scallops develop a caramel-colored crust yet remain tender, meaty morsels. See? Nothing to fear here, other than eating over a pound of irresistible scallops…in one sitting…by yourself…for lunch. Been there, done that.

DIRECTIONS

1) Pat the scallops dry with paper towel. In a large skillet, heat olive oil over medium-high heat. Add scallops in a single layer and sprinkle with salt and pepper. Without moving the scallops, cook 2 minutes, until golden brown on the bottom. Flip the scallops and cook another 2 minutes, until just cooked through, being careful not to overcook. Remove from skillet and keep warm. 2) Melt butter in the skillet and add shallots, stirring for 30 seconds. Add white wine to deglaze pan, about 1 minute. Add spinach, cooking 1 minute. Stir in lemon juice and place a portion of spinach on each serving plate. Top with seared scallops and sprinkle with basil.

Serves 4

BITE ME BIT

"Don't you know the Wizard's going to give you some courage?"

— Dorothy (actress Judy Garland) in the 1939 movie *The Wizard of Oz*

CHEF BINKLEY'S SWEET & SOUR SHRIMP

INGREDIENTS

Marinade

3 lbs medium raw shrimp, peeled and deveined

3 tbsp cornstarch

2 tbsp soy sauce

2 tbsp sherry vinegar

3 egg whites

Sweet & Sour Sauce

1¼ cups unseasoned rice vinegar (no sugar added)

6 tbsp fresh lime juice

1¼ cups sugar

3 tbsp cornstarch

2 tbsp vegetable oil, divided

1 tbsp vegetable oil

2 large garlic cloves, minced

1 tbsp grated fresh ginger

1 large green pepper, cut into 1-inch cubes

1 large red bell pepper, cut into 1-inch cubes

1 large yellow pepper, cut into 1-inch cubes

3 cups cubed fresh pineapple

2 tbsp thinly sliced fresh basil

This is my second time writing this intro. The first go-round, I praised our friend Matt Binkley for being a supremely talented chef and culinary fountain of knowledge. I lauded him for creating this delicious sweet and sour shrimp that anyone (read: me) can successfully execute. While this is all true, I recalled a few things about Binks, how he beans me with everything from red peppers to walnuts (he does have quite the arm), how he mocks my kitchen-friendly stilettos and how he giggles when I pick up a knife. Well, Chef, who's cooking with gas now? Hmm?

DIRECTIONS

1) For the marinade, in a large bowl, combine cornstarch, soy sauce and sherry vinegar, stirring until cornstarch is dissolved. Whisk in egg whites and add shrimp. Let marinate 30 minutes. 2) While shrimp marinates, prepare sweet and sour sauce. In a large saucepan, combine rice vinegar and lime juice. In a small bowl, toss together sugar and cornstarch to combine well. Whisk into saucepan. Bring to a boil over high heat continuously whisking. Reduce heat to low and simmer, stirring for 4 minutes until sauce thickens. Remove from heat and set aside. 3) To cook the shrimp, working in 2 batches, in a wok heat 1 tbsp oil over high heat. Add half the shrimp and stir-fry for approximately 2 minutes or until almost cooked through. Remove from wok, heat remaining 1 tbsp oil and repeat with remaining shrimp. Remove shrimp and wipe out wok. 4) Using the wok, heat 1 tbsp oil over medium-high heat. Add garlic and ginger and stir-fry for 10 seconds. Add green, red and yellow peppers and stir-fry for 2 minutes. Pour in the sweet and sour sauce and continue cooking for 1 minute. Add the shrimp and pineapple, reduce heat to low and simmer 2 minutes until the shrimp are coated with the sauce and heated through. Garnish with sliced basil.

Serves 6–8

Bone me

Satisfy your Meat Tooth

EXTRA BITE

PRIME RIB with CREAMY HORSERADISH SAUCE

Finish this sentence: Nothing says "party" like _____. If you said "wheatgrass," move on. However, if like us you said "10 pounds of meltingly tender Prime Rib," you're in the right place. Ideal for a celebratory meal (or just because it's Sunday), this beautiful cut of meat, rubbed with garlic, rosemary and thyme, is roasted until perfectly pink inside and browned outside. Grab the carving knife and serve up succulent slices of this old-school Prime Rib, accompanied with a tangy, creamy horseradish-and-mustard sauce. It gives new meaning to "having a rare old time," huh?

INGREDIENTS

Prime Rib Roast

1 (10lb/4 rib) bone-in Prime Rib roast

2 tbsp olive oil

2 tbsp kosher salt

1 tbsp freshly ground black pepper

4 large garlic cloves, minced

2 fresh rosemary sprigs, leaves removed and chopped

4 fresh thyme sprigs, leaves removed and chopped

Horseradish & Mustard Sauce

¼ cup buttermilk

2 tbsp white horseradish

2 tbsp mayonnaise

1 tbsp Dijon mustard

1 tbsp sour cream

½ tsp finely chopped fresh rosemary

¼ tsp kosher salt

¼ tsp freshly ground black pepper

DIRECTIONS

1) Preheat oven to 450°F. To ensure even cooking, bring roast to room temperature 30–60 minutes before roasting. Pat rib roast dry and make ½-inch slits over the top and on the sides of the roast. In a small bowl, whisk olive oil, salt, pepper, garlic, rosemary and thyme. Rub seasoning all over roast and inside the slits. Place roast in a large roasting pan, rib side down. Bake 15 minutes. Reduce oven temperature to 325°F and continue cooking 2 hours and 10 minutes until a meat thermometer inserted into the thickest portion of the roast reaches 130–135°F (for medium-rare). Remove from oven and let rest 15 minutes before carving. 2) For the horseradish sauce, in a medium bowl, whisk buttermilk, horseradish, mayonnaise, Dijon mustard, sour cream, rosemary, salt and pepper. Serve with sliced roast.

Serves 8–10

BITE ME BIT

"If we're not supposed to eat animals, how come they're made out of meat?"

— Tom Snyder, journalist, TV host

CUT-WITH-A-FORK BBQ-SAUCED BRISKET

INGREDIENTS

Brisket Rub

1 tbsp paprika

2 tsp freshly ground black pepper

2 tsp garlic powder

2 tsp chili powder

2 tsp brown sugar

¼ tsp cayenne pepper

1 (5½-6 lb) beef brisket

BBQ Sauce

2 cups ketchup

½ cup packed brown sugar

⅓ cup white vinegar

1 tbsp yellow mustard

1½ tsp chili powder

1 tsp garlic powder

1 tsp ground cumin

1 tsp fresh lemon juice

1 tsp freshly ground black pepper

½ tsp kosher salt

pinch of cayenne pepper

2 tbsp butter, cubed

2 cups beef broth

We've had our fair share of bad brisket. Leathery or slippery seemed to be the only two options for this tough cut of meat. Well, the days of trying to hide it from the hostess (note: *never* put it in your pocket) under peas and potatoes are over. Taking her cue from the Texans, Lisa goes the low-and-slow approach, baking the brisket at a low temperature for a long time. She takes tenderizing one step further, marinating the brisket overnight in a flavorful spice rub before coating it in a homemade tangy barbecue sauce. Slow cooked until meltingly tender, the only thing bad about this braised brisket is how little gets left over.

DIRECTIONS

1) For the brisket rub, in a small bowl, combine paprika, black pepper, garlic powder, chili powder, brown sugar and cayenne. Pat brisket dry and season both sides of the meat with the rub. Cover meat and let marinate refrigerated 6–24 hours. **2)** For the barbecue sauce, in a medium saucepan, combine ketchup, brown sugar, vinegar, mustard, chili powder, garlic powder, cumin, lemon juice, black pepper, salt and cayenne. Bring to a boil over high heat. Stir to dissolve sugar, reduce heat to low and simmer 20 minutes, stirring occasionally. Whisk in butter when sauce has finished cooking. Set aside. **3)** Bring brisket to room temperature before cooking. Preheat oven to 300°F. Place brisket in a large roasting pan, fat side up, and pour beef broth and ½ cup of the prepared barbecue sauce in the roasting pan and over the top of the meat. Cover pan tightly with aluminum foil and cook 4 hours until brisket is fork tender. Transfer to a carving board and let rest 20 minutes. To serve, remove fat cap and slice meat thinly against the grain. Serve with remaining barbecue sauce.

Serves 6–8

GRILLED STRIP STEAKS with PEPPERCORN SAUCE

INGREDIENTS

4 (8–10oz) boneless strip loin steaks

½ tsp kosher salt

½ tsp freshly ground black pepper

Peppercorn Sauce

2 tbsp butter

2 tbsp flour

1 cup beef broth

1 tbsp red currant jelly

1 tbsp green peppercorns, drained

1 tbsp whiskey

kosher salt to taste

To someone who, at times, avoids the kitchen, the idea of skipping a steakhouse in favor of making steak at home sounds like lunacy, right? Not after I made this 5-star recipe. So simple yet elegant enough for entertaining, these juicy, tender strip loin steaks are smothered in a velvety peppercorn sauce. The subtle zip of green peppercorns combined with rich beef broth, zesty red currant jelly and the distinctive flavor of whiskey make this sauce alone worth staying home for...that, and eating scrumptious steak while wearing sweatpants.

DIRECTIONS

1) Preheat barbecue to high heat and lightly oil grill grate. Generously season both sides of steaks with salt and pepper. Grill 4–6 minutes, turn over and grill another 4–6 minutes for medium rare. Transfer steaks to a plate and let rest 5 minutes before serving.

2) For the peppercorn sauce, in a medium saucepan, melt butter over low heat. Whisk in flour, stirring constantly until bubbling. Remove from heat and slowly whisk in beef broth. Bring back to a boil over medium heat and whisk in red currant jelly, peppercorns and whiskey. Reduce heat to low and simmer 5 minutes, stirring often. Remove from heat and season to taste with salt. Serve immediately over steak.

Serves 4

BITE ME BIT

Stu: Why are you peppering the steak? You don't know if tigers like pepper.

Alan: Tigers love pepper. They hate cinnamon.

— from the 2009 movie *The Hangover*

ZESTY BEEF & VEGETABLE KEBABS

INGREDIENTS

Marinade

¼ cup olive oil

¼ cup soy sauce

¼ cup orange juice

1 tbsp brown sugar

1 large garlic clove, minced

1½ tsp ground cumin

1 tsp ground turmeric

1 tsp ground paprika

1 tsp orange zest

2 lbs boneless rib eye steaks, cut into 1½-inch cubes

2 red bell peppers, cut into 1-inch pieces

1 medium zucchini, cut into 1-inch pieces

1 medium white onion, cut into 1-inch pieces

metal skewers for grilling

We know. Christopher Columbus beat us to it, detailing his enjoyment of grilled beef on skewers. Despite being scooped on this one, it still bears repeating – shish kebab is satisfyingly scrumptious. Lisa's voyage to discover tender, tasty kebabs led her to create this recipe, one in which chunks of rib eye steak, red pepper, zucchini and onion are marinated in a zesty mix of soy sauce, orange juice, garlic, cumin, turmeric and paprika. Once tenderized and threaded on skewers, the seasoned cubes are grilled to a juicy finish. It's only a matter of time before these flavorful kebabs spread like wildfire across backyard barbecues everywhere. All hail Lisa, The Great Grill Explorer.

DIRECTIONS

1) In a small bowl, whisk olive oil, soy sauce, orange juice, brown sugar, garlic, cumin, turmeric, paprika and orange zest. In a separate small bowl, reserve ¼ cup marinade to baste kebabs while grilling. 2) Place beef cubes, red pepper, zucchini and onion in a large resealable plastic bag. Add marinade and refrigerate 3–6 hours, turning meat several times. 3) Preheat barbecue to medium-high heat and lightly oil grill grate. On metal skewer, thread 3 or 4 beef cubes, alternating with pieces of pepper, zucchini and onion. Leave a small space between beef cubes to ensure they cook all round. Grill 8–10 minutes, turning skewers every 2 minutes. In the last few minutes of cooking, baste kebabs with reserved marinade. Remove from grill and allow to rest a few minutes before serving.

Serves 4–6

BITE ME BIT

"You know, I don't think that they have enough meat on sticks."

— Mary (actress Cameron Diaz) in the 1998 movie *Something About Mary*

PANKO-CRUSTED BEEF TENDERLOIN

INGREDIENTS

2 lbs beef tenderloin, center cut

2 tbsp olive oil

2 tbsp soy sauce

1 tsp wasabi paste

¼ tsp kosher salt

¼ tsp freshly ground black pepper

½ cup panko (Japanese breadcrumbs)

2 tbsp olive oil

Honey Teriyaki Glaze

2 tbsp soy sauce

2 tbsp honey

2 tbsp mirin

2 tbsp sake

1 tsp cornstarch

1 tbsp water

Sometimes, one word says it all. Take tenderloin, for example. A tender loin. We adore this lean, most prized cut of beef and love to haul out this recipe for celebrations. Marinated in a soy-wasabi paste and then baked in a crunchy panko crumb coating, the crisp-crusted, juicy tenderloin is drizzled with a sweet and savory honey-teriyaki glaze. Here's another word that says it all – heavenly.

DIRECTIONS

1) Place tenderloin in a large resealable plastic bag. In a small bowl, whisk olive oil, soy and wasabi paste. Pour over beef and seal bag, marinate 30 minutes on the counter. If marinating longer, refrigerate. **2)** Preheat oven to 400°F. Line a baking sheet with aluminum foil and coat with non-stick cooking spray. **3)** Remove tenderloin from marinade and sprinkle all sides with salt and pepper. Place panko crumbs on a flat dish. Roll beef back and forth in crumbs to adhere. **4)** In a large skillet, heat olive oil over high heat. Brown beef in skillet, 2 minutes per side. Remove from heat and place on prepared baking sheet. Bake 30–35 minutes. Using a meat thermometer, internal temperature will read 145°F for medium rare. Remove from oven and let stand 10 minutes before slicing. **5)** For the glaze, in a small saucepan, combine soy sauce, honey, mirin and sake over medium-low heat. Bring to a boil. In a small bowl, dissolve cornstarch in water. Whisking constantly, add cornstarch mixture to saucepan, stirring 2 minutes to thicken. Serve a small spoonful over each slice of beef.

Serves 6

BITE ME BIT

"Brevity is the soul of wit."

— William Shakespeare, playwright

GIMME FIVE!

Slapping you some Top Tips

PINCH HITTERS – Kitchen Substitutions

Lisa's a girl scout who's always prepared. I've been known to get halfway through a recipe only to realize I'm missing a key ingredient. Now, thanks to these 5 handy stand-ins, I can forgo the corner-store-run and just call up the replacement.

Buttermilk

1 cup buttermilk = 1 tbsp lemon juice or white vinegar + enough milk to make 1 cup

Baking Powder

1 tsp baking powder = ½ tsp cream of tartar + ¼ tsp baking soda

Fresh Herbs

1 tbsp fresh herbs = 1 tsp dried herbs

Italian Seasoning

2 tsp Italian seasoning = 1 tsp dried oregano + ½ tsp dried basil + ½ tsp dried thyme

Ketchup

½ cup ketchup = ½ cup tomato sauce + 2 tbsp sugar + 1 tbsp white vinegar

BRAIN FREEZE – Breaking the Ice with Your Freezer

I had no clue how to tame the icy abyss that I called my freezer. I'd stare at a knob of ginger, a half-empty bottle of vodka and an iced-over mystery freezer container and wonder what was for dinner. Those days are over. I've become an icebox hotshot. Here are some pointers on becoming freezer burns' foe and a bosom buddy of below zero.

1) Keep your **freezer temperature** below zero and don't overstuff your freezer – if it's too packed cold air won't circulate. 2) Keep meats and poultry at the **back of the freezer** where it's coldest – temperature fluctuates near the door making it only safe for juice concentrates, frozen vegetables and fruit. 3) To prevent **freezer burn**, wrap food using only thick "freezer-safe" bags and containers. The less air that reaches the food, the fresher it will taste when defrosted. 4) When **freezing meat**, double wrap it by removing it from its original packaging, wrapping it in freezer-safe plastic wrap and then in heavy-duty aluminum foil. Make sure to label contents using tape or a Sharpie. 5) Be sure to **cool cooked items** in the refrigerator before freezing to prevent big ice crystals from forming on the surface.

UP IN MY GRILL – Firing up Your Barbecue

Lisa's barbecue is her best friend. That's ok. My best friend is Lisa's barbecue too...you should taste the stuff that comes off of it. Here are some quick tips when taming the flame.

1) Your grill has reached medium heat when you can keep your hand over the grate for 3 seconds. 2) Always keep your grate clean. When barbecue is hot, close lid for 10 minutes to burn off any residue, then open and brush grill to clean. 3) Only use tongs to turn food on the grill – a fork will make holes and let the juices escape. 4) The best steaks for grilling are rib eyes, T-Bones, strip loins and sirloins. 5) Don't baste with marinades – you risk cross contamination.

GRILLED FLANK STEAK with CHIMICHURRI SAUCE

INGREDIENTS

2 lbs flank steak, trimmed

¼ cup olive oil

2 tbsp balsamic vinegar

2 tbsp fresh lemon juice

1 large garlic clove, minced

2 tsp Worcestershire sauce

1 tsp Dijon mustard

1 tsp kosher salt

½ tsp freshly ground black pepper

Chimichurri Sauce

1 cup fresh flat-leaf parsley

3 tbsp fresh oregano

2 tbsp fresh lemon juice

1 large garlic clove, minced

½ tsp ground cumin

½ tsp kosher salt

¼ tsp freshly ground black pepper

¼ cup olive oil

If you think flank steak is only good as a hat (Lady Gaga's chapeau at the 2010 MTV Video Music Awards), you've got it all wrong. Lean, flat and inexpensive, this cut of full-flavored meat is ideal for feeding a crowd. Marinated in an oil, vinegar and mustard mixture, the flank steak is then grilled to melt-in-your-mouth tenderness. Think that sounds good? The addition of chimichurri sauce, the *numero uno* Latin condiment that's a blend of fresh herbs, lemon juice, garlic and olive oil, takes grilled flank steak to new heights. Hang your hat on that, Poker Face.

DIRECTIONS

1) Score 1 side of the flank steak in a diamond pattern. In a large bowl, whisk olive oil, balsamic vinegar, lemon juice, garlic, Worcestershire and Dijon. Place flank steak in a large resealable plastic bag, add marinade and refrigerate 6–24 hours. **2)** Preheat barbecue to medium-high heat and lightly oil grill grate. Remove steak from marinade and pat dry with paper towel. Discard marinade and let flank steak come to room temperature before grilling. Season both sides with salt and pepper. Grill 6 minutes, flip the flank and grill to desired doneness, 4–5 minutes more for medium-rare. Transfer to a cutting board and let rest 10 minutes before slicing meat thinly against the grain. **3)** For the chimichurri sauce, in a blender, combine parsley, oregano, lemon juice, garlic, cumin, salt and pepper. Pulse on and off, just to chop herbs. Don't over blend the herbs. With machine running, pour in olive oil, blending just to combine. Serve drizzled over sliced flank steak.

Note: Leftover sauce can be stored in refrigerator. Shake well before serving.

Serves 6–8

JUDY'S SAUCY PEPPER STEAK

See what happens when I leave Lisa to write a recipe? Her title is almost as creative and enticing as her intro: "Mom made this steak with peppers all the time. Throw it over some rice and it's done." Well if that doesn't have you running to toss together this one-skillet, deliciously saucy, garlic and soy, tri-colored pepper steak, I don't know what will. I think my sister-scribe has put me out of a job.

INGREDIENTS

2 tbsp olive oil

1½ lbs top round steak, cut into ¼-inch wide strips

½ tsp kosher salt

¼ tsp freshly ground black pepper

Vegetables

1 tbsp olive oil

1½ cups thinly sliced white onions

1 large garlic clove, minced

1 large red bell pepper, sliced into thin strips

1 large yellow pepper, sliced into thin strips

1 large green pepper, sliced into thin strips

1 cup sliced celery

1 cup beef broth

1 cup canned whole tomatoes, drained and chopped

1 tsp sugar

2 tbsp cornstarch

2 tbsp soy sauce

¼ cup waterr

DIRECTIONS

1) In a large skillet, heat 2 tbsp olive oil over medium-high heat. Season meat with salt and pepper, add to skillet in 2 or 3 batches, cooking 1 minute per side or until browned. Remove from pan and set aside. 2) Wipe out the skillet and heat 1 tbsp olive oil over medium heat. Add sliced onion, cooking 3 minutes to soften slightly. Add minced garlic, stirring constantly for 30 seconds until fragrant. Add red, yellow and green peppers, celery, beef broth, canned tomatoes and sugar. Bring to a boil over high heat, reduce heat to low, cover and simmer 5 minutes. Return beef to skillet and stir to combine. 3) In a small bowl, blend cornstarch, soy sauce and water. Stirring constantly, add to meat mixture, raise heat to medium-high and cook 1–2 minutes until mixture has thickened and beef is cooked through.

Serves 4–6

BITE ME BIT

"Writing is the flip side of sex – it's only good when it's over."

— Hunter S. Thompson, journalist and author

BALSAMIC BEEF & SNOW PEA STIR-FRY

INGREDIENTS

Marinade

¼ cup soy sauce

1 tbsp sherry cooking wine

1 tbsp brown sugar

1 tbsp cornstarch

1 tsp grated fresh ginger

1½ lbs sirloin steak, thinly sliced

Sauce

3 tbsp balsamic vinegar

1 tbsp soy sauce

1 tbsp sherry cooking wine

2 tsp brown sugar

1 tsp sesame oil

½ tsp crushed red pepper flakes

1 tsp vegetable oil

2 cups snow peas, trimmed and cut on the diagonal

2 tbsp vegetable oil, divided

1 large garlic clove, minced

2 tsp cornstarch

2 tsp water

I thought my kids were just being smarty-pants when they started calling my stir-fry "blasé beef from her weary wok." While I appreciated their clever use of diction, that's where my pleasure ended. After a bit of digging, I discovered that Lisa had served them up a "mind-blowing meat medley." Seems she had a secret ingredient – balsamic vinegar. Out of the salad and into the stir-fry, balsamic lends a tangy kick and offers up the perfect balance of sweet and sour to this saucy, sizzling beef and snow pea stir-fry. Grab the Modena and see dinner transformed from mundane – to marvelous.

DIRECTIONS

1) For the marinade, in a medium bowl, combine soy sauce, 1 tbsp sherry, 1 tbsp brown sugar, cornstarch and ginger. Add sliced meat and set aside to marinate for 15 minutes. 2) For the sauce, in a small bowl, whisk balsamic, soy sauce, 1 tbsp sherry, 2 tsp brown sugar, sesame oil and red pepper flakes. Set aside. 3) Heat 1 tsp vegetable oil in a large wok over high heat. Add snow peas and stir continuously for 1 minute. Remove from wok and set aside. 4) Return wok to high heat and add 1 tbsp vegetable oil. Add minced garlic and stir, cooking 10 seconds. Add half the meat mixture, cooking until no longer pink, about 2 minutes. Remove from wok and repeat with remaining 1 tbsp vegetable oil and beef. Discard beef marinade. 5) In a small bowl, dissolve cornstarch in water. Add all cooked beef, snow peas and sauce to wok and bring to a boil over high heat. Add cornstarch mixture and cook 1 minute or until sauce thickens.

Serves 4–6

BLAZING BEEF & BEAN CHILI

Chili Chili Bang Bang. Fire in the Hole. Packing Heat. One of these names is going to be our moniker when we enter the chili cook-off circuit. Fame, fortune and bragging rights are inevitable – this chili is hot stuff. A dynamite mix of chili powder, red pepper flakes and cayenne, mingled with intense cocoa powder, sweet tomatoes, fiber-rich beans and well-seasoned meat, it can rival any Lone Star chili joint. Yes, we're confident. In a big bowl or piled atop a hot dog and fries, this one is a Chilympic winner.

INGREDIENTS

2 tbsp olive oil

2 medium white onions, chopped

1 large red bell pepper, diced

2 large garlic cloves, minced

¼ cup chili powder

1 tbsp ground cumin

1 tbsp paprika

1 tbsp cocoa powder

2 tsp kosher salt

1 tsp dried oregano

1 tsp crushed red pepper flakes

1 tsp brown sugar

½ tsp freshly ground black pepper

¼ tsp cayenne pepper

2½ lbs ground beef

1 (28oz) tin diced tomatoes

1 (5.5oz) tin tomato paste

1 cup beef broth

2 tbsp apple cider vinegar

2½ cups canned red kidney beans, rinsed and drained

Toppings

sour cream

shredded cheddar or Monterey Jack cheese

sliced jalapeno pepper

corn tortillas

DIRECTIONS

1) In a large soup pot, heat olive oil over medium heat. Add onions and stir often, cooking 4 minutes. Add diced red pepper, garlic, chili powder, cumin, paprika, cocoa powder, salt, oregano, red pepper flakes, brown sugar, black pepper and cayenne pepper. Cook for 1 minute to combine spices, stirring continuously. Add the ground beef and cook 10 minutes until no longer pink. Break beef up with a wooden spoon as it cooks. Add diced tomatoes, tomato paste, beef broth and cider vinegar. Bring to a boil over high heat. Reduce heat to low, cover and simmer 45 minutes, stirring occasionally. Add kidney beans and simmer uncovered for 15 minutes more. 2) Serve topped with sour cream, cheddar or Monterey Jack cheese, sliced jalapeno and/or fried tortilla strips (cut corn tortillas into thin strips, fry in 1-inch of oil for 1–2 minutes and season with a little salt). This chili tastes even better the next day.

Serves 8–10

MOM'S SWEET & SOUR MEATBALLS

INGREDIENTS

Sweet & Sour Sauce

3 tbsp vegetable oil

1 cup diced celery

1 cup diced yellow onion

3½ cups Heinz chili sauce

3 cups water

2 (28oz) tins diced tomatoes, with juices

1 cup packed brown sugar

½ cup fresh lemon juice

¼ cup honey

2 tbsp white vinegar

kosher salt and freshly ground black pepper, to taste

Meatballs

½ cup chopped Yukon Gold potato

½ cup chopped yellow onion

1 large celery stalk, chopped

½ tsp kosher salt

½ tsp freshly ground black pepper

2 lbs lean ground beef

½ cup sweet and sour sauce from above

Chicken

2 boneless, skinless chicken breast halves

If you're ever around our family table and the chant "fric, fric, fric" starts, this is the recipe we're subtly requesting. Our mom Judy is an incredible cook who has turned out hit after hit since we were wee ones. Many moons ago, when she created this fricassee, she omitted the traditional nasty giblets in favor of mini meatballs and shredded chicken in a lip-smacking sweet and sour sauce. The Jude (as we affectionately call her) is a woman who not only makes it all look easy but also knows her audience well and caters to all their wants, whims and whines. Say it with us...fric, fric, fric.

DIRECTIONS

1) For the sauce, in a large saucepan, heat oil over medium heat. Add celery and onion and cook 5 minutes, until softened. Add chili sauce, water, tomatoes, brown sugar, lemon juice, honey and white vinegar. Bring to a boil over high heat, reduce heat to low and simmer while preparing meatballs. After the sauce has finished cooking, season to taste with salt and pepper. 2) For the meatballs, in a food processor, puree potatoes, onion, celery, salt and pepper until smooth. Place ground beef in a large bowl and add vegetable puree and ½ cup of the prepared sweet and sour sauce. Mix well to combine. Using wet hands, roll meatballs into marble-sized balls and add to pot of sauce. Cook uncovered over low heat for 2 hours, shaking the pot occasionally. 3) While the meatballs cook, place the chicken breasts in a small pot of boiling water and simmer over low heat for 20 minutes until chicken is cooked through. Remove chicken from water, cool and shred. Once the meatballs have finished cooking, place in a serving dish, cover with shredded chicken and sprinkle a little sauce over top of the chicken. This dish is best made the day before. Reheat gently in a 300°F oven until heated through.

Serves 10

DAD'S (mini) MEATLOAF MADNESS

INGREDIENTS

1 tbsp olive oil

1 small yellow onion, finely chopped

1 large celery stalk, finely chopped

2 large garlic cloves, minced

2 tbsp finely chopped fresh flat-leaf parsley

1 cup plain breadcrumbs

½ cup whole milk

3 tbsp Worcestershire sauce

2 large eggs, lightly beaten

1 tsp kosher salt

1 tsp freshly ground black pepper

½ tsp dried thyme

2 lbs lean ground beef

¼ cup barbecue sauce, for topping

Our dad is still a bit steamed we dedicated a salad to him in our first book. A salad? How can the King of Carnivores be celebrated with a bowl of leafy greens? He can't, and that's why we honor him with the thing he loves most: meatloaf, a classic comfort food he orders in restaurants as an appetizer. These moist mini loaves are perfect for him because they're baked up in half the time of a full-sized meatloaf, handy when his serious hunger tests his infinite patience. As well, the smallness of these petite meat-bites makes them especially practical when he wants a nibble while on the treadmill. Go, Daddy, Go.

DIRECTIONS

1) Preheat oven to 425°F. Line a baking sheet with aluminum foil and coat with non-stick cooking spray. 2) In a medium skillet, heat olive oil over medium heat. Stir in onion and celery, cooking 5 minutes, until softened. Add garlic and parsley, cooking for 1 minute more, stirring constantly. Remove from heat and let cool slightly. 3) In a large mixing bowl, combine breadcrumbs, milk Worcestershire sauce, eggs, salt, pepper, thyme and onion mixture. Stir well to combine. Add ground beef and mix just to combine, careful not to overmix. Loosely form the mixture into 6 mini oval loaves. Place on prepared baking sheet and spread barbecue sauce evenly over each loaf. Bake 20 minutes.

Yield: 6 mini meatloaves.

BITE ME BIT

"You know, maybe if you ate more comfort food you wouldn't have to go around shooting people."

— Hurley (actor Jorge Garcia) on the TV show *Lost*

THE BLD (breakfast, lunch & dinner) BURGER

INGREDIENTS

Burger

2½ lbs medium ground beef

½ tsp kosher salt

¼ tsp kosher salt

Grilled Cheese Bun

24 slices of thinly sliced white bread

12 slices cheddar cheese

12 tbsp butter, softened

Sunny Side Up

2 tbsp butter

6 large eggs

tomato and lettuce, for garnish

OK, folks. We know this burger is fit for a glutton-bowl and won't win any nutritional awards. However, it scores big time for deliciousness, it's high in the fun-feast category and it's remarkable that the idea of this behemoth burger came to Lisa's husband in a dream. My husband jumped on the bandwagon, pointing out the practicality of it all. For breakfast, the boys promote the rise-and-shine factor of the fried egg perched atop the juicy burger. At lunch, they praise the pair of gooey grilled cheese sandwiches standing in for the usual boring bun. And finally, they say their dinner is covered with the salad ingredients of lettuce and tomato. One burger, 3 meals covered. Got to admire the men and their efficient meal planning.

DIRECTIONS

1) For the burgers, divide the meat into six 6-ounce portions. Gently form each portion into a round burger, about ¾-inch thick, careful not to overmix the meat. Season both sides of burgers with ½ tsp kosher salt. **2)** Heat a large cast iron skillet over medium-high heat. Sprinkle skillet with remaining ¼ tsp salt. Place burgers in skillet and cook 4–5 minutes per side, until slightly charred. **3)** While the burgers are cooking, prepare the grilled cheese buns by placing 1 slice of cheddar between 2 slices of bread. Spread softened butter on both sides of sandwich. Heat a frying pan over medium heat and cook 2 minutes until underside is golden brown. Flip and cook 1–2 minutes more. Remove from pan. **4)** For each fried egg, heat a non-stick pan over high heat. Add 1 tsp butter in the center of the pan and let it melt. Crack the egg into the pan over the melted butter. Cook 2 minutes for runny yolk or 3 minutes for slightly firmer. Remove from pan. **5)** To assemble, place 1 grilled cheese sandwich on a plate. Top with cooked burger, fried egg, lettuce, tomato and finish off with another grilled cheese sandwich. Serve immediately.

Serves 6

Join us in the Meat Locker for a carnivore's carnival

PAT QUINN'S IRISH BEEF STEW

Pat Quinn is our lucky charm. Along with Chef Bala, Pat has filled our pot with gold, Guinness gold. Served up at Pat's stellar Irish eateries in Toronto, P.J. O'Brien and Irish Embassy, this classic Irish stew is jam-packed with tender chunks of beef, carrot, turnip, potato and parsnip. Flavored with wine, Guinness and beef broth, this unbelievably flavorful and filling stew has us clicking our heels like Lord of the Dance. Your da would be very proud. *Erin go bragh!*

INGREDIENTS

3½ lbs stewing beef, cut into 1-inch cubes

¼ cup flour

¾ tsp kosher salt

¾ tsp freshly ground black pepper

2 tbsp canola oil

1 tbsp canola oil

4 cups diced yellow onion

2 cups sliced white mushrooms

1 cup diced celery

2 large garlic cloves, minced

½ tsp kosher salt

½ tsp freshly ground black pepper

2 dried bay leaves

10 sprigs fresh thyme, tied with kitchen string

1⅓ cups dry red wine

1⅓ cups Guinness

4 cups beef broth

2 cups carrots, peeled and cut into 1-inch cubes

2 cups turnips, peeled and cut into 1-inch cubes

2 cups red potatoes, peeled and cut into 1-inch cubes

1 cup parsnips, peeled and cut into 1-inch cubes

DIRECTIONS

1) Place beef in a large bowl and toss with flour, ¾ tsp salt and ¾ tsp pepper. In a large soup pot, heat 2 tbsp canola oil over medium-high heat. Add meat in a single layer, browning it in batches if your pot isn't big enough. Brown meat on all sides 5–6 minutes until a good crust forms. Transfer to a bowl and repeat with remaining beef. Wipe out pot when finished browning. 2) In the same pot, heat 1 tbsp canola oil over medium-high heat. Add onions, mushrooms, celery and garlic, stirring occasionally and cooking 8 minutes. Season with salt, pepper, bay leaves and thyme. Add browned beef, red wine and Guinness. Bring to a boil over medium-low heat. Add beef broth and simmer uncovered over low heat for 45 minutes. Stir in carrots, turnips, potatoes and parsnips. Simmer uncovered over low heat for 1 hour.

Serves 10–12

GRILLED LAMB CHOPS with MINT SAUCE

INGREDIENTS

Marinade & Sauce

¼ cup olive oil

¼ cup rice vinegar

¼ cup chopped fresh mint

¼ cup chopped fresh flat-leaf parsley

1 tbsp honey

1 small garlic clove, minced

½ tsp grated fresh ginger

½ tsp ground cumin

½ tsp kosher salt

½ tsp freshly ground black pepper

8 rib lamb chops, about ¾-inch thick

I love candy. When Lisa told me she was making lollipops I hightailed it over to her kitchen. Imagine my surprise when I discovered they were lamb lollies, and my delight when I discovered that I was in love at first bite with these chop pops. Marinated in a robust mixture of fresh herbs, garlic and olive oil, the lamb is grilled until super-tender and topped with a mint and parsley sauce. Impressive, easy and elegant, these delicious grilled chops are a carnivore's candy.

DIRECTIONS

1) In a food processor, combine olive oil, rice vinegar, mint, parsley, honey, garlic, ginger, cumin, salt and pepper. Pulse until mixture is finely chopped. Place lamb chops in a large resealable plastic bag and coat with only ¼ cup of the marinade. Refrigerate at least 1 hour or overnight. Save remaining marinade to serve as a sauce with the cooked lamb. 2) Bring lamb chops to room temperature. Preheat barbecue to medium-high heat and lightly oil grill grate. Grill chops 5–7 minutes per side or until desired doneness. Let the lamb chops rest for at least 5 minutes before serving. When ready to serve, top each lamb chop with a big spoonful of reserved parsley-mint sauce.

Serves 4

BITE ME BIT

"Today I'm handing out lollipops and ass whoopings and right now, I'm all out of lollipops."

— Grace (actress Debra Messing) on the TV show Will & Grace

VEAL PARMESAN

INGREDIENTS

Tomato Sauce

2 tbsp olive oil

1 medium white onion, chopped

1 large garlic clove, minced

1 (28oz) tin diced tomatoes, with juices

3 tbsp tomato paste

1 tsp sugar

½ tsp dried oregano

½ tsp kosher salt

¼ tsp freshly ground black pepper

8 (2oz) veal cutlets, pounded to ⅛-inch thickness

¼ tsp kosher salt

¼ tsp freshly ground black pepper

¼ cup flour

2 large eggs

½ cup plain breadcrumbs

½ cup freshly grated Parmesan cheese

½ tsp dried oregano

½ tsp kosher salt

4 tbsp olive oil, divided

8 tbsp shredded provolone cheese

8 tbsp freshly grated Parmesan cheese

I would kiss the cook but Lisa only lets me on her birthday. So, instead, I'll blow her a kiss. She deserves it. She has taken a classic Italian menu item I never ordered (too greasy or too tough to cut) and transformed it into my daily special. Lisa's Veal Parmesan is like a veal pizza – a golden-crusted, tender cutlet is topped with a smooth marinara sauce, followed by bubbly provolone and melted Parmesan cheese. Really, other than Lisa letting me bear hug her, what could be better? I figured out how to eat this for lunch too…nothing like a drool-worthy Veal-Parm Hero.

DIRECTIONS

1) In a large skillet, heat 2 tbsp olive oil over medium-high heat. Season meat with salt and pepper, add to skillet in 2 or 3 batches, cooking 1 minute per side or until browned. Remove from pan and set aside. 2) Wipe out the skillet and heat 1 tbsp olive oil over medium heat. Add sliced onion, cooking 3 minutes to soften slightly. Add minced garlic, stirring constantly for 30 seconds until fragrant. Add red, yellow and green peppers, celery, beef broth, canned tomatoes and sugar. Bring to a boil over high heat, reduce heat to low, cover and simmer 5 minutes. Return beef to skillet and stir to combine. 3) In a small bowl, blend cornstarch, soy sauce and water. Stirring constantly, add to meat mixture, raise heat to medium-high and cook 1–2 minutes until mixture has thickened and beef is cooked through.

Serves 4–6

BITE ME BIT

"I'd love to kiss you, but I just washed my hair."

— Madge (actress Bette Davis) in the 1932 movie *The Cabin in the Cotton*

VITELLO TONNATO

INGREDIENTS

1 (2½–3½ lb) veal roast, top round, tied with kitchen twine

3 cups dry white wine

2 large carrots, peeled, cut into 3 pieces

2 large celery stalks, cut into 3 pieces

1 medium yellow onion, quartered

4 fresh sage leaves

2 dried bay leaves

10 whole black peppercorns

1 tsp kosher salt

Tuna Sauce

3 large eggs

1½ cups oil-packed, solid white canned tuna, drained

½ cup olive oil

2 tbsp capers, rinsed and drained

2 tbsp fresh lemon juice

2 tbsp white wine vinegar

¼ cup reserved veal broth

¼ tsp kosher salt

¼ tsp freshly ground black pepper

Garnish

2 tbsp chopped fresh flat-leaf parsley

1 lemon, cut into 8 wedges

When Lisa started going on about Vitello, I pictured a seductive Casanova, an elegant Mastroianni, a gorgeous Cannavaro. I was off the mark, but not totally. You see, while this sophisticated Vitello can't whisk us away in a red Ferrari, it leaves us totally satisfied and grinning ear to ear. In this Italian classic, a veal (aka *vitello*) roast is simmered in an aromatic broth, chilled and cut into thin slices. Served cold, the tender, delicate pieces are topped with a swoon-worthy puree of tuna, olive oil, capers and lemon. *Amiamo* Signor Vitello Tonnato.

DIRECTIONS

1) For the veal, pat dry with paper towel. In a large, heavy pot, combine white wine, carrots, celery, onion, sage, bay leaves, peppercorns and salt. Add enough water to come ¾ of the way up the pot. Bring to a boil over high heat. Reduce heat to low, add veal roast and simmer covered 40–45 minutes, until the roast reaches an internal temperature of 135°F. Remove from heat and transfer veal to a plate to cool. Strain the broth through a fine mesh sieve, reserving ¼ cup of the broth for the tuna sauce. Cover veal and refrigerate until chilled, at least 4 hours. **2)** Remove twine from veal, slice thinly against the grain and arrange on a platter. **3)** For the tuna sauce, in a small saucepan, cover eggs with cold water. Bring to a boil over medium-high heat. Turn heat to low, cooking 3–4 minutes. Drain and cool slightly in cold water. Cut the top off each egg and scoop out the soft yolk. Place yolks in a food processor along with tuna, olive oil, capers, lemon juice, white wine vinegar, 2 tbsp reserved veal broth, salt and pepper. Puree until smooth, adding more veal broth to achieve desired consistency. Refrigerate covered until ready to use. To serve, spoon over sliced veal, sprinkle with parsley and garnish platter with lemon wedges.

Serves 8–10

GRILLED VEAL CHOPS with MUSHROOM SHERRY SAUCE

INGREDIENTS

4 veal rib chops, well trimmed, about 1 inch thick

3 tbsp olive oil

3 tbsp fresh lime juice

2 tbsp honey

1 tsp lime zest

¼ tsp kosher salt

¼ tsp freshly ground black pepper

Mushroom Sherry Sauce

1 tbsp olive oil

1 tbsp butter

2 cups sliced white mushrooms

1 small shallot, diced

2 tbsp sherry cooking wine

1 tbsp coarse grain mustard

½ cup chicken broth

1 tbsp butter

¼ tsp kosher salt

In past interviews, we've been billed as "The Saucy Sisters." It's appropriate given that we love sauce, we constantly hit the sauce and we're always supremely sauced. In fact, we refuse to lay off the sauce, so it shouldn't come as any great surprise that topping this incredibly tender veal chop is an immensely drinkable mushroom sherry sauce. The chop, a prime cut of veal, is marinated in lime and honey and then grilled until juicy and crusted. Mushrooms and diced shallots are sautéed, along with sherry and broth, to create a delicate-yet-deeply-flavored sauce that is served atop the hearty veal chop. Don't even think of staging a saucervention...we're never giving up the stuff.

DIRECTIONS

1) Place veal chops in a large glass baking dish. In a small bowl, whisk olive oil, lime juice, honey and lime zest. Pour over chops, making sure to coat each side. Cover and refrigerate 4 hours, turning occasionally. Bring veal chops to room temperature before grilling. 2) Preheat barbecue to medium-high heat and lightly oil grill grate. Remove veal from marinade and season with ¼ tsp salt and pepper. Grill veal 6–8 minutes per side for medium doneness. Remove from grill and let rest at least 5 minutes before serving. 3) For the mushroom sherry sauce, in a large saucepan, heat olive oil and 1 tbsp butter over medium-high heat. Add mushrooms and shallots, and cook 3 minutes, stirring often. Add the sherry and mustard, stirring for 1 minute. Add chicken broth, reduce heat to low and simmer 3 minutes. Remove from heat and add 1 tbsp butter and salt. Serve with veal chop.

Serves 4

BITE ME BIT

"I want you to be happy. Would you like Smiley Sauce with that?"

— Lester (actor Kevin Spacey) in the 1999 movie *American Beauty*

Spread me

Putting Out a First-Rate Brunch

FRESH CINNAMON BREAD FRENCH TOAST

INGREDIENTS

Cinnamon Quick Bread

1¾ cups flour

2 tsp ground cinnamon

1¼ tsp baking powder

¼ tsp kosher salt

¼ tsp baking soda

1 cup sour cream

½ cup butter, softened

¾ cup sugar

2 large eggs

1 tsp vanilla extract

Topping

⅓ cup packed brown sugar

2 tbsp flour

⅛ tsp ground cinnamon

1 tbsp butter

French Toast

2 large eggs

½ cup milk

½ tsp vanilla extract

2 tbsp butter

maple syrup, for serving

Lisa is an extraordinary baker. I often get a whiff of *eau de Fresh Baked Bread* as she walks by. It's a marketable scent, but unfortunately doesn't come in a bottle or in a cellophane bag of store-bought bread. No amount of dough can buy that smell. I desperately wanted my baking to match the aroma of Lisa's, but was intimidated by the prospect of leavening loaves. With that in mind, she created this easy cinnamon quick bread (the word "quick" comforted me) for me to get my feet wet. Now, I'm no *boulanger* but I must say that this bread was a breeze to make and even more delicious when turned into thick-sliced French toast. I can get this double cinnamon loaf from pantry to oven in less than 15 minutes. It takes me 30 minutes to get to the grocery store, buy cinnamon bread and return home. Huge bonus. That, and I now get to walk around with a spritz of cinnamon bread behind my ears.

DIRECTIONS

1) For the cinnamon bread, preheat oven to 350°F. Coat a 9x5-inch loaf pan with non-stick cooking spray. In a medium bowl, combine flour, cinnamon, baking powder and salt. In a small bowl, combine baking soda and sour cream. 2) Using an electric mixer, cream butter and sugar until light and fluffy. Add eggs one at a time, mixing until well beaten. Add vanilla. On low speed, alternate adding flour and sour cream mixtures, beginning and ending with the flour. Mix just until flour disappears. Pour batter into prepared loaf pan. 3) For the topping, in a small bowl, mix together brown sugar, flour and cinnamon. Cut in butter until mixture resembles coarse meal. Sprinkle over cinnamon loaf and bake 1 hour, until a toothpick inserted in the center comes out clean. Remove from oven and let loaf cool. 4) For the French toast, preheat oven to 400°F. Line a baking sheet with aluminum foil and coat with non-stick cooking spray. Cut cooled loaf into 8 thick slices. In a medium bowl, combine eggs, milk and vanilla. Heat butter in a flat skillet over medium-high heat. Dip cinnamon bread slices in egg mixture and brown 1–2 minutes per side. Transfer to prepared baking sheet and bake 12 minutes. Serve with maple syrup.

Yield: 8 slices French toast

BANANA-STUFFED FRENCH TOAST SOUFFLÉ

INGREDIENTS

1 (1lb) egg bread (challah)

Caramelized Bananas

1 cup packed brown sugar
½ cup butter
2 tbsp corn syrup
¼ tsp ground cinnamon
6 bananas, ripe yet still firm, sliced into ¼-inch rounds

Batter

6 large eggs
2½ cups whole milk
2 tbsp sugar
1 tsp vanilla extract
½ tsp ground cinnamon
½ tsp kosher salt

Streusel Topping

½ cup quick cooking oats
½ cup flour
½ cup packed brown sugar
¼ cup butter, softened

Vive le French toast! *Oui*, I know that it's neither French nor toast, but I wanted to make this battle cry in honor of my sister. No one amours French toast quite like Lisa, and when given carte blanche (by *moi*, of course), she took her favorite comfort food to new heights. Stuffed with caramelized bananas and topped with a brown sugar streusel, this French toast bake hits all the right notes. Perfect for company because it's prepared in advance, this crowd pleaser has a golden crisp crust and sweet, soft banana center. French toast never tasted so *délicieux*. Encore! Encore!

DIRECTIONS

1) Coat a 13x9-inch baking dish with non-stick cooking spray. Slice bread into ½-inch thick slices. Arrange half of the slices in prepared dish. The bread can overlap a little. 2) For the caramelized bananas, in a medium saucepan, combine brown sugar, butter and corn syrup over medium heat. Cook and stir until butter is melted and brown sugar dissolved. Add cinnamon and sliced bananas, cooking for 2 minutes. Evenly cover bread in baking dish with banana mixture. Top with remaining slices, squishing to fit them in. 3) For the batter, in a medium bowl, whisk eggs, milk, sugar, vanilla, cinnamon and salt. Pour over bread, cover and refrigerate 4–24 hours. 4) When ready to bake, preheat oven to 350ºF. 5) For the streusel topping, in a medium bowl, combine oats, flour, brown sugar and butter, mixing with a fork or fingers until crumbly. Set aside. 6) Place French toast in oven for 40 minutes. Remove and sprinkle with streusel topping. Bake 20 minutes more or until golden and puffy. Let stand 10 minutes before serving.

Serves 10

BIT ME BIT

"She was so wild that when she made French toast she got her tongue caught in the toaster."

— Rodney Dangerfield, comedian

BREATHTAKING CINNAMON BUNS

INGREDIENTS

Dough

1 cup whole milk, warmed

½ tsp sugar

1 (¼oz) package active dry yeast

½ cup sugar

½ tsp vanilla extract

2 large eggs

4 cups flour

1 tsp kosher salt

⅓ cup butter, softened, cut into pieces

extra flour for dusting

Filling

1 cup packed brown sugar

2 tbsp ground cinnamon

⅓ cup butter, melted

Cream Cheese Glaze

½ cup cream cheese, softened

½ cup butter, softened

1¾ cups icing sugar

1 tsp vanilla extract

I really don't have to do much of a sell job on these, but here are the adjectives that best describe these fluffy, gooey, rich, warm, blissful, sweet pastries swirled with buttery, cinnamon-brown sugar and smothered with a creamy cream cheese frosting: amazascrumptabulous. If that doesn't sell these to you, the intoxicating aroma of these finger lickin' rolls of kryptonite will certainly seal the deal.

DIRECTIONS

1) For the dough, in the bowl of an electric mixer, combine warm milk and ½ tsp sugar. Sprinkle in yeast and let sit 10 minutes, until foamy. 2) Using the dough hook, add ½ cup sugar, vanilla and eggs on low speed. Add flour and salt on low speed. Once incorporated, turn mixer to medium-high, allowing it to knead dough for 4 minutes. Add butter and continue on medium-high speed for 6 minutes, until dough is smooth and pulls away from the sides of the bowl. With floured hands, remove dough from mixer and roll into a large ball. Place it in a large bowl that has been coated with non-stick cooking spray. Cover with plastic wrap and let rise in a warm spot until doubled in size, about 1 hour 15 minutes. 3) Line 2 large baking sheets with parchment paper. On a lightly floured surface, roll dough into a ¼-inch thick rectangle that measures 16x21 inches. 4) For the filling, in a small bowl, combine brown sugar and cinnamon. Brush the melted butter on the surface of the dough leaving a ½-inch border around the edges. Sprinkle brown sugar mixture over melted butter. Roll the dough into a fairly tight cylinder and press along the edges to seal. Cut into 12 equal pieces. Place on prepared baking sheets, cover with a cloth and let rise in a warm area for 1 hour. 5) Preheat oven to 400°F. Bake buns 10 minutes or until golden. 6) For the glaze, in an electric mixer, cream together cream cheese and butter on medium-high speed until well blended. On low speed, add icing sugar and vanilla. Once combined, raise speed to medium and mix well. Spread on warm cinnamon buns.

Yield: 12 cinnamon buns

BIT ME BIT

"I really don't think I need buns of steel. I'd be happy with buns of cinnamon."

— Ellen DeGeneres, comedian and TV host

LEMON RICOTTA PANCAKES with BLUEBERRY SAUCE

INGREDIENTS

Lemon Ricotta Pancakes

3 large eggs

1 cup ricotta cheese

¼ cup milk

¼ cup fresh lemon juice

½ tsp vanilla extract

¾ cup flour

2 tbsp sugar

1 tsp lemon zest

½ tsp baking powder

¼ tsp kosher salt

Blueberry Sauce

1 tbsp cornstarch

⅓ cup fresh lemon juice

1½ cups fresh or frozen blueberries

½ cup sugar

Lisa may be our resident French toast fanatic but I'm a flapjack freak. When I'm happy, I eat pancakes. When I'm sad, I eat pancakes. From silver-dollar sized to full-dish dimensions, I eat pancakes. To say I have a finely tuned pancake palate would be an understatement. So, too, would be calling a stack of these luscious pancakes "good." They're divine, with ricotta cheese adding a light, creamy touch and zesty lemon providing a refreshing tang. Blanketed in a warm, homemade blueberry sauce, these are first-rate, fluffy and flavorful pancakes.

DIRECTIONS

1) For the pancakes, separate eggs and place yolks in a large mixing bowl and whites in the bowl of an electric mixer. 2) To create batter, add ricotta, milk, lemon juice and vanilla to the egg yolks. Whisk well to combine. Add flour, sugar, lemon zest, baking powder and salt, mixing gently just to combine. 3) Using the electric mixer, beat egg whites on high speed until soft peaks form. Fold egg whites into pancake batter bowl. 4) Coat griddle or skillet with non-stick cooking spray and heat over medium heat. Drop batter by the heaping tablespoon, cooking pancakes 2 minutes per side or until golden. 5) For the blueberry sauce, in a small bowl, dissolve cornstarch in lemon juice. Set aside. In a medium saucepan, stir fresh or frozen blueberries with sugar over high heat. Once mixture comes to a boil, reduce heat to low, add cornstarch mixture and simmer until slightly thickened. Serve with pancakes.

Yield: approximately 30 pancakes

BITE ME BIT

"I don't get why people like brunch. What's the benefit of combining break dancing and lunch?"

— Tracy Jordan (actor Tracy Morgan) on the TV show *30 Rock*

BLUEBERRY BUCKLE

INGREDIENTS

Lemon Crumb Topping

1 cup flour

½ cup sugar

2 tsp lemon zest

¼ tsp kosher salt

6 tbsp butter, softened

Blueberry Cake

1 cup sugar

½ cup butter, softened

2 large eggs

1 tsp vanilla extract

1 tsp lemon zest

1 cup sour cream

1 tsp baking soda

2 cups flour

1 tsp baking powder

½ tsp kosher salt

1½ cups fresh blueberries

Have you ever wondered why it's called a buckle cake? The real reason is that it collapses (aka buckles) as the batter sinks to the bottom while baking. My reason, equally valid, is that I have to loosen my belt buckle as I make my way through this moist, crumb-topped blueberry cake. Much like a gigantic 9-inch-square muffin, this old-fashioned buckle is topped with zesty lemon crumble and loaded with plump, juicy blueberries. Take it from me – elastic-waist pants are the way to go when you bake up this delicious, knee-buckling buckle.

DIRECTIONS

1) Preheat oven to 375ºF. Coat a 9-inch square baking pan with non-stick cooking spray. 2) For the topping, in a small bowl, combine flour, sugar, lemon zest and salt. Add butter and mix with your fingers until crumbly. Set aside. 3) For the cake, in an electric mixer, cream sugar and butter until light and fluffy. Add eggs, one at a time, beating well after each addition. Add vanilla and lemon zest, mixing to combine. In a small dish, combine sour cream and baking soda and add to butter mixture. On low speed, add flour, baking powder and salt. Fold in fresh blueberries. Pour batter in prepared pan and sprinkle with crumb topping. Bake 40–45 minutes until cake is lightly browned around the edges.

Serves 10

ALPINE ASPARAGUS & MUSHROOM STRATA

INGREDIENTS

2 tbsp butter

2 cups asparagus, trimmed and cut into 2-inch pieces

¼ tsp kosher salt

¼ tsp freshly ground black pepper

2 cups sliced mushrooms

1 large garlic clove, minced

1 tsp minced fresh thyme

6 large eggs

2¼ cups whole milk

½ tsp kosher salt

¼ tsp freshly ground black pepper

9 cups (approx. 1lb) French bread, cut into 1-inch cubes

2 cups shredded Swiss cheese

¼ cup freshly grated Parmesan cheese

I have to send Lisa packing more often. While vacationing in the Alps, the little Swiss Miss was yodeling on a mountaintop when she came up with this breakfast bake of woodsy mushroom, asparagus, thyme and savory Swiss cheese. Assembled a day in advance and baked off just before guests arrive, the soft, custardy bread, the nutty-flavored, gooey cheese and the earthy vegetables pave the way for an easy-yet-breathtaking brunch. And, this strata isn't the only thing that will leave guests speechless...Lisa flittering about in a dirndl is a crowd pleaser too. Can't wait to see what happens when I ship her off to Patagonia.

DIRECTIONS

1) Coat a 13x9-inch baking dish with non-stick cooking spray. 2) In a large skillet, melt butter over medium-high heat. Add asparagus, cooking 2 minutes, until slightly softened. Sprinkle asparagus with ¼ tsp each salt and pepper. Add mushrooms, cooking 4–5 minutes until softened and liquid evaporates. Add garlic and thyme, cooking 1 minute. Remove from heat and let cool slightly. 3) In a medium bowl, whisk eggs, milk, ½ tsp salt and ¼ tsp pepper. 4) To assemble, spread half the bread cubes in the prepared baking dish. Top with half the egg mixture, followed by half the asparagus/mushroom mixture and then half the shredded Swiss cheese. Repeat with remaining bread, egg mixture, asparagus/mushroom mixture and Swiss cheese. Sprinkle top with Parmesan cheese, cover with plastic wrap and refrigerate 4–24 hours. 5) When ready to bake, preheat oven to 325°F. Let strata sit at room temperature until oven is heated. Bake 45 minutes, until strata sets and the top browns. Let cool 10 minutes before cutting into squares.

Serves 8

MINI ZUCCHINI & PROVOLONE FRITTATAS

INGREDIENTS

1 tbsp olive oil

1½ cups chopped zucchini

1 large garlic clove, minced

8 large eggs

½ tsp kosher salt

¼ tsp freshly ground black pepper

¾ cup freshly grated Parmesan cheese

¾ cup shredded provolone cheese

2 tbsp thinly sliced fresh basil

½ cup flour

½ tsp baking powder

As a kid, "Little Lisa" was always having her chubby cheeks pinched. I wasn't. She wore head-to-toe Hello Kitty, while I was more into safety pinning jeans and clomping around in Doc Martens. While she can still be spotted sporting the occasional "precious" outfit, she's no longer the only one who can bring the cute – I successfully rock these super-adorable mini frittatas. Filled with zucchini, Parmesan and provolone, these easy, protein-packed eggs are made in muffin tins. Charming for brunch, delicious served at any temperature and perfect for a grab-and-go breakfast or packed lunch, these minis are darling. Enjoy, and feel free to pinch my cheeks next time you see me.

DIRECTIONS

1) Preheat oven to 350°F. Coat a 12-cup muffin tin with non-stick cooking spray. **2)** In a medium skillet, heat olive oil over medium-high heat. Add zucchini and cook 4 minutes, until lightly golden. Add minced garlic, cooking 30–60 seconds, until fragrant. Remove from heat and set aside to cool slightly. **3)** In a large bowl, lightly whisk eggs, salt and pepper. Stir in Parmesan, provolone, basil and cooked zucchini. Gently fold in flour and baking powder just until flour disappears. Divide mixture evenly among prepared muffin cups. Bake 18–20 minutes until frittatas feel firm to the touch and appear slightly golden. Remove from oven and allow to sit 5 minutes before removing from tin.

Yield: 12 mini frittatas

THE LET (lettuce, egg & tomato) BREAKFAST BURRITO

INGREDIENTS

8 slices turkey bacon

1 tbsp butter

4 large eggs

4 tbsp milk

1 cup shredded sharp cheddar cheese

4 (10-inch) flour tortillas

2 large tomatoes, each cut into 4 slices

¼ tsp kosher salt

¼ tsp freshly ground black pepper

1 cup shredded iceberg lettuce

Lisa isn't a jealous person. However, I find it rather interesting that she created this breakfast wrap centered around her childhood initials (her middle name is Ellen, but I call her Esther), when the filling combinations could have just as easily been mine, JLT (juicy tomatoes, lovely lettuce and terrific eggs). A tad telling, but let's give her her moment in the sun... when the sun has barely risen, when your eyes are only half open and you're hungry for a warm breakfast burrito. A toasted tortilla stuffed with cheesy scrambled eggs, turkey bacon, sliced tomato and shredded lettuce, this LET is totally JLT (jam-packed, luscious, tasty).

DIRECTIONS

1) Place turkey bacon in a dry skillet over medium heat and cook until golden and crisp. Remove from heat and set aside. 2) For the scrambled eggs, in a large non-stick frying pan, melt butter over medium heat. In a medium bowl, vigorously whisk eggs and milk. Add to frying pan and allow eggs to set slightly. As soon as eggs begin to solidify, sprinkle with cheddar. Using a spatula, begin to scrape eggs from side of the pan and fold over into the middle, breaking up any large pieces of egg as you do this. Cook 3–4 minutes, until all runny liquid has disappeared. Remove from heat. 3) To assemble, place tortillas on a work surface and divide eggs evenly among them. In each tortilla, place 2 slices of turkey bacon over the eggs, top with 2 slices of tomato, season with salt and pepper and finish each wrap with ¼ cup shredded lettuce. Fold the edges over to form a wrap and place seam side down in a hot skillet set over high heat. Cook 1–2 minutes on each side until golden.

Serves 4

BITE ME BIT

"I'm not Lisa, my name is Julie."

— from the 1975 Jessi Colter song "I'm Not Lisa"

OLD SCHOOL MAC and CHEESE

INGREDIENTS

1 lb macaroni pasta

Breadcrumb Topping

6 slices white bread, crusts removed

3 tbsp butter, melted

¼ cup freshly grated Parmesan cheese

¼ cup grated sharp white cheddar

¼ tsp kosher salt

Cheese Sauce

¼ cup butter

¼ cup flour

½ tsp kosher salt

3 cups milk, warmed

3 cups grated sharp white cheddar

2½ cups grated Gruyere cheese

¾ cup Velveeta cheese, cubed

kosher salt and pepper to taste

We're all for following food trends and applauding culinary innovation. However, we're sick and tired of blue cheese, bacon, tomatoes and truffles messing with mac and cheese. For us, "gourmet" and "comfort food" don't belong in the same breath, let alone bite. Here, our mac and cheese lets the cheese do the talking, the creamy goodness of melted Gruyere, white cheddar and Velveeta nestled beneath a crunchy golden crust speaks volumes. This homemade classic of cheesy and buttery simplicity will take you on a welcome trip down memory lane, ketchup bottle in tow.

DIRECTIONS

1) Preheat oven to 350°F. Coat a 9-inch baking dish with non-stick cooking spray. In a large pot of lightly salted boiling water, cook noodles until tender. Drain well and set aside. **2)** For the topping, pulse the bread in the food processor until coarse crumbs. Place in a medium bowl and toss with melted butter, Parmesan, ¼ cup cheddar and salt. Set aside. **3)** For the cheese sauce, in a large saucepan, melt butter over low heat. Remove from heat and whisk in flour and salt until smooth. Return to low heat, cooking for 1 minute. Pour in half the milk whisking constantly. Raise the heat to medium and add remaining milk. Continue to whisk 6–8 minutes until mixture has thickened and coats the back of a spoon. Remove from heat, stir in cheddar, Gruyere, Velveeta and cooked macaroni. Season to taste with salt and pepper. Transfer to prepared baking dish, top with breadcrumb mixture and bake uncovered for 30 minutes or until heated through and top is lightly browned.

Serves 6–8

NOODLE PUDDING with CARAMELIZED APPLES

INGREDIENTS

Caramelized Apples

4 large Granny Smith apples, peeled and cored

2 tbsp butter

¼ cup sugar

½ tsp ground cinnamon

Noodle Pudding

1 (1lb) bag broad egg noodles

2 cups cottage cheese

1 (8oz) package cream cheese, softened

2 cups sour cream

½ cup sugar

6 large eggs

1½ tsp vanilla extract

Graham Topping

2 cups graham crumbs

½ cup butter, melted

¼ cup sugar

We know some people who are fiercely territorial and loyal to their "secret" noodle pudding (aka kugel) recipe. "My Morrie says mine is better than his mother's," and, "You can't beat my 7-generation-old recipe," are only a few of the phrases that have been lobbed during kugel combat. I'll leave the fighting to others and let you know that this dairy delight, this sweet, old-fashioned noodle pudding dotted with caramelized apples, is *the* best, *the* greatest, *the* one-and-only version that will kick all others' kugel to the curb. Egg noodles are tossed with cottage cheese, sour cream and cream cheese and topped with a crumbly graham cracker topping, resulting in a taste much like that of a sweet cheesecake. Put up your dukes, Aunt Dottie. We're ready to rumble.

DIRECTIONS

1) For the apples, quarter each apple and slice each quarter into thirds. In a large skillet, melt butter over medium-high heat. Stir in apples and sprinkle with sugar and cinnamon. Cook 4 minutes without stirring. After that time, stir apples gently and cook 4 minutes more until softened and golden. Remove from heat. 2) Preheat oven to 350°F. Coat a 13x9-inch baking dish with non-stick cooking spray. In a large pot of lightly salted boiling water, cook noodles until tender. Rinse and drain. 3) In a large bowl, blend together cottage cheese and cream cheese until smooth. Mix in sour cream, sugar, eggs and vanilla, blending well. Add cooked noodles, tossing to coat. Pour half the noodle mixture into prepared baking dish. Layer the apples on top and cover with remaining noodle mixture. 4) For the topping, in a small bowl, combine graham crumbs with melted butter and sugar. Sprinkle topping evenly over noodle pudding. Cover and bake 30 minutes. Remove cover and continue baking 15 minutes more. Cool before slicing.

Serves 8–10

APRICOT RUGELACH

Easy to say (rug-a-lah), but a challenge to spell (variations include rugelakh, ruggalah, rogelach), these ruggies (only one spelling for that) are perfection. A Yiddish word meaning "little twists," rugelach are tiny crescent rolls that are traditionally served during Jewish holidays. We say "feh" to that – every day should be celebrated with a tray of these soft-centered, flaky-crusted, apricot jam and sweet cream cheese dough rugelach. These addictive twists will make a baleboste...balebusteh...ech...an A-1 homemaker out of anyone.

INGREDIENTS

2¼ cups flour

½ cup icing sugar

½ tsp kosher salt

1 cup cold butter, cut into cubes

1 (8oz) package cold cream cheese, cut into cubes

extra flour for dusting

6 tbsp apricot jam

2 tbsp sugar

½ tsp ground cinnamon

¼ cup milk

DIRECTIONS

1) For the dough, place flour, icing sugar and salt in a food processor. Pulse to blend. Add butter and cream cheese cubes. Pulse just until the dough starts to come together. Remove dough from food processor and gather into 1 large ball. Divide the dough into 4 equal pieces. Shape each piece into a round, flat disk and wrap in plastic wrap. Refrigerate at least 1 hour. 2) Preheat oven to 350°F. Line a baking sheet with parchment paper. Working with 1 piece of dough at a time, on a lightly floured surface use a rolling pin to roll dough into a 9-inch circle about ⅛-inch thick. Dust with additional flour as needed when rolling out dough. Using a spatula, spread 1½ tbsp apricot jam all over the surface of the dough. Cut into 8 wedges and roll from the wide end toward the point. Place on prepared baking sheet. Repeat with remaining dough. 3) In a small bowl, combine sugar and cinnamon. Lightly brush tops of each rugelach with milk and sprinkle with sugar-cinnamon mixture. Bake 18–20 minutes, until golden.

Yield: 32 cookies

CHOCOLATE, CARAMEL & CINNAMON COFFEE CAKE

INGREDIENTS

Caramel Bottom

¾ cup packed brown sugar

6 tbsp butter

2 tbsp corn syrup

Chocolate Cinnamon Streusel

1 cup chopped milk chocolate

½ cup packed brown sugar

½ cup flour

1 tbsp cocoa powder

½ tsp ground cinnamon

¼ cup cold butter, cut into 1-inch pieces

Sour Cream Coffee Cake

1½ cups flour

½ tsp baking powder

½ tsp baking soda

½ tsp kosher salt

½ cup butter, softened

¾ cup sugar

2 large eggs

½ tsp vanilla extract

¾ cup sour cream

I always thought I wanted to be a coffee drinker. They gather, gulp and gossip over steaming java and pieces of crumble-topped cake. Sounds nice, huh? I thought so too until I drank a cup of Joe and began dancing on the ceiling. However, for the sake of the cake, I was willing to pound back the grinds. Turns out, I don't have to because I now have my very own coffee cake, one that's going to make all those "venti half-caff extra-hot ristretto soy latte in two paper cup" drinkers boil over with envy. A moist sour cream coffee cake, it's layered with chunky chocolate cinnamon streusel and a decadent caramel coating. I welcome you all to join me for a scrumptious slab and a bit of banter, but only if you grab me a mug of Earl Grey.

DIRECTIONS

1) Preheat oven to 350ºF. Coat a 9-inch round cake pan with non-stick cooking spray. 2) For the caramel, in a small saucepan, whisk brown sugar, butter and corn syrup over medium heat until sugar is completely dissolved. Remove from heat and pour evenly over the bottom of the baking pan. 3) For the streusel, in a medium bowl, mix together chopped chocolate, brown sugar, flour, cocoa powder and cinnamon. Add butter and crumble in with your fingers until mixture looks like coarse meal. Set aside. 4) For the cake, in a large bowl, combine flour, baking powder, baking soda and salt. Set aside. Using an electric mixer, cream butter and sugar on medium speed until light and fluffy, scraping down the side of the bowl occasionally. Add the eggs one at a time, beating well after each addition. Add vanilla and sour cream on low speed just until incorporated. Add the flour mixture on low speed, mixing just until flour disappears. Do not overmix. Pour ½ the cake batter over the caramel bottom in the cake pan. Sprinkle ½ chocolate streusel over the batter, covering the entire surface. Evenly spread the remaining batter over the streusel and sprinkle with remaining streusel. Place on baking sheet and bake 50 minutes until a toothpick inserted comes out clean. Let cake cool 5 minutes. Run a butter knife around the edges of the cake to loosen it from the pan. Place serving plate over top of cake and carefully flip it while still hot so caramel doesn't harden before coming out of the pan. Let cool slightly and serve.

Serves 10–12

BITE ME BIT

"In Seattle you haven't had enough coffee until you can thread a sewing machine while it's running."

— Jeff Bezos, founder of Amazon.com

title Cherry Cake

from the kitchen of Bubby

time not

time much notes Delicious

ingredients Cherries

BUBBY'S CHERRY CAKE

INGREDIENTS

Topping

¼ cup sugar

1 tsp ground cinnamon

Cherry Cake

2 cups sugar

1 cup vegetable oil

½ cup orange juice

4 large eggs

1 tbsp vanilla extract

3 cups flour

1 tbsp baking powder

¼ tsp kosher salt

2 cups canned
cherry pie filling

Lisa delivered big-time on this one. Bubby Anne, our late grandmother, was a dynamo, often cooking for her 23 grandchildren. The instant her cherry cake showed up, elbows flew and punches were thrown in efforts to get a piece of the cinnamon and sugar-topped cake. A traditional Bubby, she fed us, remembered our birthdays and didn't write down a single recipe. When she was gone, so was her cherry cake, or so we thought. Cousins, aunts and uncles…it's time to rejoice because Lisa, with her bionic sense of taste, smell and gastronomical recall, has unlocked the secret and taken us all back to the delectable days of cherry cake combat.

DIRECTIONS

1) Preheat oven to 350°F. Line a 9-inch square baking pan with parchment paper and coat with non-stick cooking spray. 2) For the topping, in a small bowl, combine ¼ cup sugar and 1 tsp cinnamon. Set aside. 3) For the cake, in a large bowl, combine 2 cups sugar, vegetable oil, orange juice, eggs and vanilla, whisking until sugar is dissolved and ingredients blended. Gently fold in flour, baking powder and salt, mixing just until flour disappears. Pour half the batter into prepared baking pan. Evenly spread cherry filling over top. Top with remaining batter and sprinkle with sugar-cinnamon mixture. Bake 55 minutes or until cooked through.

Serves 6–8

MUGSY'S CLASSIC SCONES

INGREDIENTS

Scone

2 cups flour

¼ cup sugar

1 tbsp baking powder

½ tsp kosher salt

½ cup cold butter, cut into pieces

1 large egg

½ cup whole milk

extra flour for dusting

Egg Wash

1 large egg

pinch kosher salt

1 tbsp sugar

strawberry jam, fresh berries, clotted cream, for serving

When we asked our good friend, chef and food stylist Ian Muggridge, for a recipe that would best reflect his UK upbringing, we were gobsmacked by his suggestions. Kippers, bubble and squeak and spotted dick were all a tad too authentic for us. Then came something that we were chuffed to bits about: scones. Forget those precious teatime sandwiches. We fancy tucking into these soft, buttery and flaky gems straight from the oven. Split open, spread with jam and Devon cream, these superb scones are smashing. Ta, old chap.

DIRECTIONS

1) Preheat oven to 425ºF. Line a baking sheet with parchment paper.
2) In a large bowl, combine flour, sugar, baking powder and salt. Cut in cold butter with a pastry blender or your fingers until coarse crumbs. In a small bowl, whisk 1 egg and milk. Add to flour mixture and stir with a wooden spoon until moistened. Gather into a ball and transfer to a lightly floured surface. Knead several times and pat dough into an 8-inch-round circle. Cut into 8 wedges and place on prepared baking sheet. In a small bowl, whisk 1 egg and pinch of salt. Using a pastry brush, lightly brush tops of scones with egg wash and sprinkle with 1 tbsp sugar. Bake 12 minutes until golden brown. Remove from oven and cool on a wire rack. Serve with jam, fruit and clotted cream.

Yield: 8 scones

STEVE ZOLPER'S BREAKFAST COOKIES

INGREDIENTS

1 cup quick cooking or old-fashioned oats

¾ cup whole-wheat flour

¼ cup ground golden flax seed

½ tsp baking soda

½ tsp baking powder

⅛ tsp salt

1 tsp ground cinnamon

¼ tsp ground nutmeg

1 tbsp grated fresh ginger

¼ cup canola oil

½ cup lightly packed brown sugar

2 tbsp honey

1 large egg

¼ cup plain low-fat yogurt

1 tsp vanilla extract

½ cup organic Thompson raisins

¾ cup shredded carrot

½ cup chopped pecans

½ cup chopped dates

Though I exercise more for my hips than my health, I love breaking the occasional sweat. I've tried everything (Tae Bo) and everyone (Jane Fonda) under the sun, but no one shines brighter than Steve Zolper, a trainer with boundless energy, knowledge and positivity. As I grumbled and groaned my way through his challenging workouts, I oft wondered where all his dynamism came from. Power naps? Ginseng? Chocolate? Nope. The answer is in his nutrient packed, energy boosting breakfast cookies that are easy to make and will add muscle to your morning routine. I now eat one of these tastes-like-carrot-cake healthy cookies and I'm good for at least 10 sit-ups before lunch. Thanks, Zolps. Now drop and give me 20.

DIRECTIONS

1) Preheat oven to 350ºF. Line a baking sheet with parchment paper. **2)** In a medium bowl, combine oats, flour, flax, baking soda, baking powder, salt, cinnamon, nutmeg and ginger. Set aside. **3)** Using an electric mixer, beat canola oil, brown sugar and honey. Beat egg, yogurt and vanilla. Gradually stir in oat mixture, just until blended. Stir in raisins, carrots, pecans and dates. Chill dough in refrigerator for 30 minutes, up to 24 hours. **4)** Using a large spoon, scoop dough balls (slightly larger than a golf ball) on to prepared baking sheet, leaving 2 inches between cookies. Bake 20–25 minutes, until edges are golden and centers are set. Allow to cool. Store in refrigerator.

Yield: 8 large cookies or 15 smaller, golf ball-sized cookies

The trainer brings the heat to the kitchen

FUDGY CHOCOLATE BREAD with CHOCOLATE-COFFEE GLAZE

INGREDIENTS

Chocolate Bread

1 cup flour

½ cup + 2 tbsp cocoa powder, sifted

½ tsp ground cinnamon

½ tsp kosher salt

½ tsp baking powder

½ tsp baking soda

2 tbsp hot water

2 tsp instant coffee

½ cup buttermilk

½ cup butter, softened

1 cup sugar

2 large eggs

½ tsp vanilla extract

Chocolate Coffee Glaze

½ cup semi-sweet chocolate chips

3 tbsp butter

1 tsp instant coffee

1 tsp hot water

1 tbsp icing sugar, sifted

Lisa is a self-professed chocaholic. When she was little, she buried a chocolate bar in the backyard, hoping to grow a cacao tree. Now that she's older, a bit crankier and short one chocolate forest, I do drive-by bonbons, pegging bars at her and running. And, well, since she's not a morning person (she might dispute this, but take my word), I'm thrilled she created this decadent and dense chocolate loaf cake that undoubtedly lifts her spirits sky high. With a 1-2–chocolate punch, this coffee-glazed bread will leave you with a sweet chocolate high… one slice and Lisa's euphoric.

DIRECTIONS

1) Preheat oven to 350ºF. Line a 9x5-inch loaf pan with parchment paper, draping it over the edges to cover the sides. Lightly coat with non-stick cooking spray. **2)** In a medium bowl, combine flour, cocoa powder, cinnamon, salt, baking powder and baking soda. Set aside. **3)** In a small bowl, combine hot water and instant coffee stirring well to dissolve. Add buttermilk and stir to combine. Set aside. **4)** In an electric mixer, cream butter and sugar on medium speed, until light and fluffy, about 2 minutes. Add eggs one at a time, beating well after each addition. Add vanilla extract. On low speed, alternate adding flour mixture and buttermilk mixture, beginning and ending with the flour. Beat just until flour disappears, careful not to over mix. Pour into prepared loaf pan and bake 42–45 minutes. Let cool 20 minutes before removing from pan. **5)** For the glaze, in a small, microwave-safe bowl, melt the chocolate chips and butter. In a separate small bowl, dissolve coffee in hot water and then stir into chocolate mixture along with sifted icing sugar. Stir well to combine and evenly spread on top of cooled chocolate loaf.

Serves 10–12

CARAMELIZED BANANA BREAD

INGREDIENTS

Caramelized Bananas

½ cup sugar

2 tbsp water

2 tbsp butter

1 large banana, ripe yet still firm,
thinly sliced

Banana Bread

1¼ cups flour

1 tsp baking soda

¼ tsp kosher salt

2 large eggs, lightly beaten

½ tsp vanilla extract

½ cup vegetable oil

¾ cup sugar

1 cup ripe bananas (2–3),
mashed

When we were little, I wanted my MTV while Lisa whined until she could watch Captain Caveman pull a wrench out of his fur. Lisa's still a cartoon kid and lately has been calling me B1 and herself B2, like the freaky huge, walking, talking, pajama-wearing bananas that live on Cuddles Avenue. The only good thing to come out of this recent gone-bananas phase is this double-dose banana bread, a superb banana-laden loaf topped with caramelized bananas. I'm so thankful for this moist, flavorful twist on the classic banana bread, but I'm equally grateful she's moved on from her Josie and The Pussycats (no, I won't purr) period.

DIRECTIONS

1) Preheat oven to 350ºF. Coat a 9x5-inch loaf pan with non-stick cooking spray and dust bottom and sides with flour, tapping out any excess. 2) For the caramelized bananas, in a large skillet, bring sugar and water to a boil over medium-high heat. Stir to dissolve at first, then stop stirring and cook until the mixture starts to turn amber. Remove from heat and swirl in butter. Add sliced bananas and stir for 1 minute over low heat. Evenly spread the caramelized bananas along the bottom of the prepared loaf pan. 3) For the banana bread, in a medium bowl, stir together flour, baking soda and salt. In another bowl, whisk eggs, vanilla, oil, sugar and mashed bananas. Add the banana mixture to the flour mixture, stirring just until the flour disappears. Pour the batter over the caramelized bananas. Place pan on a baking sheet and bake 50 minutes until a toothpick inserted in the center comes out clean. After cooling for 10 minutes, invert loaf on a platter and let cool completely.

Serves 10–12

APPLE BREAD with BUTTERSCOTCH GLAZE

INGREDIENTS

Apple Bread

2½ cups flour

1 tsp cinnamon

1 tsp baking soda

½ tsp baking powder

½ tsp kosher salt

¾ cup sugar

½ cup packed brown sugar

½ cup vegetable oil

¼ cup buttermilk

2 large eggs

½ tsp vanilla extract

2 cups peeled and coarsely chopped Granny Smith apples

1 cup butterscotch chips

Butterscotch Glaze

2 tbsp milk

2 tbsp butter

½ cup icing sugar

½ cup butterscotch chips

How do you like them apples? I love the shiny orbs because they can't be compared to oranges, they're forbidden *and* they keep the doctor away. Lisa adores this fruit for more relevant reasons – aromatic, succulent and crunchy, apples lend themselves beautifully to baking. To further her point, she created this chunky apple bread laced with creamy butterscotch chips. With a cup of tea, at the Thanksgiving table or in the Garden of Eden, a slice of this luscious bread will have you, too, declaring Lisa the apple of your eye.

DIRECTIONS

1) Preheat oven to 350ºF. Coat a 10-inch loaf pan with non-stick cooking spray. 2) For the apple bread, in a medium bowl, combine flour, cinnamon, baking soda, baking powder and salt. In a large bowl, whisk sugar, brown sugar, oil, buttermilk, eggs and vanilla. Add flour mixture, chopped apples and butterscotch chips, stirring just until combined. Transfer to prepared loaf pan. Bake 65 minutes until a toothpick inserted comes out clean. Cool 15 minutes in the pan before removing to a wire rack. Cool completely before glazing. 3) For the glaze, in a medium saucepan, bring milk and butter to a boil over medium heat. Remove from heat and whisk in icing sugar and butterscotch chips. Allow glaze to sit for 20 minutes before spreading on the loaf.

Serves 12–15

BITE ME BIT

"Ducking for apples – change one letter and it's the story of my life."

— Dorothy Parker, author and satirist

SOUR CREAM COFFEE CAKE MUFFINS

INGREDIENTS

Crumble Topping

1 cup flour

½ cup packed brown sugar

½ tsp ground cinnamon

¼ tsp kosher salt

¼ cup butter, softened

Sour Cream Coffee Cake Muffins

2 cups flour

1 tsp baking powder

½ tsp baking soda

½ tsp kosher salt

½ tsp ground cinnamon

½ cup butter, softened

1 cup sugar

2 large eggs

1 tsp vanilla extract

¾ cup sour cream

Sweet Glaze

½ cup icing sugar

1 tbsp milk

¼ tsp vanilla extract

Shh. Don't tell anyone, but you can have your cake *and* eat it too. Really. Lisa has taken her scrumptious streusel coffee cake and disguised it by transforming it into mouthwatering muffins. These handy, single-serving breakfast "muffins" (nudge, nudge) are topped with a brown sugar and cinnamon crumble. As the icing on the cake (wink, wink), each domed top is drizzled with a gorgeous glaze. These moist muffins really do take the cake (say no more, say no more) alongside a cup of steaming coffee.

DIRECTIONS

1) For the crumble topping, in a medium bowl, combine flour, brown sugar, cinnamon and salt. Cut in butter with your fingers until mixture is crumbly. Set aside. 2) For the muffins, preheat oven to 350°F. Line a 12-cup muffin tin with paper muffin cups. In a medium bowl, combine flour, baking powder, baking soda, salt and cinnamon. Set aside. 3) In an electric mixer, cream butter and sugar on medium speed until well blended. Add eggs one at a time, beating well after each addition. On low speed, add vanilla and sour cream, beating just until combined. Add flour mixture, mixing just until flour is incorporated. 4) To assemble muffins, place a spoonful of batter in the bottom of each muffin cup. Top each with a small spoonful of crumble topping followed by dividing remaining batter among cups. Finish each muffin sprinkled with crumble topping. Bake 24 minutes. Allow muffins to cool before glazing. 5) For the glaze, in a small bowl, stir together icing sugar, milk and vanilla until smooth. Drizzle on cooled muffins.

Yield: 12 muffins

MAPLE PANCAKE MUFFINS

I adore pancakes. Oops. Let me rephrase. I adore pancakes especially when I don't have to make them. Standing, sweating and flipping batch after batch morphs me from Morning Glory to Dragon Lady. Lisa couldn't take standing at my stove any longer so she conjured up these portable pancakes. Good for morning, noon and night, these pancake muffins, infused with liquid gold (aka pure maple syrup) and topped with a maple glaze, instantly stop my short-stack sniveling. A snap to throw together, these sweet maple pancakes come without the griddle grind. Only thing missing is the side of home fries and bacon, Lisa. Lisa? Hey, where'd Lisa go?

INGREDIENTS

Maple Muffins

½ cup butter, melted
½ cup sugar
½ cup pure maple syrup
1 large egg
1 tsp vanilla extract
½ cup milk
1¼ cups flour
½ cup quick cooking oats
2 tsp baking powder
½ tsp kosher salt

Maple Glaze

½ cup icing sugar
1 tbsp butter, softened
1 tbsp pure maple syrup

DIRECTIONS

1) Preheat oven to 400°F. Line 10 muffin cups with paper muffin liners. 2) For the muffins, in a medium bowl, whisk melted butter, sugar, syrup, egg, vanilla and milk. In a large bowl, combine flour, oats, baking powder and salt. Make a well in the center of the flour mixture and pour in the egg mixture. Stir only until dry ingredients are moistened. Don't over mix, batter will be lumpy. Spoon batter into muffin cups and bake 16–18 minutes. Cool 10–15 minutes before glazing. 3) For the glaze, in a small bowl, combine icing sugar, butter and maple syrup. Stir until smooth. Spread glaze on cooled muffins.

Yield: 10 muffins

BITE ME BIT

"What did you do, Romeo? Did you pour maple syrup all over your body and ask her if she was in the mood for a short stack?"

— Howard Wolowitz (actor Simon Helberg) on the TV show *The Big Bang Theory*

PUMPKIN CUPCAKES with CREAM CHEESE ICING

INGREDIENTS

Pumpkin Cupcakes

1½ cups canned pumpkin puree

1½ cups sugar

⅔ cup packed brown sugar

¾ cup butter, melted

⅓ cup buttermilk

2 large eggs

1 tsp vanilla extract

2 cups flour

1½ tsp baking soda

1½ tsp ground cinnamon

½ tsp kosher salt

¼ tsp ground ginger

Cinnamon Cream Cheese Icing

1 (8oz/250g) package cream cheese, softened

½ cup butter, softened

½ tsp vanilla extract

¼ tsp ground cinnamon

4½ cups icing sugar

How did the muffin industry manage to take a dense cake the size of a UFO and brand it as "healthy" breakfast food and the sensible accompaniment to coffee and a newspaper? All the while, the poor, poor cupcake, all light, small and fluffy, got tagged as a "treat" to be consumed only as dessert. Not at our brunches, where we serve up these delicious cupcakes loaded with the ultimate in morning fare: fruit, eggs, flour, buttermilk, cinnamon and cream cheese. Join us in our crusade to bring cupcakes to the brunch buffet.

DIRECTIONS

1) For the cupcakes, preheat the oven to 350°F. Line muffin tins with 20 cupcake liners. In a large bowl, whisk pumpkin, sugar, brown sugar, melted butter, buttermilk, eggs and vanilla. In a small bowl, combine flour, baking soda, cinnamon, salt and ginger. Add flour mixture to egg mixture, stirring gently just until combined. Fill muffin cups approximately ¾ full. Bake 22–24 minutes until a toothpick inserted in the center comes out clean. Let the cupcakes cool on a wire rack before icing. 2) For the icing, in an electric mixer, combine cream cheese, butter, vanilla, cinnamon and icing sugar. Mix at low speed until blended. Scrape down the sides of the bowl and beat on medium speed for 30 more seconds until smooth and creamy. Frost cupcakes once they're cooled.

Yield: 20 cupcakes

Tempt me

Seductive Desserts

PILED PAVLOVA with BERRIES & CREAM

INGREDIENTS

Meringues

4 egg whites

pinch of kosher salt

1 cup sugar (divided)

1 tsp cornstarch

1 tsp white vinegar

Filling

1½ cups whipping cream

½ cup icing sugar

3 cups assorted fresh berries; sliced strawberries, raspberries, blueberries, blackberries

Don't tell us to "go big or go home." We'll do both, as we did with this dramatic dessert. We took the traditional, measly, single-layered Pavlova and turned it into a meringue masterpiece. All that, and we did it at home. Egg whites were beaten stiff; crisp-on-the-outside, soft-on-the-inside shells were baked and cream was whipped, resulting in stacked layers of airy, marshmallow-like meringue, mounded with sweet clouds of cream and fresh berries. "Going big" worked out great on this one…just don't ask us what happened when we got perms in the '80s.

DIRECTIONS

1) Preheat oven to 300°F. Line 2 baking sheets with parchment paper. Trace three 8-inch circles on the sheets of paper. Flip the parchment over so your meringue won't touch the ink. **2)** For the meringues, place the egg whites and salt in the clean, dry bowl of an electric mixer. Using the whisk attachment, whip on medium speed until soft peaks form. Increase speed to high and gradually add ¾ cup sugar, mixing until stiff peaks form. In a small bowl, combine ¼ cup sugar with cornstarch. Lightly fold cornstarch mixture and vinegar into the egg whites. Spread meringue into pre-drawn circles approximately ¼-inch thick. Level the tops of each circle with the back of a spoon. Bake for 1 hour, turn oven off and open door slightly, allowing meringues to cool inside the oven for 30 minutes. **3)** For the filling, using the whisk attachment of an electric mixer, whip cream and icing sugar on high speed until thickened. **4)** To assemble, place 1 meringue layer on serving dish. Spread evenly with ¾ cup whipped cream followed by 1 cup mixed berries. Repeat with remaining meringue layers, finishing with whipped cream and berries on top.

Serves 8–10

Watch this cover-worthy shot being photographed

EXTREME CHOCOLATE CAKE with PEANUT BUTTER FROSTING

We all know that Lisa loves chocolate madly, deeply. That's the primary reason this outrageously chocolaty chocolate cake exists – a rich, dense and fudgy wonder that fulfills her daily chocolate yen. Why the peanut butter frosting, you ask? Lisa was appalled to witness me lick a PB-smeared, chocolate-topped knife. Hey, we all have our cravings and one of mine happens to be for this classic combination of sweet and salty. Lisa's creation of this creamy peanut-butter frosted, decadent and moist chocolate cake delivers major stick-to-your-mouth satisfaction – the only thing you'll be licking clean is your plate.

INGREDIENTS

Chocolate Cake

2 cups sugar

1¾ cups flour

1 cup cocoa powder, sifted

1½ tsp baking soda

1½ tsp baking powder

½ tsp kosher salt

1 tsp (heaping) instant coffee

1 cup boiling water

½ cup vegetable oil

2 large eggs

1 tsp vanilla extract

1 cup milk

Peanut Butter Frosting

1 cup smooth peanut butter

1 cup butter, softened

2 tbsp cream

2 tsp vanilla extract

4 cups icing sugar

DIRECTIONS

1) Preheat oven to 350ºF. Coat two 9-inch round cake pans with non-stick cooking spray. 2) For the cake, using the whisk attachment of an electric mixer, combine sugar, flour, cocoa powder, baking soda, baking powder and salt on low speed. In a small bowl, combine instant coffee with boiling water. In a large bowl, whisk vegetable oil, eggs, vanilla, milk and coffee mixture. Add to dry ingredients and beat at medium speed for 2 minutes, making sure to scrape down the sides of the bowl during mixing. Divide batter evenly between prepared pans and bake 23–25 minutes. Remove from oven and let cool slightly before removing from pans. Let layers cool completely on a wire rack before frosting. 3) For the frosting, using an electric mixer, cream peanut butter and butter on medium speed until combined. On low speed, add cream, vanilla and icing sugar. Raise speed to medium and beat until icing sugar is incorporated. 4) To assemble, place 1 layer on a serving plate and top with 1 cup frosting, spreading evenly. Top with cake layer and frost sides and top with remaining frosting.

Serves 10

BIT ME BIT

"I'd rather be dead than singing 'Satisfaction' when I'm forty-five."

— Mick Jagger, musician

LAYERED TOFFEE CRUNCH CAKE

INGREDIENTS

Toffee Cake

2 cups sugar

3 large eggs

1 cup vegetable oil

2 tsp vanilla extract

1 cup sour cream

2½ cups flour

1 tsp baking powder

½ tsp baking soda

½ tsp kosher salt

1 (200g) package SKOR or Heath bar bits

Toffee Frosting

½ cup vegetable shortening

½ cup margarine

3 cups icing sugar

1 tsp vanilla extract

2 tbsp milk

½ cup SKOR or Heath bar bits

A quick Internet search for a recipe like this and you'll find thousands that involve store-bought angel food cakes sliced in half and filled with whipped topping and chopped up chocolate bars. I thought this sounded pretty good until I dug into Lisa's homemade version, a confectionery cake where buttery toffee bits are baked into moist vanilla cake and folded into creamy frosting. One bite and you too will discover that the *Gnat*net is the only place to search for drool-worthy desserts.

DIRECTIONS

1) Preheat oven to 350°F. Coat two 8-inch round cake pans with non-stick cooking spray and cover the bottom of each pan with parchment paper. **2)** For the cake, using the whisk attachment of an electric mixer, beat sugar and eggs on medium speed for 2 minutes, until thickened. On low speed, add the vegetable oil, vanilla and sour cream, mixing until blended. Add the flour, baking powder, baking soda, salt and toffee bits, mixing just until combined. Divide batter evenly into prepared pans. Bake 33–35 minutes or until a toothpick inserted in the center comes out clean. Remove from oven and let cool for 10 minutes before transferring cakes from pans to wire racks. Make sure layers are completely cooled before frosting. **3)** For the frosting, in an electric mixer, cream vegetable shortening and margarine on medium speed until well combined. On low speed, add icing sugar, vanilla and milk. Once incorporated, turn mixer to medium speed and blend until icing is smooth. Fold in toffee bits. **4)** To assemble the cake, place 1 cake layer on a serving dish and top with ¾ cup frosting. Spread evenly over cake. Top with remaining layer and spread the remaining frosting on the top and sides of the cake.

Serves 10

LEMONADE LAYER CAKE

INGREDIENTS

Lemonade Cake

2½ cups flour

1 tbsp lemon zest

1½ tsp baking powder

½ tsp baking soda

½ tsp kosher salt

¾ cup butter, softened

2 cups sugar

3 large eggs

2 tsp vanilla extract

3 tbsp thawed frozen-lemonade concentrate

1 cup buttermilk

¼ cup fresh lemon juice

Lemonade Frosting

1 (8oz) package cream cheese, softened

½ cup butter, softened

1 tbsp thawed frozen-lemonade concentrate

2 tsp lemon zest

½ tsp vanilla extract

4½ cups icing sugar

Lisa and I have had our fair share of lemonade stand-offs. We set up shop 15 paces apart and see who's the superior street salesperson. Her stand always has a lineup down the block. Could be because I sell for a buck a cup while she gives it away. Or it might be that while I pour warm lemonade from a carton, hers is icy cold and hand-squeezed. Fine. Lisa understands lemonade and has proven it with this zingy cake, moist layers infused with all things lemon and topped with a lemon-cream-cheese frosting. Hope Lisa can keep up with the demand because I'm going to be charging at least $10 a slice for her masterful lemonade layer cake.

DIRECTIONS

1) For the cake, preheat oven to 350ºF. Coat two 9-inch round cake pans with non-stick cooking spray. In a small bowl, combine flour, lemon zest, baking powder, baking soda and salt. Set aside. 2) Using an electric mixer, cream butter and sugar on medium speed, until light and fluffy. Beat in eggs one at a time. Mix in vanilla and lemonade concentrate. 3) In a small bowl, combine buttermilk and lemon juice. Alternate adding flour mixture and buttermilk mixture to mixer, beginning and ending with the flour. Mix just until combined. Divide batter evenly between prepared pans and bake 20–24 minutes until a toothpick inserted in the middle comes out clean. Cool in pans for 10 minutes before removing to wire racks. Cool cakes completely before frosting. 4) For the frosting, in an electric mixer, beat cream cheese and butter until well combined. On low speed, add lemonade concentrate, lemon zest, vanilla and icing sugar. Scrape down the sides of the bowl and beat for 30 seconds on medium speed until smooth and creamy. 5) To assemble the cake, place 1 layer on a serving plate and spread with 1 cup frosting. Top with cake layer and spread remaining frosting over the top and sides of the cake.

Serves 10–12

BITE ME BIT

"At my lemonade stand I used to give the first glass away free and charge five dollars for the second glass. The refill contained the antidote."

— Emo Phillips, comedian

WHITE CHOCOLATE CHEESECAKE with FRESH BLUEBERRY GLAZE

INGREDIENTS

Vanilla Wafer Crust

2 cups vanilla wafer crumbs

½ cup butter, melted

2 tbsp sugar

pinch of kosher salt

Cheesecake Filling

1½ cups chopped white chocolate, melted

4 (8oz) packages cream cheese, softened

2 tbsp flour

⅛ tsp kosher salt

1¼ cups sugar

1 tbsp vanilla extract

1 tbsp lemon zest

4 large eggs

Blueberry Glaze

1 cup sugar

2 tbsp cornstarch

1 cup water

½ cup fresh blueberries

Topping

1½ cups fresh blueberries

Lisa knows me better than I know myself. She knows I loathe fluffy things (e.g. pillows, hair), yet went ahead and created a cloud-like, airy white chocolate cheesecake perched atop a vanilla wafer crust. A calculated risk on her part, but this rich, silky smooth cheesecake stunned me into silence. Once again, sister knows best. Sigh.

DIRECTIONS

1) Preheat oven to 375°F. 2) For the crust, in a medium bowl, combine vanilla wafer crumbs with butter, sugar and salt, until mixture clumps together. Press evenly on the bottom and up the sides of a 9-inch springform pan. Bake 9 minutes. Remove from oven and let cool before filling. Reduce oven temperature to 300°F. 3) For the filling, to melt the white chocolate, put water in the bottom ¼ of a double boiler and bring to a boil over medium-high heat. Reduce heat to low and place white chocolate in the top of the double boiler. Stir frequently and remove as soon as chocolate has melted. 4) Using the paddle of an electric mixer, beat cream cheese on medium speed until smooth, scraping down sides and bottom of bowl often. On low speed, add melted white chocolate, flour, salt and sugar, mixing until combined. Increase speed to medium and beat until mixture is smooth and fluffy. Add vanilla and lemon zest, mixing well. Add eggs one at a time, scraping down the bowl to make sure there are no lumps, careful not to over mix eggs, mixing just until combined. Pour batter evenly in cooled crust and bake 65–70 minutes. The center will still be wobbly but will firm up after chilling. Once the cheesecake has cooled to room temperature, cover and refrigerate at least 6 hours before topping with blueberries and glaze. 5) For the blueberry glaze, in a medium saucepan, whisk sugar and cornstarch. Gradually whisk in water. Add ½ cup blueberries to sugar mixture. Place over medium heat, stirring constantly until mixture comes to a boil. Boil 3 minutes more, whisking continually. Remove from heat and cool completely. 6) To assemble cheesecake topping, arrange remaining 1½ cups blueberries over the top of the chilled cheesecake. Pour cooled glaze over blueberries.

Serves 10–12

LEMON CREAM PIE with GINGERSNAP CRUST

INGREDIENTS

Gingersnap Crust
1½ cups finely ground gingersnap cookies

2 tbsp sugar

1 tsp lemon zest

5 tbsp butter, melted

Creamy Lemon Filling
2 cups sweetened condensed milk

3 egg yolks

¾ cup fresh lemon juice

2 tbsp sugar

1 tbsp lemon zest

Sweet Whipped Cream
1 cup whipping cream

2 tbsp icing sugar

½ tsp vanilla extract

I'm a bit slow with the whole texting thing. Until recently, I thought LOL was short for "lots of love." Imagine my embarrassment when I replied with "Love you too." :S (Awkward). This pie from C=:-) (Chef) Lisa will have you :-& (tongue-tied) with its silky, tart lemon filling piled atop a spicy gingersnap crust. The result is like taking a big bite of ((o)) (sunshine) piled with fluffy, :-9 (lip-licking) whipped cream. This luscious dessert will get all (Y) (thumbs up...I don't get this one), will have everyone :)~~ (drooling) and full of :D (big grins). ;-) (so happy, I'm crying) that this intro is done. @:-) (goodbye).

DIRECTIONS

1) Preheat oven to 350ºF. **2)** For the crust, in a large bowl, combine gingersnap crumbs, sugar and lemon zest. Add melted butter and stir until crumbs are moistened. Press crumbs evenly on the bottom and sides of a 9-inch pie plate. Bake 8–9 minutes. Cool crust slightly before filling. **3)** For the filling, in an electric mixer, beat the condensed milk and egg yolks on medium speed for 3 minutes until light and fluffy. Add lemon juice, sugar and zest, continuing to beat 2 minutes. Pour filling into cooled crust. Bake at 350ºF for 10 minutes. Remove from oven and cool before refrigerating. Cover and refrigerate 4 hours. **4)** For the whipped cream, in an electric mixer, beat the cream on high speed until soft peaks form. Add icing sugar and vanilla, continuing to beat for 1 minute until medium peaks form. Serve with slices of pie.

Serves 8–10

BITE ME BIT

"Our store is called 'The Pie Hole.' As in, shut your. Or, in this case, 'Open Your,' because it's real good."

— Olive Snook (actress Kristin Chenoweth) on the TV show *Pushing Daisies*

BANOFFEE PIE with CRUNCHY CHOCOLATE TOPPING

INGREDIENTS

Graham Crust

1½ cups graham cracker crumbs

⅓ cup butter, melted

¼ cup sugar

Filling

2 (300ml/10.5oz) cans sweetened condensed milk

3 large bananas, ripe yet still firm

Chocolate Toffee Graham Topping

16 graham crackers

¼ cup butter

2 tbsp sugar

2 tbsp brown sugar

¾ cup milk chocolate chips

½ cup SKOR or Heath bar bits

For those of you who aren't from the UK, yes, it's "banoffee," a slurring of the words banana and toffee. As classically British as 007 and a stiff upper lip, banoffee is a sticky, seductive pie of creamy toffee and slices of sweet banana. Lisa, a longtime Spice Girls fan, wanted to add a little oomph to this already decadent dessert so she crowned it with a toe-tapping, hip-wiggling, spirit-lifting crunchy top layer of graham crackers coated in milk chocolate and toffee bits. This brill, smashing golden pie is the bee's knees...Rule, Britannia (and Lisa)!

DIRECTIONS

1) Preheat oven to 350°F. Coat a 9-inch pie plate with non-stick cooking spray. 2) For the crust, in a small bowl, combine graham crumbs, melted butter and sugar. Press mixture into the bottom and up the sides of pie plate. Bake 10 minutes. Set aside to cool. Leave oven on at 350°F to bake chocolate graham topping. 3) For the filling, remove labels from cans of condensed milk. Place cans in a medium saucepan and submerge the unopened cans in water. Place saucepan over medium heat and bring water to a boil. Partially cover and boil 2½ hours, making sure to keep cans covered by water the entire time, adding more water as it evaporates. When done, remove cans from pot and cool 30 minutes before opening. 4) For the topping, line a baking sheet with aluminum foil and coat with non-stick cooking spray. Arrange graham crackers in a single layer, edges touching. In a medium saucepan, melt butter over medium heat. Add sugar and brown sugar, stirring to combine. Once mixture comes to a boil, turn heat to low, stop stirring and let gently bubble for 2–3 minutes. Remove from heat and immediately pour over graham crackers. Bake 8 minutes. Remove from oven and sprinkle with chocolate chips. As they start to melt, gently spread over graham crackers and sprinkle evenly with toffee bits. Once cooled to room temperature, refrigerate 1–2 hours, until firm enough to break into 1- to 2-inch irregular shaped pieces. 5) To assemble pie, pour cooked condensed milk over prepared crust, spreading evenly. Allow to cool completely. Slice bananas over the filling. Top with chocolate toffee graham cracker pieces. Refrigerate. Serve chilled.

Serves 10

BITE ME BIT

"You never know where to look when eating a banana."

— Peter Kay, comedian

CHOCOLATE COCONUT PECAN PIE

INGREDIENTS

Crust

1¼ cups flour

½ tsp kosher salt

½ tsp sugar

½ cup cold butter, cut into ½-inch cubes

2–3 tbsp ice water

extra flour for dusting

Filling

2 cups pecan halves

⅓ cup butter, melted

1 cup corn syrup

¾ cup packed brown sugar

3 large eggs

1 tsp vanilla extract

½ tsp kosher salt

1 cup sweetened flaked coconut

1 cup semi-sweet chocolate, cut into chunks

Do you spend the holidays hiding Schnapps from Aunt Edna, dodging too-tight hugs from Uncle Sal and juggling dinner dishes? Predictable, huh? Here's something no one is going to see coming, a holiday staple all stirred up. Yes, Lisa has taken the humdrum pecan pie and elevated it to heavenly heights. While this divine dessert has the golden gooey filling, it also has the bonus of a blissfully buttery and crisp crust topped with tasty toasted pecans, fanciful flaked coconut and scrumptious semi-sweet chocolate. So scrumptious and surprising, this pie will even take the sting out of your kid announcing she's dropping out of school for her eat-pray-love year.

DIRECTIONS

1) For the crust, in a food processor, combine flour, salt and sugar, pulsing once to mix. Add butter and process with quick on/off pulses until the mixture resembles small peas. Add ice water to machine while it's running. Process 10 seconds, just until the dough gathers into a ball. Remove dough and press into the shape of a circular disk, about 1-inch thick. Wrap in plastic wrap and refrigerate at least 1 hour before rolling. **2)** Preheat oven to 350°F. On a lightly floured surface, roll dough into a 12-inch circle. To lift the dough, roll it lightly around a rolling pin and transfer it to a 9-inch pie plate, pressing it gently into the corners without stretching the dough. Trim off overhang, leaving approximately 1-inch excess. Fold excess dough under and decorate edges by either pressing with fork tines or fluting. Place crust in freezer while preparing filling. **3)** Place pecan halves on a baking sheet and toast in preheated oven for 5–8 minutes and watch carefully to avoid burning. When cool enough to handle, coarsely chop 1 cup of the pecan halves and combine with remaining uncut toasted pecan halves. **4)** For the filling, in a large bowl, whisk melted butter, corn syrup, brown sugar, eggs, vanilla and salt. Remove crust from freezer, place pecans on the bottom of the piecrust, followed by the coconut and chocolate chunks. Pour corn syrup mixture over top. To prevent over-browning, wrap the edges of the piecrust with aluminum foil. Place pie on a baking sheet and bake 30 minutes. Remove foil from edges and bake 23–25 minutes more until the center is set. Cool completely before serving.

Serves 8–10

APPLE PIE à la CRISP

INGREDIENTS

Pie Crust

1¼ cups flour

1 tbsp sugar

½ tsp kosher salt

½ cup butter, cut into 1-inch cubes, chilled

3–4 tbsp ice cold water

extra flour for dusting

Apple Filling

8 Granny Smith apples, peeled, cored and thinly sliced

½ cup sugar

4 tbsp flour

1 tsp ground cinnamon

Crumb Topping

1¼ cups flour

½ cup packed brown sugar

½ cup butter, cut into 1-inch cubes, chilled

½ tsp ground cinnamon

¼ tsp kosher salt

People often ask us how we manage to work together and still love each other. The answer is simple – compromise. I tell Lisa what I want and then harass her until she agrees. That's kind of what happened in the case of her perfectly traditional, all-American apple pie. While we both love the stacked, cinnamon-sugared apples, I missed the buttery, crunchy topping that covers apple crisps. I repeated myself ad nauseam and *voilà*, the result is the best of both worlds – a hybrid of sweet apples mounded atop a tasty, flaky bottom crust and hidden under a golden streusel topping. Yes, cooperation is the key to eternal happiness and sisterhood.

DIRECTIONS

1) For the crust, in a food processor, combine flour, sugar and salt, pulsing once to mix. Add butter and process with quick on/off pulses until the mixture resembles small peas. Add ice water to machine while it's running. Process 10 seconds, just until the dough gathers into a ball. Remove dough and press into the shape of a circular disk, about 1-inch thick. Wrap in plastic wrap and refrigerate at least 1 hour before rolling. **2)** Preheat oven to 425ºF. On a lightly floured surface, roll dough into a 12-inch circle. Fold the circle in half and transfer to a 9-inch pie plate. Trim off overhang, leaving approximately 1-inch excess. Fold under excess dough and decorate edges. Place crust in freezer while preparing filling. **3)** For the apple filling, in a large bowl, combine sliced apples, sugar, flour and cinnamon, tossing until apples are evenly coated. Spoon mixture into pie crust. **4)** For the crumb topping, in a medium bowl, mix together flour and brown sugar. Add in butter, cinnamon and salt, using a fork or your fingers to mix until crumbly. Sprinkle on top of apples. **5)** Bake 20 minutes and then lower heat to 375ºF and continue to bake 35–40 minutes more, until apples are tender and crust and topping are golden. If the top of the pie is getting too browned during baking, tent with aluminum foil. Remove from oven and allow to cool before slicing.

Serves 8–10 people

BITE ME BIT

"When you die, if you get a choice between going to regular heaven or pie heaven, choose pie heaven. It might be a trick, but if it's not, mmmmm, boy."

— "Deep Thoughts" by Jack Handy on the TV show *Saturday Night Live*

APPLE CINNAMON COBBLER

INGREDIENTS

Apple Mixture

8 Golden Delicious apples, peeled, cored and cut into ½-inch slices

¾ cup sugar

2 tbsp flour

¼ tsp ground cinnamon

¼ tsp kosher salt

2 tbsp butter

Cobbler Topping

2 cups flour

6 tbsp sugar

1 tbsp baking powder

½ tsp kosher salt

½ cup butter, cold

½ cup whole milk

2 large eggs, lightly beaten

2 tsp sugar, for topping

It's easy to do my job when the star of the dessert is called Golden Delicious. This old-fashioned dessert, a deep-dish inverted pie of sweet apples, cinnamon and buttery crust, is golden *and* delicious. Crisp and juicy, Golden Delicious are the perfect baking apple. In this cobbler, slices are cooked with cinnamon and sugar until slightly softened, and topped with a sweet drop batter until caramelized and bubbly. Golden-crusted and deliciously fuss-free (no kneading, rolling or fluting required), this dessert is as tasty and easy as pie.

DIRECTIONS

1) Preheat oven to 400ºF. **2)** For the apple mixture, in a large bowl, toss apples with sugar, flour, cinnamon and salt. In a large skillet, melt butter over medium heat. Add apple mixture and cook 7 minutes until apples are slightly tender. Transfer to a 9-inch pie plate.
3) For the cobbler topping, in a large bowl, combine flour, sugar, baking powder and salt. Cut the butter in until the mixture resembles coarse crumbs. Using a wooden spoon or your hands, stir in the milk and eggs, just until batter is moistened, careful not to over mix. Taking large spoonfuls, drop the batter over the apples and sprinkle with 2 tsp sugar. Place pie plate on a baking sheet and bake 30 minutes until top is nicely browned.

Serves 6–8

STRAWBERRY & CRANBERRY DOUBLE CRISP

INGREDIENTS

Top & Bottom Crust

2 cups flour

2 cups large oat flakes

1½ cups packed brown sugar

pinch kosherof salt

pinch cinnamon

¾ cup butter, softened

Filling

3 cups fresh or frozen cranberries

3 tbsp cornstarch

¼ cup water

4 cups hulled and sliced strawberries

½ cup sugar

1 tsp vanilla extract

My idea of overachieving is doing a push-up, sewing a button and brushing my hair. Lisa's of a totally different mindset – a run-of-the-mill day for her might involve rotating tires, wielding an axe, hooking up a home theater, and, of course, baking an off-the-charts dessert. What fun would it be for her to put down the jumper cables and make a humdrum crisp? None at all, so she gives us a bottom *and* top crust bookending a strawberry-cranberry filling. Sweet strawberries are simmered, crushed into a jam and paired with fresh cranberries sandwiched between a cookie-like top and bottom crust. Really, sometimes I think she's just a big show off.

DIRECTIONS

1) Preheat oven to 350°F. Coat a 13x9-inch baking dish with non-stick cooking spray. **2)** For the top and bottom crust, in a large bowl, combine flour, oats, brown sugar, salt and cinnamon. Cut in the butter with your fingers, until topping is crumbly. Press half the mixture on the bottom of the prepared baking dish. Scatter cranberries evenly over the bottom crust. **3)** For the strawberry mixture, in a small bowl, combine cornstarch and water. Place strawberries and sugar in a medium saucepan. Using a potato masher, crush the berries. Bring to a boil over medium heat. Stir in cornstarch mixture and keep cooking, stirring continuously for 3 minutes. Remove from heat and stir in vanilla. Pour strawberries over the cranberries and sprinkle with remaining crumble. Place crisp on a baking sheet and bake 40–45 minutes.

Serves 8–10

BITE ME BIT

"I took a speed reading course and read *War and Peace* in 20 minutes. It involves Russia."

— Woody Allen, writer, actor and director

S'MORES BREAD PUDDING

INGREDIENTS

8 cups cubed French bread

2 cups roughly crushed graham crackers, about 20

2 cups miniature marshmallows

2 cups coarsely chopped milk chocolate

2 cups milk

2 cups half-and-half cream

4 large eggs

½ cup packed brown sugar

¼ cup sugar

1 tsp vanilla extract

½ tsp ground cinnamon

We live in a S'More-galore world, a place where everything from protein bars to vodka has gone crazy for the combination of graham, marshmallow and chocolate. Though the treat has left the fire pit, you don't have to get your real S'More fix by licking the S'More-flavored Lip Gloss you're wearing. Oozing with gooey melted marshmallows, creamy melted chocolate and crunchy graham crackers, this is one S'More-we-adore bread pudding that has even us holding hands and singing Kumbaya.

DIRECTIONS

1) Preheat oven to 350°F. Coat a 13x9-inch baking dish with non-stick cooking spray. 2) In a large bowl, combine bread cubes and graham crackers. In another bowl, combine marshmallows and chocolate. 3) In a medium bowl, whisk together milk, cream, eggs, brown sugar, sugar, vanilla and cinnamon. Pour over bread mixture, gently tossing to make sure all the bread is covered. Let stand for 30 minutes, tossing bread occasionally. After 30 minutes, mix in all but 1 cup of marshmallow chocolate mixture. Place in prepared baking dish and sprinkle top evenly with remaining cup of marshmallows and chocolate. Bake for 45 minutes. Let cool 10 minutes before serving.

Serves 8–10

SUGAR COOKIES & PUDDING for PENNY

INGREDIENTS

Sugar Cookie Crust

2 cups flour

¼ cup icing sugar

1 cup butter, softened

Cream Cheese Layer

1 cup icing sugar

1 (8oz) package
cream cheese, softened

½ tsp vanilla extract

2 cups frozen
whipped topping, thawed

2½ cups mini marshmallows

Pudding Layer

3 cups milk

1 (3.9oz/113g) package
instant chocolate pudding mix

1 (3.4oz/102g) package
instant vanilla pudding mix

1 cup frozen whipped topping,
thawed

I'm not talking about the shiny copper coin. What I am telling you is that this fast and easy, nut-free (her grandkids have allergies) marshmallow-studded chocolaty pudding sitting atop a sugar cookie crust is for a priceless woman named Penny Offman. Penny always has her hands full either feeding hordes of hungry ones or proofreading our books and helping me solve crosswords. Mom to my oldest friend, Penny has always been so warm and welcoming to all of us. Pen – thanks for all the feeding and the reading.

DIRECTIONS

1) Preheat oven to 350°F. Line a 13x9-inch baking pan with parchment paper and coat with non-stick cooking spray. **2)** For the crust, in a large bowl, combine flour and icing sugar. Cut in butter with your fingers until well combined. Press crust into the bottom of the prepared pan. Bake 20–22 minutes until golden around the edges. Cool completely before filling. **3)** For the cream cheese layer, using an electric mixer, combine icing sugar, cream cheese and vanilla on medium speed until smooth. Fold in 2 cups whipped topping. Spread mixture evenly over cooled crust. Sprinkle with mini marshmallows. For the pudding layer, using whisk attachment of an electric mixer, combine milk, chocolate and vanilla pudding mixes on medium speed for 2 minutes. Spread over the marshmallows and top the pudding with the remaining 1 cup of whipped topping. Cover and refrigerate at least 2 hours or overnight.

Serves 12

COOKIE DOUGH FUDGE BROWNIES

INGREDIENTS

Fudge Brownies

1 cup butter

6 oz unsweetened chocolate, chopped

3 cups sugar

5 large eggs

1½ cups flour

⅓ cup cocoa powder, sifted

½ tsp kosher salt

1 cup semi-sweet or milk chocolate chips

Cookie Dough

½ cup butter, softened

½ cup packed brown sugar

¼ cup sugar

2 tbsp milk

½ tsp vanilla extract

1 cup flour

¼ tsp kosher salt

½ cup mini semi-sweet chocolate chips

Despite having a bad hair day (read: any day), I was recently asked by a fist-pumping gentleman to give him some sugar. To that I responded, "Ask my sister." Sweet I'm not, but make no mistake about it, Sugarplum (aka Lisa) and I have gigantic sweet teeth. In fact, we take great pride that neither of us has ever uttered the phrase, "Too sweet for me." Grab a giant glass of milk because you're about to have the sugar rush of a lifetime when you dig into these rich chocolate brownies that are topped with soft chocolate-chip cookie dough. Clearly our idea of dessert isn't a bowl of applesauce.

DIRECTIONS

1) Preheat oven to 350ºF. Coat a 13x9-inch baking dish with non-stick cooking spray. Line with parchment paper and lightly spray with cooking spray. **2)** For brownie layer, in a microwave safe bowl, combine 1 cup butter and unsweetened chocolate. Melt on high heat for 1 minute, stir and melt for 30 seconds more or until the chocolate and butter are melted and smooth. **3)** In a large bowl, whisk sugar and eggs. Whisk in melted chocolate mixture. Stir in flour, cocoa powder, salt and chocolate chips just until flour disappears. Pour batter into prepared pan. Bake 30 minutes. Remove from oven and cool in pan for 1 hour. **4)** For cookie dough layer, in an electric mixer, cream butter, brown sugar and sugar on medium speed, until light and fluffy. Beat in milk and vanilla. On low speed, add flour, salt and mini chocolate chips, mixing just until flour disappears. Spread over cooled brownies, pressing the dough out with your hands. Refrigerate until firm.

Yield: 24 brownies

BITE ME BIT

"Who discovered we could get milk from cows and what did he think he was doing at the time?"

— Billy Connolly, comedian

CARAMEL, CHOCOLATE & PECAN BLONDIE BLITZ

Sis Boom Bah. That sis of mine has done it again. Despite not being able to somersault, throw a ball or ride a bike, Lisa has captured the golden trophy for game-winning blondies. Perfectly moist and chewy, these reverse brownie bars infused with creamy caramel, milk chocolate and crunchy toasted pecans will leave you blind-sided. She may be compromising your tight end but Lisa will make a Superfan out of all of you with these decadent and delicious blondies.

INGREDIENTS

2 cups flour
½ tsp kosher salt
¼ tsp baking soda
2 cups packed brown sugar
¾ cup butter, softened
2 large eggs
2 tsp vanilla extract

1½ cups pecan halves

Caramel Sauce

1 (14oz) package caramels
½ cup evaporated milk
¼ tsp kosher salt

1 cup milk chocolate chips

DIRECTIONS

1) Preheat oven to 350°F. Coat a 13x9-inch baking pan with non-stick cooking spray. Line the bottom and sides with parchment paper.
2) In a small bowl, combine flour, salt and baking soda. In an electric mixer, cream together brown sugar and butter until light and fluffy. Beat in eggs and vanilla, adding eggs one at a time until combined. Add flour mixture, mixing on low speed just until flour disappears. Spread half the batter evenly in the prepared pan. Bake for 8 minutes and let cool slightly while toasting pecans and preparing caramel sauce. 3) For the pecans, spread in a single layer on a baking sheet. Bake at 350°F for 8–10 minutes, tossing once during cooking. Coarsely chop pecans once they're crisp and lightly browned.
4) For the caramel sauce, in a small saucepan, melt caramels and evaporated milk over low heat until smooth, stirring frequently. Stir in ¼ tsp salt and pour caramel sauce over baked blondie layer. Top caramel layer with toasted pecans and chocolate chips. Drop remaining batter by the tablespoon over the pecans and chocolate. You will not be able to spread it, but it will spread while baking. Bake 24–26 minutes more until lightly browned on top. Let cool for at least 1 hour before removing from pan.

Yield: 24 squares

STUFFED-WITH-FLUFF MARS BAR CUPCAKES

INGREDIENTS

Chocolate Cupcake

¾ cup boiling water

¾ cup cocoa powder, sifted

¾ cup butter, softened

2 cups sugar

3 large eggs

1 tsp vanilla extract

2½ cups cake flour

1 tsp baking soda

1 tsp baking powder

½ tsp kosher salt

1 cup buttermilk

1 cup chopped Mars bars

Chocolate Icing

1 cup butter, softened

½ cup cocoa powder, sifted

2½ cups icing sugar

3 tbsp milk

Filling

24 tbsp marshmallow fluff

Lisa and I have many confectionary pet names for one another. I'm Butterfinger, she's Mounds; I'm Chuckles, she's Chunky; I'm Jelly Belly, and so on. We thought it high time we brought a third musketeer in on the act. Since he's older than us, we thought we'd christen our brother "Mr. Big." Yikes. Shouting Mr. Big across the table was uncomfortable. He's athletic so we moved on to the Marathon Bar, but it just didn't roll off our tongues. Finally, we settled on Mars, a bar that has a good hard shell, a nice sweet center and exists in outer space. Earth-to-Mars, these infinity-and-beyond chocolate marshmallow cupcakes are for you.

DIRECTIONS

1) For the cupcakes, preheat oven to 350°F. Line 24 muffin cups with paper liners and spray with non-stick cooking spray. 2) In a small bowl, combine boiling water and cocoa powder. Set aside. In a medium bowl, sift together cake flour, baking soda, baking powder and salt. 3) Using an electric mixer, cream butter and sugar until light and fluffy. Add eggs one at a time, beating well after each addition. Continue creaming on medium speed and add vanilla extract. On low speed, alternate adding flour mixture and buttermilk, beginning and ending with the flour. Add cocoa mixture and chopped Mars bars, continuing on low speed, just until all ingredients are combined. Spoon batter into prepared cupcake liners until each is ¾ full. Bake 22–24 minutes or until tops feel firm and a toothpick inserted in the center comes out clean. Cool cupcakes completely before filling and icing. 4) For the icing, in an electric mixer, combine butter, cocoa powder and icing sugar on low speed. Once combined, on medium speed, add milk 1 tbsp at a time to achieve desired consistency. 5) To assemble the cupcakes, using a paring knife, cut out a small cone from the center of each cupcake. Spoon 1 heaping tbsp of marshmallow fluff into each cupcake. Replace cut-out piece of cupcake. Spread cupcake top with chocolate icing and serve.

Yield: 24 cupcakes

Meet Mars
(aka our Big Bro)

FROSTED COCONUT CUPCAKES

INGREDIENTS

Coconut Cupcakes

1⅓ cups flour
1 tsp baking powder
1 tsp baking soda
¼ tsp kosher salt
½ cup sour cream
½ cup coconut milk
½ cup butter, softened
1 cup sugar
2 large eggs
½ tsp vanilla extract

Coconut Frosting

½ cup coconut milk
½ cup butter, softened
3 cups icing sugar
1 tsp vanilla extract
¾ cup sweetened
shredded coconut,
to garnish tops

Hey, cupcake cynics. You can put away your crystal ball and stop lamenting the future death of this delicious dessert. These moist mini cakes aren't a "trend" – they've been around since 1902 and are here to stay. I'll never part with these baked beauties that look like snowballs and taste like they just fell off a palm tree. All sweet, buttery and white, these cupcakes are infused with coconut milk, topped with a creamy coconut frosting and rolled in shredded coconut. Cupcakes have some serious staying power. Think you'll be eating whoopie pies or cake pops into the next century? Not a snowballs chance...

DIRECTIONS

1) Preheat oven to 350ºF. Line 12 muffin cups with paper liners and spray with non-stick cooking spray. 2) For the cupcakes, in a medium bowl, combine flour, baking powder, baking soda and salt. In a small bowl, combine sour cream and coconut milk. Set aside. 3) Using an electric mixer, cream butter and sugar on medium speed until light and fluffy. Add eggs one at a time, beating well after each addition. Mix in vanilla. On low speed, alternate adding flour mixture and sour cream mixture, beginning and ending with the flour, mixing just until flour disappears. Do not over mix. Fill prepared muffin cups ¾ full with batter. Bake 18 minutes, until golden. Cool completely before frosting. 4) For the frosting, in a small saucepan, bring coconut milk to a boil over medium heat. Reduce heat to low and cook 5 minutes, stirring often. Remove from heat and cool before continuing with frosting. 5) Using an electric mixer, combine butter, icing sugar, vanilla and cooled coconut milk, beating until desired consistency. Place shredded coconut in a small bowl. Spread frosting on cooled cupcakes and gently roll the frosted top in the shredded coconut.

Yield: 12 cupcakes

BITE ME BIT

"We're so trendy we can't even escape ourselves."

— Kurt Cobain, musician

LEMON MERINGUE CUPCAKES

INGREDIENTS

Lemon Filling

⅓ cup fresh lemon juice

3 large eggs

1 egg yolk

½ cup sugar

½ cup butter, cut into chunks

1 tsp lemon zest

Cupcake Batter

2 cups flour

3 tsp baking powder

½ tsp kosher salt

1½ tsp lemon zest

1 cup sugar

4 large eggs

1 cup vegetable oil

1 cup buttermilk

1 tsp vanilla extract

Meringue

6 egg whites

1 tsp cream of tartar

1 cup sugar

I don't have an "inner child" because, according to others, I'm still a child. Ha. As if. Lisa is too, y'know. A while ago I had to pull her off the swing set and advise her that her polka dot short shorts weren't age appropriate. After blowing bubbles in my face, she hauled me inside to try a dessert that would surely tickle my kid-like fancy. She was right. Again. These portable pies-turned-cupcakes are killer, filled with pucker-up, smooth lemon curd and topped with fluffy meringue clouds. What's even better is I can gobble these one-handed delights while playing marbles. Awesome.

DIRECTIONS

1) For the lemon filling, in a medium heatproof bowl, whisk lemon juice, eggs, egg yolk and sugar until combined. Place bowl over a pot of simmering water and add chunks of butter, whisking continuously 15–18 minutes until thickened. Remove from heat and press through a fine mesh strainer. Fold in lemon zest and cover with plastic wrap. Refrigerate until ready to use, cooling completely. 2) For the cupcakes, preheat oven to 350ºF. Line muffin pans with 16 cupcake liners. 3) In a medium bowl, whisk flour, baking powder, salt and lemon zest. In a large bowl, whisk sugar, eggs, oil, buttermilk and vanilla and gently stir into flour mixture just until blended. Divide batter evenly among muffin cups and bake 16–18 minutes until cake springs back when gently pressed. Remove and cool cupcakes completely. 4) For the meringue, using an electric mixer, beat egg whites and cream of tartar on medium speed until foamy. Increase speed to high and gradually beat in sugar until stiff, glossy peaks form. 4) To assemble the cupcakes, preheat oven to 400ºF and place cupcakes on a baking sheet. Using a paring knife, cut out a small cone from the center of each cupcake. Spoon a heaping tablespoon of the lemon filling into each cupcake. Mound top of cupcake with meringue, lifting spoon to create decorative peaks. Bake 4–5 minutes until tops of meringues brown.

Yield: 16 cupcakes

THIN & CRISP CHOCOLATE CHIP COOKIES

INGREDIENTS

1 cup butter, softened

1 cup sugar

1 cup packed brown sugar

1 large egg

1 tsp vanilla extract

1½ cups flour

1 tsp baking soda

1 tsp kosher salt

1½ cups semi-sweet chocolate chips

Lisa either misheard me or wasn't listening. I said I wanted a box of Cookie Crisp, the deliciously chocolaty breakfast cereal, so we could play our childhood game of Cookie Crook (me) and Officer Crumb (her). Well, good thing she ignored me and made a batch of these crisp cookies, the perfect balance of crunchy edges and soft centers. Chocolaty and buttery, these easy-to-make, wafer-thin cookies are even more perfect for playing Bakery Bandit – I won't be able to stop myself from swiping the milk and robbing the cookie jar blind, regardless of Law-woman Lisa making a citizen's arrest.

DIRECTIONS

1) Preheat oven to 350°F. Line 2 baking sheets with parchment paper. 2) Using an electric mixer, cream butter, sugar and brown sugar on medium speed until blended. Beat in egg and vanilla, mixing until light and fluffy. On low speed, add flour, baking soda, salt and chocolate chips, mixing just until flour disappears. Drop batter by rounded tablespoon on prepared baking sheets, at least 2 inches apart. Bake 10 minutes until edges are golden brown. Remove from oven and allow to cool a few minutes before transferring cookies to a wire rack.

Yield: 35 cookies

CHOCOLATE CHIP, COCONUT & OATMEAL COOKIES

INGREDIENTS

1 cup butter, softened

¾ cup sugar

¾ cup packed brown sugar

1 large egg

1 tsp vanilla extract

1½ cups flour

½ tsp baking soda

½ tsp kosher salt

3 cups old-fashioned large-flake oats (not quick cooking)

1½ cups sweetened flaked coconut

1½ cups semi-sweet chocolate chips

I'm a goal suck. I dawdle around the crease, waiting for someone to pass me the puck. Not Lisa – she's all about shooting and scoring. Once again, The Sniper (call her that when you see her, OK?) has pulled off a veritable hat trick, combining 3 incredible elements in a single winning cookie. Oatmeal, chocolate chips and coconut work together to make these unbeatable cookies simultaneously soft, chewy and crisp-edged.

Trust me when I tell you, one bite and there will be a bench-clearing brawl over the last cookie.

DIRECTIONS

1) Preheat oven to 350ºF. Line a baking sheet with parchment paper. 2) In an electric mixer, cream butter, sugar and brown sugar on medium speed until light and fluffy. Add egg and vanilla, beating until well mixed. Add flour, baking soda, salt, oats, coconut and chocolate chips, mixing on low speed just until flour disappears. 3) Drop heaping tablespoons of dough on prepared baking sheet, pressing dough down to flatten slightly. Bake 10 minutes, until edges begin to brown. Cool completely on a wire rack.

Yield: 48 cookies

BITE ME BIT

"You do that, you go to the box, you know. Two minutes, by yourself, you know and you feel shame, you know. And then you get free."

— Denis Lemieux (actor Yvon Barrette) in the 1977 movie *Slap Shot*

DOUBLE BUTTERSCOTCH PUDDING COOKIES

INGREDIENTS

1 cup butter, softened

¾ cup packed brown sugar

¼ cup sugar

1 (3oz) pouch instant butterscotch pudding mix

2 large eggs

1 tsp vanilla extract

2¼ cups flour

½ tsp baking soda

½ tsp kosher salt

2 cups butterscotch chips

We love to celebrate. On the last Monday in January we make a ruckus in honor of National Bubble Wrap Appreciation Day, on April 16 we fête Eggs Benedict, and we jump for joy on the November 15 Clean Out Your Fridge Day. Yet, none of these festivities holds a candle to September 19, National Butterscotch Pudding Day. While I rejoice by eating butter and drinking scotch, Lisa whips up a batch of these prize-winning sweet and creamy butterscotch cookies.

DIRECTIONS

1) Preheat oven to 350°F. Line a baking sheet with parchment paper. 2) In an electric mixer, cream butter, brown sugar and sugar on medium speed. Add butterscotch pudding, mixing to combine. Add eggs one at a time, beating until fluffy. Mix in vanilla extract. On low speed, add the flour, baking soda, salt and butterscotch chips, mixing just until the flour disappears. Do not over mix. 3) Drop heaping tablespoons of batter on prepared baking sheet. Flatten cookie batter slightly. Bake 10–12 minutes, until the edges begin to brown. Cool cookies on wire rack.

Yield: 33–35 cookies

WHITE CHOCOLATE BERRY THUMBPRINTS

INGREDIENTS

Thumbprint Cookies

1 cup butter, softened

⅔ cup icing sugar

1 tsp vanilla extract

½ tsp kosher salt

2¼ cups flour

½ cup finely chopped white chocolate

Jam Filling

6 tbsp strawberry jam

6 tbsp raspberry jam

½ cup chopped white chocolate, for drizzling on top

Want to get teachers, bosses and mother-in-laws under your thumb? Forget brute force, blackmail or bitchiness. You need our 2 Bs – baking and butter. These shortbread-like thumbprint cookies are loaded with sweet white chocolate and mounded high with berry jam. Not only are these scrumptious, crunchy cookies simple to make (I had time to twiddle my thumbs), but they're also excellent festive fare. These mouthwatering weapons will have friend and foe eating out of your hand.

DIRECTIONS

1) Preheat oven to 350ºF. Line a baking sheet with parchment paper. 2) For the thumbprint cookies, using an electric mixer, combine butter and icing sugar on medium speed, until well blended and smooth. On low speed, add vanilla, salt, flour and white chocolate, mixing 1 minute or until dough forms. Using 2 teaspoons of dough, roll into a ball. Place on prepared baking sheet and, using a ½ tsp measuring spoon, make a depression in the center of each ball. Bake 15–16 minutes or until light brown around the edges. Remove to a wire rack and cool completely before filling. 3) For the jam filling, in a small bowl, combine strawberry and raspberry jam. Fill each indentation with approximately 1 tsp of jam mixture. 4) For the white chocolate drizzle, use a double boiler or place a heatproof bowl across the top of a small pan with a small amount of water in it. Bring the water to a simmer over low heat. Place the ½ cup chopped white chocolate in the bowl and stir frequently until melted, making sure no water touches the chocolate. Remove bowl from heat and, using a fork, drizzle melted white chocolate over each cookie.

Yield: 35–40 cookies

HOT CHOCOLATE COOKIES

INGREDIENTS

¾ cup butter, softened

1¼ cups sugar

¼ cup packed brown sugar

2 large eggs

1 tsp vanilla extract

2 cups flour

⅔ cup cocoa powder, sifted

½ tsp baking soda

¼ tsp kosher salt

¼ cup marshmallow fluff

1½ cups semi-sweet chocolate chips

We started skiing when we were really little. While our brother was a steep-and-deep hot-dogger, Lisa and I were busy cruising down beginner runs and traversing into the trees. Don't tell our dad, but the truth is we hated the cold and regularly cried under our goggles. Other than the ski lifts shutting down, what cheered us up? Hot chocolate, of course. It thrilled us to huddle in the ski lodge sipping from Styrofoam cups of marshmallow-crammed cocoa. Imagine how much more ecstatic we would have been had we had our numb fingers on these hot chocolate cookies? Today, bring on the sub zero temps...we've got our super-soft, chocolaty and marshmallow-infused hot chocolate cookies to warm us up.

DIRECTIONS

1) Preheat oven to 350ºF. Line a baking sheet with parchment paper.

2) Using an electric mixer, cream butter, sugar and brown sugar on medium speed until light and fluffy. Add eggs one at a time, beating well after each addition. Add vanilla. On low speed, add flour, cocoa powder, baking soda, salt, marshmallow fluff and chocolate chips. Mix just until combined, careful not to over mix. Drop the batter by rounded tablespoon on prepared baking sheet. Bake 9–10 minutes. Cool slightly on baking sheet before moving to cooling rack.

Yield: 32–34 cookies

BITE ME BIT

"Skiing combines outdoor fun with knocking down trees with your face."

— Dave Barry, author and columnist

SOFT & CHEWY GINGER COOKIES

INGREDIENTS

2 cups flour

1½ tsp baking soda

1 tsp ground ginger

1 tsp ground cinnamon

½ tsp kosher salt

¾ cup butter, softened

1 cup sugar

1 large egg

¼ cup molasses

1 tsp vanilla extract

¼ cup sugar

I have 3 wishes. First is that I get to be Ginger when we play Gilligan's Island (Lisa's *so* Mary Ann and our brother is Thurston Howell, III). Second is the invention of a cookie that fights off colds. Third is that Lisa recreate Starbucks' moist, chewy ginger cookies I drop a fortune on daily. So lucky, all my wishes have been granted. These classic cookies are pure gingery greatness – soft and chewy, like gingersnaps without the snap. I think it's appropriate I wear my very best sequined, desert island evening gown while I devour a batch of these ginger-spiced molasses cookies...now if only Mary Ann would brew me a cup of tea, I'd be set.

DIRECTIONS

1) Preheat oven to 350°F. Line a baking sheet with parchment paper. 2) In a large bowl, combine flour, baking soda, ginger, cinnamon and salt. In the bowl of an electric mixer, cream together butter and 1 cup sugar on medium speed until smooth and creamy. Beat in egg. Add molasses and vanilla and mix well until combined. On low speed, add flour mixture, mixing just until incorporated. Place remaining ¼ cup of sugar into a small bowl. 3) Scoop a heaping teaspoon of dough and roll into a ball. Drop into reserved bowl of sugar and roll ball around. Place on baking sheet, spaced 2 inches apart. Bake 8–10 minutes, just until tops crack and cookies are flat. Allow to cool on baking sheet 5 minutes before removing to wire rack to cool completely. Repeat with remaining cookie dough.

Yield: 40–45 small cookies

RSVP
me

Parties Everyone Can Throw

EXTRA BITE

See us throw
7 parties
in 6 hours

"Laughter is an instant vacation."

— Milton Berle, comedian

SURF (ON HOME) TURF BEACH PARTY

Tired of complaining about the weather? Wishing for a vacation? Get ready to make a quick getaway...at home. Grab the lime, the coconut and stir it all up – your friends will be thrilled to get their buns toasted Hang(ing) Ten and drinking like fish at your Beach Ball.

STAYCATION SPREAD

TGTBT Salad Rolls (BITE ME, p. 14)

Green Bean, Tomato & Arugula Salad   59

Asparagus & Edamame Orzo Salad   65

Primo Fish Tacos with Chipotle Lime Dressing   175

Lemonade Layer Cake   241

Caramel, Chocolate & Pecan Blondie Blitz   254

Trip Tips

✈ Hand deliver invitations created on coconuts or messages in a bottle

✈ Greet guests wearing a wet suit and snorkel

✈ Make some boozy popsicles

✈ Have *Baywatch* playing in the background

BONBON BIRTHDAY BASH

SUGARCOATED CROONING

"Sugar Daddy"
Yerba Buena

"Sweet Emotion"
Aerosmith

"Shake Your Bon-Bon"
Ricky Martin

"Gum Drop"
The Crew-Cuts

"Cotton Candy Land"
Elvis Presley

"Sweet Child O' Mine"
Guns N' Roses

"I Want Candy"
Bow Wow Wow

"Candy Girl"
The Four Seasons

"Lollipop"
Mika

"Choo'n Gum"
Dean Martin

If someone knocks on your door and says "Candy Gram," answer it. You're going to be a kid in a candy store at our gumball gala and sweet-tooth extravaganza. Trust us, no one is too old (or young) for some Lik-M-Aid fun.

SKITTLES & VITTLES MENU

Caramelized Onion & Gruyere Pizza   18

Sky-High Potato Skins (BITE ME, p. 20)

Fiery Oven Fries   84

The BLD Burger   197

Layered Toffee Crunch Cake   239

S'Mores Bread Pudding   251

Eye Candy

- Rim glasses with Pop Rocks and put frozen gummy bears in cocktails
- Tie together candy necklaces to swag across table edge
- Create Candy Land path on the floor with colored paper
- Send everyone home with a loot bag and a toothbrush

"We elves try to stick to the four main food groups: candy, candy cane, candy corn and syrup."

— Buddy (actor Will Ferrell) in the 2003 movie *Elf*

JULIE

"It's the eye of the tiger, it's the cream of the fight/Risin' up to the challenge of our rival."

— from the 1982 Survivor song "Eye of the Tiger"

ROLL THE DICE GAME NIGHT

While Lisa loves a night of fun and games (ooh...Boggle!), I'm more about engaging in some friendly competition (think: Vince Lombardi's "Show me a good loser, and I'll show you a loser.") Whichever way you play it, put all your chips on the table and throw this winner-of-a-party.

CHECK MATE MENU

Polenta Crostini with Roasted Red Peppers & Olives   20

Minestrone Soup with Pesto Drizzle (BITE ME, p.49)

Parmesan-Crusted Chicken & Arugula Salad   76

Roasted Vegetable Manicotti with Chunky Tomato Sauce   110

Extreme Chocolate Cake with Peanut Butter Frosting   238

Frosted Coconut Cupcakes   257

Bonus Round

$ Use game boards as serving platters or place mats

$ Hit the dollar store for trophies, dice and marbles

$ Scrabble letters are great for spelling out names

$ A glue gun is the secret to building a towering house of cards

Sometimes I like to call Lisa by her real name: Barkeep. She can mix up carousing cocktails like nobody's business. These tasty liquid assets are a bonus at any liquid lunch, tipplers' tea or sauced soiree.

P.S. Lisa has no sympathy for the hooch hangover. Trust me.

Bottoms Up

Life of the Party Libations

BLOODY MARY

1 oz vodka

3 oz tomato juice

2 dashes red-hot sauce

1 dash Worcestershire sauce

½ oz fresh lemon juice

pinch salt

pinch freshly ground black pepper

1 stalk celery, for garnish

Stir together all ingredients and pour into a chilled highball glass. Garnish with celery stick.

MOJITO

4 fresh mint leaves

½ lime, cut into 4 wedges

1 tbsp sugar, or to taste

1 cup ice cubes

1½ oz white rum

½ cup club soda

Place mint leaves and 1 lime wedge in a highball glass. Using a wooden spoon, crush mint and lime to release mint oils and lime juice. Add 2 more lime wedges and the sugar and muddle again with wooden spoon. Fill the glass with ice. Stir in the rum and top off with the club soda. Stir and add more sugar if desired. Garnish with remaining lime wedge.

BUTTERSCOTCH APPLETINI

1 lime wedge

1 package sour apple Pop Rocks

2 oz Absolut vodka

1 oz Sour Apple Pucker

½ oz butterscotch schnapps

Start with a chilled cocktail glass and rub rim with lime wedge. Rim the glass with sour apple Pop Rocks. In a cocktail shaker filled with ice, add vodka, Sour Apple Pucker and schnapps. Shake and strain into prepared glass.

LEMON DROP

1 lemon wedge

1 tsp sugar

2 oz lemon vodka, or unflavored vodka

2 tsp fresh lemon juice

1 tsp sugar

lemon slice

Rub the rim of a chilled cocktail glass with the lemon wedge and dip in 1 tsp sugar to frost the rim. In a cocktail shaker filled with ice, add vodka, lemon juice and sugar. Shake and strain into prepared glass and garnish with lemon slice.

STRAWBERRY DAIQUIRI

1 oz light rum

½ oz triple sec

2 tbsp fresh lime juice

1 tsp sugar

1 cup ice

6 fresh strawberries, stems removed

In a blender, combine rum, triple sec, lime juice, sugar, ice and strawberries. Blend well at high speed. Serve in highball glass.

PEACH MARGARITA

1½ oz tequila

1 oz peach schnapps

½ oz triple sec

1 tbsp fresh lime juice

1 fresh peach, peeled and chopped

1 cup ice

In a blender, combine tequila, schnapps, triple sec, lime juice, peach and ice. Blend well at high speed. Serve in chilled margarita glass.

Wonder Women Wienie Roast

Put down the *Water for Elephants* and grab on to the "Vodka for Ladies." It's time for a girls' night in, a chance to let your hair down and blab with your besties. Get ready for a riotous time that won't be over 'til the fat lady sings…and we're not singing so fast.

GIRL GRUB

Quinoa, Roasted Red Pepper & Feta Wraps   28

Orange, Jicama & Spinach Salad   62

Girl-Meets-Grill Vegetable Pasta Salad   81

Sesame Roasted Salmon with Wasabi Dip   168

Fudgy Double Chocolate Layer Cake (BITE ME, p.235)

Thin & Crisp Chocolate Chip Cookies   260

Fabio Ideas

♥ Make makeup verboten and dress code sweatpants

♥ In addition to dessert, serve tubs of ice cream with spoons

♥ Start a round of truth-dare, double-dare, promise-to-repeat

♥ Give out copies of Judy Blume's *Forever* as guests leave

"I am woman, hear me roar."

— from the 1972 Helen Reddy song "I am Woman"

> **"Are you the lady who doesn't realize she's pregnant until she's sitting on the toilet and the kid pops out?"**
>
> — Debbie (actress Leslie Mann) in the 2007 movie *Knocked Up*

NEW KID ON THE BLOCK BABY SHOWER

DIAPER DITTIES

"Teach your Children"
Crosby, Stills, Nash & Young

"Forever Young"
Soweto Gospel Choir

"Barefoot and Pregnant"
Joan Armatrading

"Lullabye"
Billy Joel

"Hold my Hand"
Hootie & The Blowfish

"I'm So Tired"
The Beatles

"Mother and Child Reunion"
Paul Simon

"Daughters"
John Mayer

"Isn't She Lovely"
Stevie Wonder

"Born to Run"
Bruce Springsteen

Her back aches, she has heartburn and she can't see her toes. Do you really want to add deer-in-the-headlights panic to her woes? Booties and bottles and bibs, oh my! Throw the mom-to-be a shower short on labor stories and long on laughs. It's time to do some major kidding around.

BUNS IN THE OVEN

Mini Zucchini & Provolone Frittatas   214

Lemon Ricotta Pancakes with Blueberry Sauce   210

Banana-Stuffed French Toast Soufflé   207

Noodle Pudding with Caramelized Apples   218

Fudgy Chocolate Bread with Chocolate-Coffee Glaze   226

Apple Streusel Muffins (BITE ME, p.218)

Child's Play

- Use doll bathtubs as serving bowls and supply guests with kid-sized utensils
- Use pregnancy sticks as stir sticks in drinks
- Decorate with packages of Sugar Babies candy
- As guests leave, give them jars of homemade pickles

IN-HOUSE OFFICE BLOWOUT

TEAMWORK TUNES

"9 to 5"
Dolly Parton

"I Don't Like Monday's"
The Boomtown Rats

"Longest Days"
John Mellencamp

"Staple It Together"
Jack Johnson

"Straight Lines"
Silverchair

"Big Brother"
Stevie Wonder

"That's it, I Quit, I'm Movin' On"
Adele

"Trashcan"
Delta Spirit

"The Underdog"
Spoon

"She Works Hard for the Money"
Donna Summer

Your friend just got hired, fired or retired. Head up the social committee and throw this "out of the box" office party that'll have everyone gathering 'round the water cooler.

CORPORATE CHOW

Super Cool Chicken Nachos   15

Prime Rib with Creamy Horseradish Sauce, made into sandwiches   180

Hoisin Chicken Tortilla Wraps   157

Grilled Corn, Tomato & Avocado Salad   61

Sara Lisa's Iced Banana Cake (BITE ME, p.240)

Double Butterscotch Pudding Cookies   263

Suggestion Box

☐ Get wigs and replicate Donald Trump's hairdo

☐ Write invitation like a memo

☐ Laminate ID badges and awards

☐ Put pictures of random kids in frames alongside potted plants and "easy" buttons from Staples

> **"You moon the wrong person at an office party and suddenly you're not 'professional' anymore."**
>
> — Jeff Foxworthy, comedian

"It's Thanksgiving. Some people bake pies. We bake ourselves."

— Michael Kelso (actor Ashton Kutcher) on the TV show *That '70s Show*

EASY AS PIE
THANKSGIVING FEAST

DANKE, GRACIAS, MERCI MELODIES

"Sweet Potato Pie"
James Taylor & Ray Charles

"Praise You"
Fatboy Slim

"Thank You"
Led Zeppelin

"Young Pilgrims"
The Shins

"Gravy"
Dee Dee Sharp

"Come On-A My House"
Rosemary Clooney

"Thanks a Lot"
Johnny Cash

"Free Bird"
Lynyrd Skynyrd

"Mashed Potatoes"
Rufus Thomas

"Give Thanks and Praise"
Bob Marley

We love this holiday. We have much giving to be thankful for, as our cornucopias overfloweth with incredible family, delectable eats and semi-effective slimming garments. Race you for the wishbone.

FOODATHALON FARE

Butternut Squash Soup with Parmesan Sage Croutons   42

Lickity Split Stuffing (BITE ME, p. 156)

Oven Roasted Turkey Breast with Gravy   158

Airy Carrot Soufflé with Crunchy Pecan Topping   91

Apple Bread with Butterscotch Glaze   229

Pumpkin Cupcakes with Cream Cheese Icing   233

Holiday Harvest

 Stick candles in bottles of Wild Turkey

🍽 Place white candles in clear vases filled with candy corn

🍽 Mix up cranberry or pumpkin pie martinis

🍽 Fresh cranberries at the bottom of vases will hold flowers in place

"I feel a very unusual sensation – if it is not indigestion, I think it must be gratitude."

— Benjamin Disraeli, Prime Minister of the UK, 1874–1880

We Greatly Appreciate

Kim McArthur and crew at McArthur & Company, photographer Michael Alberstat, food stylist Ian Muggridge, filmmaker Andrew Nisker, recipe tester Sarah Ramsey, überhelpful Martha Snyder, cheeky Naomi Finlay, grammar goddess Penny Offman, BITE ME's top promoters (Dara Willow, The Allen Boys, Cheryl Louvelle, Karen Haber, Brenda Goldstein and Marty Handelman), siblings Kenny and Jen Tanenbaum, grandmother extraordinaire Alice Lieberman, and, of course, Larry and Judy Tanenbaum, parents who continue to inspire and tolerate us.

Julie Greatly Appreciates

Kenny A. for his boundless kindness, humor and encouragement; Jamie for being "proud" of me; Perry for making me laugh; Benjy for wishing I was done so I could play; my left (Carolyn Offman) and right (Dahra Granovsky) hands while writing this book; and, of course, all the friends I adore and who continue to bite me.

Lisa Greatly Appreciates

Jordan for his endless support and eating his way through 176 recipes, Emmy for her encouragement and motherly advice, Alex "flambé" because her nose knows, Lauren for tasting everything with a smile and to all the poker buddies for devouring anything and everything.

**"Don't cry because it's over.
Smile because it happened."**

— Dr. Seuss

INDEX

Page numbers of illustrated recipes are shown in bold type.

CREDITS

Design
Counterpunch Inc. / Peter Ross

Design Concept
Julie Albert

Printing
Trigraphik LBF

Copy editor
Becky Toyne

Food Photography
Michael Alberstat

Food Styling
Ian Muggridge

Indexing
Linda Lefler

PHOTO CREDITS